Analyzing the Media

Analyzing the Media
A Systemic Functional Approach

Edited by Martin Kaltenbacher and Hartmut Stöckl

SHEFFIELD UK   BRISTOL CT

Published by Equinox Publishing Ltd.

UK Office 415, The Workstation, 15 Paternoster Row, Sheffield,
    South Yorkshire S1 2BX
USA ISD, 70 Enterprise Drive, Bristol, CT 06010

www.equinoxpub.com

First published 2019

© Martin Kaltenbacher, Hartmut Stöckl and contributors 2019

All rights reserved. No part of this publication may be reproduced or transmitted in any form or by any means, electronic or mechanical, including photocopying, recording or any information storage or retrieval system, without prior permission in writing from the publishers.

British Library Cataloguing-in-Publication Data

A catalogue record for this book is available from the British Library.

ISBN-13 978 1 78179 625 2 (hardback)
         978 1 78179 626 9 (paperback)
         978 1 78179 627 6 (ePDF)

Library of Congress Cataloging-in-Publication Data

Names: Kaltenbacher, Martin, 1966- editor. | Stöckl, Hartmut, 1965- editor.
Title: Analyzing the media : a systemic functional approach / edited by
   Martin Kaltenbacher and Hartmut Stöckl.
Description: Sheffield, UK ; Bristol, CT : Equinox Publishing Ltd, 2019. |
   Includes bibliographical references and index.
Identifiers: LCCN 2018032328 (print) | LCCN 2018050663 (ebook) | ISBN
   9781781796276 (ePDF) | ISBN 9781781796252 | ISBN 9781781796252 q(hardback)
   | ISBN 9781781796269 q(paperback) | ISBN 9781781796276 q(ePDF)
Subjects: LCSH: Mass media and language. | Functionalism (Linguistics) |
   Systemic grammar.
Classification: LCC P96.L34 (ebook) | LCC P96.L34 A53 2019 (print) | DDC
   302.2301/4--dc23
LC record available at https://lccn.loc.gov/2018032328

Typeset by Sparks – www.sparkspublishing.com

Contents

Acknowledgements		vii
List of Figures		ix
List of Tables		xi
1	Introduction *Martin Kaltenbacher and Hartmut Stöckl*	1
2	Media and education: A functional view on simplification criteria of news articles in the second language classroom *Ana María Coria, María Cristina Spínola † and Ann Montemayor-Borsinger*	13
3	Personalization as cultural practice: the interpersonal component of language in the opinion discourse of the British, German, and Italian quality press *Melanie Kerschner*	31
4	Generic structures, rhetorical relations and thematic patterns in English and Spanish journalistic texts: a comparative study *Julia Lavid-López and Lara Moratón Gutiérrez*	49
5	Popular science articles in broadsheet newspapers, consumer magazines, and specialized magazines: Engagement resources from a translation perspective *Marina Manfredi*	67
6	The interpersonal metafunction of *and*-parenthetical clauses in English journalism *Carlos Prado-Alonso*	91
7	Packaging voices in the British press: aspects of the logogenesis of science dissemination *Miriam Pérez-Veneros*	111

8 English news texts in the light of authorial orientation: a classification of subjective and objective text types based on the system of modality 131
Martin Kaltenbacher

9 Interpersonal aspects of an English language Internet travel forum 149
David Banks

10 Blending SFL and Activity Theory to model communication and artefact use: examples from Human-Computer Interaction 167
Rebekah Wegener and Jörg Cassens

11 Smell as social semiotic: on the deployment and intersemiotic potential of smell 189
Daniel Lees Fryer

Author index 205

Subject index 209

Acknowledgements

Our special thanks go to David Schönthal from Cardiff University for his meticulous proofreading and language editing, for his valuable comments on many earlier drafts of the chapters included in this volume and for designing Figures 4.1–4.4.

Thanks go to Franz Frommann for designing the book cover and to Jana Pflaeging for designing the conference logo for ESFLC 2016.

Thanks also go to OLMS Verlag for giving permission to publish an English version of the book chapter Kaltenbacher, M. (2017) "Was macht den Kommentar zum Kommentar? Auktoriale Orientierung als Textsortenindikator in englischen Zeitungstexten." In: Lenk, Hartmut & Giessen, Hans (eds.) *Persuasionsstile in Europa III: Linguistische Methoden zur vergleichenden Analyse von Kommentartexten in Tageszeitungen europäischer Länder*. Hildesheim: OLMS, 57-75.

Thanks are also due to Anders Kofod-Petersen for giving us permission to use the photos in Figure 10.1.

Finally, thanks are due to Springer Nature for giving permission to reprint Figure 11.1, reprinted/adapted by permission from Springer Nature: Springer eBook, *Essential Oils as Psychotherapeutic Agents*, by Tisserand, R. © (1988).

List of Figures

Figure 3.1	Overview of frequencies of 1st and 2nd person personal, possessive and reflexive pronouns per news culture	38
Figure 3.2	Detailed distribution of frequencies of 1st and 2nd person personal, possessive and reflexive pronouns ordered according to news culture	39
Figure 4.1	Simple linear progression	52
Figure 4.2	Split Rheme progression	52
Figure 4.3	Constant progression	53
Figure 4.4	Derived Hyperthematic Progression	53
Figure 4.5	Generic structure of News Reports (English and Spanish)	54
Figure 4.6	Rhetorical structure of News Reports (English and Spanish)	55
Figure 4.7	TP patterns and Moves in a Spanish News Report	56
Figure 4.8	TP patterns and Moves in an English and a Spanish News Report	57
Figure 4.9	Summary of textual structures in News Reports	57
Figure 4.10	Generic structure of Editorials (English and Spanish)	58
Figure 4.11	TP patterns and Moves in an English Editorial	59
Figure 4.12	TP patterns and Moves in an English and a Spanish Editorial	60
Figure 4.13	Comparison of generic structures in the three newspaper genres	61
Figure 4.14	Summary of textual structures in Letters to the editor	61
Figure 6.1	Normalized distribution of *and*-parenthetical clauses in Press Reportage, Press Editorial and Press Review	97
Figure 6.2	Mean scores of Dimension 1: Involved vs. Informational Production (cf. Biber 1988: 128)	100
Figure 6.3	Distribution of the *and*-parenthetical construction in the journalistic textual categories of the corpora	101
Figure 8.1	The system of Modality (after Halliday and Matthiessen 2014: 182)	133
Figure 8.2	Results for categories of modal orientation per text type in absolute numbers	139
Figure 8.3	Relative results for categories of modal orientation per text type in percent	139

List of Figures

Figure 10.1	Behaviour-aware sliding doors: demonstrator (Solem 2011)	177
Figure 10.2	Meeting activity at a whiteboard: conversation with audience and writing on the board	177
Figure 10.3	Central concepts from CHAT	180
Figure 10.4	Integrating CHAT and SFL	181
Figure 11.1	'Mood cycle' (after Tisserand 1988: 180, Fig. 9.3)	196
Figure 11.2	System network for Mood (based on Tisserand 1988: 180)	197

List of Tables

Table 2.1	Simplification by unpacking a nominalization in Theme position	17
Table 2.2	Simplification of a clause acting as Subject in Theme position	18
Table 2.3	Simplification of nominalization in Theme by adding parataxis	18
Table 2.4	Simplification and deletion of thematic equative	19
Table 2.5	Simplification of non-finite hypotaxis in Text 1	21
Table 2.6	Simplification of non-finite hypotaxis in Text 2	21
Table 2.7	Simplification of finite hypotaxis in Text 1	22
Table 2.8	Simplification of finite hypotaxis in Text 2	22
Table 2.9	Simplification of non-finite expansion	23
Table 2.10	Preservation of finite expansion	24
Table 2.11	Preservation of projection, with simplification	25
Table 2.12	Examples of lexical changes in Text 1	26
Table 2.13	Examples of lexical changes in Text 2	26
Table 3.1	1st and 2nd person personal, possessive and reflexive pronouns considered in the analysis	38
Table 3.2	Frequencies of 1st and 2nd person pronoun forms in all editorials, normalized and absolute	39
Table 5.1	The corpus of feature articles on the basis of the *Revised Field of Science and Technology (FOS) Classification* (OECD 2007)	76
Table 5.2	Instances of Engagement in STs and TTs	77
Table 6.1	Sources and distribution of the corpus texts from LOB, Brown, FLOB and FROWN, BE06, AmE06	92
Table 6.2	Pearson correlation coefficient for the distribution of *and*-parenthetical clauses and Biber's (1988: 122-124) mean scores on Dimension 1	101
Table 7.1	Corpus of articles used in the study (*Proj_Sci* corpus)	117
Table 7.2	The ten different types of projection of Things	119
Table 7.3	Tokens of projected Propositions, Facts and Things in the *Proj_Sci* corpus	122
Table 7.4	Types and tokens of Things in the *Proj_Sci* corpus	123

List of Tables

Table 8.1	Objective versus subjective description (based on Kane 1988: 254–263)	132
Table 8.2	Modalizations of the type 'probability' with high, median and low value	134
Table 8.3	Modalizations of the type 'usuality' with high, median and low value	134
Table 8.4	Modulations of the type 'obligation' with high, median and low value	134
Table 8.5	Modulations of the type 'inclination' with high, median and low value	135
Table 8.6	Modal expressions according to explicit-subjective, implicit-subjective, implicit-objective and explicit-objective orientation	136
Table 8.7	Word count for each text within each text type	138
Table 8.8	Results for all categories of modal orientation across text types in absolute numbers (normalized to reflect the sample size of the text type 'comment')	138
Table 9.1	Northumbria: exchanges and turns	152
Table 9.2	Namibia: exchanges and turns	153
Table 9.3	Other countries represented in the Namibia sample	153
Table 9.4	Modal expressions	157
Table 9.5	Modal functions	159
Table 9.6	Process types	160

1 Introduction

Martin Kaltenbacher and Hartmut Stöckl
University of Salzburg, Austria

1.1 Systemic Functional Linguistic Theory

In addition to its decidedly anti-structuralist and anti-formalist stances, Systemic Functional Linguistic Theory (SFL) has mainly gained the solid ground it now occupies in modern linguistics thanks to its focus on context and situation and its insistence on dealing with authentic text and communication. These orientations have allowed SFL to be applicable to many diverse fields and to flexibly shift research perspectives in its view of language, text and discourse. The power of SFL is, as it seems to us, rooted in four vital perspectives of language as a social semiotic:

(1) Pro-Contextualism/Situationalism: Turning against some of the major hallowed assumptions in traditional language theory meant functionalists had cleared the way for setting different priorities. The utmost priority in a systemic functional approach to language clearly has been given to context in its widest cultural and situational sense. This means that, ultimately, language and context are inseparable: you can only study language through context and you can only capture context through language and other social semiotic activity. This very strong kind of contextualism led to the emergence of such widely recognized notions as register or genre (Halliday & Hasan 1989). Both seek to model the dependency of linguistic/textual form on various parameters of the context.

(2) Text/Communication-Centrism: Thanks to this contextual orientation, systemic functionalist linguistics is also a rather holistic enterprise geared at macro-level structures situated in text and discourse. These two entities are primarily viewed as medium-independent notions of highest-level units. They are the practical site where function-driven structures are placed and enacted in communicative situations. Matthiessen (2015: 143) says, quite aptly, that language system and text are 'one phenomenon' – a continuum where

'system and text are conceptualized as different "phases" of the same phenomenon'. Halliday (1985: 10) himself characterizes this relationship in a very succinct and almost judgemental way: 'For a linguist, to describe language without accounting for text is sterile; to describe text without language is vacuous.' Not surprisingly, SFL fits in well with modern-day pragmatics and text linguistics and also has a natural connection to corpus linguistics as it places a 'high value on naturally occurring text instances' (Matthiessen 2015: 143).

(3) Pro-Applicationism: SFL has been thriving, not least because it is essentially a truly applicable theory of language and communication. This inherent applied linguistics stance shows itself most clearly in approaches to the teaching of literacy in educational linguistics, in corpus linguistics and in sociolinguistics (*Language as Social Semiotic*; Halliday 1978) as well as in cognitive linguistics, translation studies or media linguistics. More recently, it has also surfaced in social semiotics and multimodality, where the fundamental notions of meta-functions, meaning potential, semiotic resources and choice carry over very well and can be applied to different signing modes (e.g. music, image) as well as to the intermodal meaning making or intersemiotic textures of multimodal artefacts (Jewitt 2014, Jewitt & Henriksen 2016).

(4) Multi-Perspectivism: Finally, SFL is so powerful because it can elegantly account for some of the central problems in any theory of language, e.g. how languages are acquired or how languages change. In terms of language acquisition, Halliday's (1975) *Learning How to Mean* suggests that it is the development of situated communicative needs and contextual functionality in children along with their general socio-cognitive development that drive the learning of forms. As for language change, Halliday and Matthiessen (1999) have described it as changes in the paradigmatic choices and their meaning potentials. Such changing choices can be related to texts, individual users and language communities, i.e. communities of practice or cultures.

As a holistic and universalistic theory of language, text and communication, SFL also allows for the shifting of perspectives within the theoretical framework. Seen from above, functions might be in focus; seen from below, structures might be given prominence; and seen from all sides, resources as organized in system networks might gain visibility. These multiple viewpoints that SFL affords are a methodological and theoretical strength that is born out in all applications of the theory.

1.2 Linguistically viable notions of 'the media'

Perhaps with the exception of spoken (and signed) face-to-face conversation, all physical transmission of meaning and communication is dependent on the use of a technology, be it a primitive stone table and a chisel, a papyrus scroll and a reed pen, paper and a printing press, or a more modern communication technology, like a postcard, a telephone, or a computer keyboard and screen. This being so, it is no surprise that SFL with its focus on the study of authentic language could not have grown to its current state-of-the-art position without intensive study of language and meanings manifested in and shaped by media and their related technologies. Appraisal Theory serves as a prototypical example of a substantial element of SFL theory that has evolved in a mutually stimulating process of media research and theory building. The original theory was built by Iedema et al. (1994) in a project that studied newspaper, TV and radio texts in order to develop tools and strategies for the teaching of media literacy in secondary schools. It was then, most prominently, Peter White, who studied the language in broadsheet newspapers to develop Appraisal Theory into the fully fledged theory it is today, first in his doctoral dissertation (White 1998), then on his Appraisal Website (White 2002–2015) and finally, together with Jim Martin, in *The Language of Evaluation: Appraisal in English* (Martin & White 2005).

Beyond their current social hype, the media have long before been of major concern to linguists, in general, and to SFL, in particular. Rooted in rhetorical notions of effectiveness and appropriateness, featuring in early models of communication (e.g. Jakobson 1960), surfacing in the principled division of speech and writing, and generating a key idea in text theory and language variation (e.g. register/mode, Halliday & Hasan 1976), the concept of medium has recently been gaining ground in discourse and text linguistics and general linguistic theory (Cotter & Perrin 2018). Some would go as far as to claim independent disciplinary status to an ever-growing field of media linguistics (Luginbühl 2015, Schmitz 2018). Despite the wealth of notions of medium, there would seem to be linguistic consensus on at least three relevant key elements of the concept:

(1) A technological element: Media are primarily seen as the technological means and infrastructure enabling and shaping the use of language. Technical frameworks like radio, TV, printing, new and social media leave traces in the linguistic styles and the texture of the discourse constructed. Each medium comes equipped with its own material-situational constraints and affordances. The new and social media compound, refine and fuse communicative potentials (Page et al. 2014).

(2) A semiotic element: Viewing media as affording and realizing sign systems or semiotic modes opens up a multimodal approach to text and discourse which seeks to describe the patterns of mode co-operation, combination and integration. In this view, one can look at medium-specific multimodal patterns of texture. But fundamental mode differences, i.e. modal affordances of, for instance, images vs. language/text and the question of the autonomy or interdependence of speech and writing, also come to the fore here (Stöckl 2014, 2016).

(3) A socio-cultural and pragmatic element: From a sociolinguistic and pragmatic point of view, media can be recast as socially constituted routines and forms of textual practice. In this view, media institutions as agents of semiotic production and their social orientations are highlighted, which invent, adopt and remake pragmatic routines and patterns of text design that in their turn affect genres and their linguistic and multimodal styles (Luginbühl 2018). Here one can also ask how relations between communicators are shaped by the medium used.

1.3 Analyzing the media: A systemic functional approach

Based on these multi-dimensional ideas of medium, the present volume looks at currently popular media genres from an SFL perspective. The majority of the chapters address different news genres (reports, popular science articles, analyses, editorials, comments, reviews, letters/emails to the editor) and analyze them from a wide range of theoretical perspectives, such as generic, thematic and rhetorical structures, the distribution and function of pronouns and of *and*-parentheticals, engagement, projection and the packaging of voices, modality and authorial voice, etc. Two chapters focus on the lexicogrammatical and functional changes that affect journalistic texts when they are translated for re-publication in a different news culture or adapted for use in the second language classroom. Other chapters discuss the integration of interpersonal meanings in online travel discussion forums, the multimodal exploitation of smell in open-house viewings and the modelling of communication and artefact use in human–computer interaction.

In Chapter 2, Ana María CORIA, María Cristina SPÍNOLA and Ann MONTEMAYOR-BORSINGER analyze the lexicogrammatical simplification strategies applied to newspaper texts to make them applicable for use in second language classrooms at different levels of proficiency (elementary, immediate and advanced). Their analyses show that the simplified text versions exhibit a decrease in the logical complexity of subordination and a resolution of the complex structures of experiential grammatical metaphor. These changes go hand in hand with a replacement of more 'contentful' with more 'content-light' themes (Berry 2013) and of abstract with more concrete grammatical subjects (Halliday & Mathiessen 2014). At the same time, typical genre features like catchy headlines, the declarative mode and writer invisibility are preserved.

In Chapter 3, Melanie KERSCHNER examines the role of national news cultures in the personalization of news events. To this end, she investigates the effect of personalization strategies exhibited in the use of personal, possessive and reflexive pronouns in newspaper editorials taken from British, German and Italian newspapers. She argues that German editorials, and to a limited extent also Italian editorials, contain 1st person pronouns (*I, my* and inclusive *we*) to express solidarity with the readership, while British writers keep more personal distance to their readers, avoiding the *I* completely and favouring the 'exclusive *we*' over the more inclusive 'patriotic *we*'.

Julia LAVID and Lara MORATÓN (Chapter 4) conduct a corpus-based comparative study of the relationship between generic structures, rhetorical relations and thematic patterns in a bilingual corpus of editorials, reports and letters to the editor in English and Spanish quality newspapers. In a detailed analysis of the types of generic structures and the distribution of their typical moves therein, they show that generic structures are generally longer and more explanatory in Spanish than in English. They also demonstrate that the distribution of thematic and rhetorical structures is not a matter of random individual choices in discourse but can be interpreted functionally as indicative of the genre under study.

Marina MANFREDI (Chapter 5) looks at instantiations of writers' subjective voice in Italian popular science feature articles translated from articles that were originally published in English broadsheet newspapers, consumer magazines and specialized science magazines. In particular, she investigates 'evaluation shifts' that occur in the translation of interpersonal meanings realized through the resource of Engagement, a subsystem of Appraisal Theory (Martin & White 2005). She finds that the original English feature articles are more addressee-oriented, leaving room for alternative views, while the Italian translations tend to reduce explicit indicators of Engagement either through shifts towards a higher degree of certainty or through omissions.

In Chapter 6, Carlos PRADO-ALONSO investigates the interpersonal metafunction of *and*-parenthetical constructions in British and American newspapers in a corpus study on the three news genres press reportage, editorial and review, included in the LOB, Brown, FLOB, FROWN, BrE06 and AmE06 corpora (Hofland et al. 1999, Baker 2009). He shows that *and*-parentheticals – and we are including one as an example between the two hyphens here – are frequently to be found in the more subjective text types editorial and review, where they function as interpersonal discourse markers of persuasion that express addressor involvement in the discourse. In addition, he argues that they provide the reader with background information expressing the writer's degree of commitment, judgment or opinion in the context of the main utterance.

Miriam PÉREZ-VENEROS (Chapter 7) explores the dynamics of projection in popular science articles throughout the logogenetic growth of the article in the British press. Following Thompson (1994), she examines the packaging of scientific knowledge either as Proposition, as Fact or as Thing, and she looks at the effects of the applied type of packaging on the cohesive development or conversion of participants. She argues that in popular science articles, projections are mainly realized through Propositions and Facts. Projections that are realized as Things only occur at the beginning of articles and frequently become the participants of new projections evolving into either Propositions or Facts. The type of packaging chosen by journalists also reflects the way they position themselves towards the scientific information delivered in the projections.

In Chapter 8, Martin KALTENBACHER investigates the prevalent use of subjective and objective authorial voice in different journalistic text types. To this end, he analyzes the manifestation of modal orientation in terms of explicit subjective, implicit subjective, explicit objective and implicit objective modality (Halliday & Matthiessen 2014: 692–693) in a small corpus of reports, editorials, comments, analyses and emails to the editor published in British newspapers in March 2013 on the so-called 'Cyprus bailout'. He shows that, in spite of frequently heard claims that news reports are becoming more and more subjective, the boundaries between informing and commenting newspaper genres remain solid and intact. The formerly distinct commenting text types editorial and comment, however, seem to merge into one prototypical form of commentary.

David BANKS (Chapter 9) conducts a culture-contrastive study of two English-language Internet travel forum communities – one from Northumberland, UK, the other from Namibia – in which he examines their exploitation of interpersonal meaning making resources. He investigates Mood structures in direct and indirect questions, the form and function of modal expressions, and the distribution of process types, which he relates to the interpersonal stratum of the message as they affect the speakers' relationship with their audience. He shows that questions have a greater tendency to be indirect in the Namibia sample. Modal expressions are more likely to be epistemic in the Namibia sample and dynamic in the Northumberland sample; deontic modality is rare in both, but more common in the Namibia sample. Also rare are affective mental processes; nevertheless, they are more frequent in the Northumberland sample. Overall, the participants in the Namibia sample seem more involved and closer to forming a virtual community than the participants in the Northumberland sample.

In Chapter 10, Rebekah WEGENER and Jörg CASSENS blend Systemic Functional Linguistics and Activity Theory to set up a model of communication and artefact use in human–computer interaction. They argue that it is possible to integrate the two theories at abstract levels and apply them to instances of human–computer interaction in order to model communication between, e.g. humans and automated sliding doors which recognize a person's intention to walk through the door. In a second application, they show how their model can be applied to interactive whiteboards. These boards can interpret different presenter actions and adjust their behaviour accordingly so that, for example, a video feed showing a user drawing on the whiteboard is displayed only if the presenter is facing the audience but not when facing the whiteboard.

Daniel Lees FRYER (Chapter 11) investigates the deployment and intersemiotic potential of smell as a multimodal meaning making resource in open-house viewings organized by real-estate agents to attract potential buyers. In such events, specific smellscapes are created, e.g. by brewing coffee and baking cinnamon buns, and integrated with other semiotic systems to make meanings that are potentially complementary to those conveyed verbally, visually and spatially. He explores the interpersonal meaning making potential of different smells (both pleasant and unpleasant) in such events and shows how they combine with other visual, tactile or auditory experiences to unfold their potential. In addition, he demonstrates the potential of smells to evoke feelings of comfort and homeliness but also to serve as icebreakers to get a conversation going.

The book brings together theoretical and methodological approaches that have the power to inform future media genre analysis, systemic functional linguistics as well as multimodal theory and analytical methods. The chapters go back to the 26th European Systemic Functional Linguistics Conference, which took place at Salzburg University in 2016 with the thematic orientation of 'Functional and Social Semiotic Approaches to the Media' and which was organized by a team around the editors of this volume. All contributions demonstrate and highlight – in one way or another – the significance of the basic tenets set up by the functionalist founding fathers and re-developed in recent decades of SFL work. In this fashion, the chapters provide a showcase of current SFL work on media-related issues in the widest sense. The four principles sketched out above set the agenda and explain it through the volume's individual contributions: they focus on clear registers or genres and are concerned with the interplay between medial factors, grammatical resources of the language systems under investigation and textual structure. Their foci are invariably concerned with selected linguistic or semiotic functions, with specific language structures or textual patterns and with particular multimodal resources.

About the authors

Martin Kaltenbacher studied English and Classics in Salzburg and Oxford. Since completing his doctoral dissertation on *Universal Grammar and Parameter Resetting in Second Language Acquisition* (2001, Frankfurt: Peter Lang), he has held a post-doc research position at the University of Salzburg. While he has kept a keen interest in Syntax and Language Acquisition, he soon shifted his scholarly focus onto Systemic Functional Linguistics, Discourse Analysis and Social Semiotics, within which fields he has conducted studies on web-design, on the discourse of tourism and, more recently, on journalism. He co-edited books on Multimodality (Ventola, E., Charles, C. & Kaltenbacher, M. (2004) *Perspectives on Multimodality*, Amsterdam: Benjamins) and on Discourse Studies (Gruber, H., Kaltenbacher, M. & Muntigl, P. (2007) *Empirical Approaches to Discourse Analysis*, Frankfurt: Peter Lang).

Hartmut Stöckl studied English and Russian languages and literatures at Leipzig University and completed his PhD in English linguistics with a thesis on English advertising language and its cohesive ties with images

(1995). From 1995 to 2007, he held a post-doc research position at Chemnitz University, where he completed his Dr. phil. habil. in 2003 with a book on the semiotic resources and textual interplay of language and image. In 2007, he was appointed full professor of English and Applied Linguistics at the University of Salzburg. His main research areas are in semiotics, text linguistics and stylistics, pragmatics and multimodal/visual communication. A recurrent theme surfacing in most of his work is a concern with a functional-linguistic theory of the multimodal text and effective analytical methods for uncovering its structures and styles. He is particularly interested in the linkage of language and image in modern media, typography and an aesthetic appreciation of advertising. His latest (co-)edited volumes are: *Bildlinguistik* (2011, Berlin: Erich Schmidt), *Medientheorien und Multimodalität* (2011, Köln: Herbert von Halem) and *Werbung – Keine Kunst!?* (2012, Heidelberg: Winter). He is the co-editor of the *Handbook Language in Multimodal Contexts* (2016, Berlin/Boston: de Gruyter) in the 21-volume series *Sprachwissen*.

References

Baker, P. (2009) *Contemporary Corpus Linguistics*. London: Continuum.

Berry, M. (2013) 'Contentful and contentlight Subject Themes in informal spoken English and formal written English'. In: O'Grady, G., Fontaine, L. & Bartlett, T. (eds.) *Choice in Language: Applications in Text Analysis*. London: Equinox, 243–268.

Cotter, C. & Perrin, D. (eds.) (2018) *The Routledge Handbook of Language and Media*. London/New York: Routledge.

Hofland, K., Lindebjerg, A. & Thunestvedt, J. (1999) *ICAME Collection of English Language Corpora*. 2nd edition. CD-ROM version. Bergen: The HIT Centre.

Matthiessen, C.M.I.M. (2015) 'Halliday on Language'. In: Webster, J.J. (ed.) *The Bloomsbury Companion to M.A.K. Halliday*. London/New York: Bloomsbury, 137–202.

Halliday, M.A.K. (1975) *Learning How to Mean*. London: Edward Arnold.

Halliday, M.A.K. (1978) *Language as Social Semiotic: The Social Interpretation of Language and Meaning*. London: Edward Arnold.

Halliday, M.A.K. (1985) 'Systemic background'. In: Benson, J.D. & Greaves, W.S. (eds.) *Systemic Perspectives on Discourse. Vol. 1: Selected Theoretical Papers from the 9th International Systemic Workshop*. Norwood, N.J.: Ablex, 1–15.

Halliday, M.A.K. & Hasan, R. (1976) *Cohesion in English.* London: Longman.

Halliday, M.A.K & Hasan, R. (1989) *Language, Context and Text: Aspects of Language in a Social-semiotic Perspective.* London: Oxford University Press.

Halliday, M.A.K. & Matthiessen, C.M.I.M. (1999) *Construing Experience Through Meaning: A Language-based Approach to Cognition.* London: Continuum.

Halliday, M.A.K. & Matthiessen, C.M.I.M. (2014) *An Introduction to Functional Grammar.* 4th edition. London: Arnold.

Iedema, R., Feez, S. & White, P.R.R. (1994) *Media Literacy. Write It Right Industry Research Monograph Vol. II.* Sydney: Disadvantaged Schools Program (NSW Department of School Education).

Jakobson, R. (1960) 'Linguistics and poetics'. In: Sebeok, T. (ed.) *Style in Language.* Cambridge, MA: M.I.T. Press, 350–377.

Jewitt, C. (2014) 'Different approaches to multimodality'. In: Jewitt, C. (ed.) *The Routledge Handbook of Multimodal Analysis.* London/New York: Routledge, 31–43.

Jewitt, C. & Henriksen, B. (2016) 'Social semiotic multimodality'. In: Klug, N.-M. & Stöckl, H. (eds.) *Handbuch Sprache im multimodalen Kontext.* Berlin/Boston: de Gruyter, 145–164.

Luginbühl, M. (2015) 'Media linguistics: On mediality and culturality'. *1plus10. Living Linguistics*, 9–26.

Luginbühl, M. (2018) 'Routinizing communication. Text production and cultural significance in media genres'. In: Cotter, C. & Perrin, D. (eds.) *The Routledge Handbook of Language and Media.* London/New York: Routledge, 461–474.

Martin, J.R. & White, P.R.R. (2005) *The Language of Evaluation: Appraisal in English.* London/New York: Palgrave.

Page, R., Barton, D., Unger, J.W. & Zappavigna, M. (2014) *Language and Social Media. A Student Guide.* London/New York: Routledge.

Schmitz, U. (2018) 'Media linguistic landscapes. Alle Linguistik sollte Medienlinguistik sein'. In: *jfml – Journal for Media Linguistics.* Discussion Paper 1 (2018). http://dp.jfml.org/2018/05/17/open-peer-review-media-linguistic-landscapes/

Stöckl, H. (2014) 'Semiotic paradigms and multimodality'. In: Jewitt, C. (ed.) *The Routledge Handbook of Multimodal Analysis.* London/New York: Routledge, 274–286.

Stöckl, H. (2016) 'Multimodalität – Semiotische und textlinguistische Grundlagen'. In: Klug, N.-M. & Stöckl, H. (eds.) *Handbuch Sprache im multimodalen Kontext.* Berlin/Boston: de Gruyter, 3–35.

Thompson, G. (1994) 'Propositions, Projection, and Things'. Paper presented at the *21st International Systemic Functional Conference*. Gent, 1–5 August, 1994, 1–22.

White, P.R.R. (1998) *Telling Media Tales: The News Story as Rhetoric*. Unpublished doctoral dissertation. Sydney: University of Sydney.

White, P.R.R (2002–2015) *The Appraisal Website*. http://grammatics.com/appraisal.

2   Media and education: A functional view on simplification criteria of news articles in the second language classroom

Ana María Coria, María Cristina Spínola † and Ann Montemayor-Borsinger
Universidad Nacional de La Plata, Argentina &
National University of Rio Negro, Argentina

2.1   Introduction

From the early stages of learning a foreign language, students need to deal with a range of discourse genres to help them develop comprehension skills in real contexts. One of these genres, the news article, is considered of particular interest for this purpose. Since difficulties in understanding a text in a foreign language are the result of different factors involving lexicogrammatical, discourse-semantic and genre-related aspects (Christie & Derewianka 2008; Christie & Martin 1997; Martin & Rose 2008; Rose & Martin 2012), teaching materials often make use of simplified versions of news articles.

This chapter looks at three different versions (elementary, intermediate and advanced) of two news articles, using Systemic Functional Linguistics. It analyzes how the texts were simplified, focusing in particular on the comparison of linguistic expressions involved in construing experiential meanings and their logical-semantic associations (cf. Martin & Rose 2007). The original versions of the texts (advanced level) are two articles from the *Guardian* newspaper – the main source of news articles used by a major publisher on its website *www.onestopenglish.com* for teachers of English. The simplified versions were published on the same website. Text 1 'Food shortages could force world into vegetarianism, warn scientists' (*Guardian* 2012) elaborates on the growth of vegetarianism as a consequence of future food shortages, and Text 2 'Warning: extreme weather ahead' (*Guardian*

2011) deals with extreme weather situations as a result of climate change. (Links to the original versions of the articles are given in the References Section.)

2.2 Discourse-semantic and genre aspects of simplification

Before discussing the lexicogrammatical level of analysis in detail, let us briefly examine some discourse-semantic and genre aspects of the news articles and their simplified versions. Interestingly, the headlines were not changed in the simplified versions of either article. For Text 1, the headline is *Food shortages could force the world into vegetarianism, warn scientists*, and for Text 2, *Warning: extreme weather ahead*. Lexical items such as *warn* or *shortage* in Text 1 or *warning* or *extreme* in Text 2 are left unchanged, probably because their function is to indicate the nature of the articles. Indeed, a news article headline is the core of text structure and texture, and each new added event acts as a satellite revolving around this initial core (see Butt et al. 2003: 228; van Dijk 1983: 71). Moreover, in addition to encapsulating the story, a headline endeavours to attract the reader with words carrying strong emotional weight (Reah 2002:13).

Another discourse-semantic aspect is the length of the simplified versions, which is reduced by various means. Text 1 is shortened at both elementary and intermediate level by leaving out the lead as well as an additional report at the end of the original article. The lead (*Water scarcity's effect on food production means radical steps will be needed to feed population expected to reach 9bn by 2050*) shows high grammatical intricacy. The Theme is a nominalization, and the Rheme is a clause complex which is difficult to process. This construction at the beginning of the article would affect elementary and intermediate level reader comprehension. Omitting the additional report shortens the simplified versions significantly without affecting their coherence. In addition, the elementary version omits four paragraphs which discuss other options for resolving the problem of hunger, thereby further shortening it without affecting its coherence.

Text 2 is also shortened by omitting the lead at elementary level. However, because of its low grammatical intricacy, the lead is retained at intermediate level with a minor lexical change and an additional note explaining the meaning of the coinage 'global weirding': *Tornados, wildfires, droughts and floods were once seen as freak conditions. But the environmental disasters we now see around the world are shocking signs of 'global weirding' (because of global warming, our weather has become strange/unusual)*. Some specific technical information is deleted from both simplified versions, e.g. the reference to the phenomena of 'El Niño' and 'La Niña', while other specific technical information is removed from the elementary text only, e.g. the effect of climate change on rich countries as opposed to poor countries.

The declarative mode is respected throughout the simplified versions of both articles, where many clauses include figures and percentages, such as the number of people suffering from food scarcity (Text 1) or temperature registers (Text 2). Figures and percentages are typical resources in the news article genre and are included to prove that the news is factually correct. However, the two texts deal differently with the voices of authority which appear in the original versions, i.e. scientists and institutions specializing in food or climate. The simplified versions of the food shortage article (Text 1) retain most instances of voices of authority. Text 1 thematizes these voices in the very first sentence: *Leading water scientists have issued one of the sternest warnings yet about global food supplies*. It is therefore not surprising that these voices are frequently used throughout the text and are preserved in the simplified versions. In contrast, in the first seven sentences of Text 2, events 'speak for themselves', and the need for voices of authority is not essential to meaning realization. This may explain why voices of authority are often omitted in the simplified versions of this latter text.

2.3 Lexicogrammatical aspects of simplification

The following sections analyze the simplification criteria used in Theme (Section 2.4), Rheme (Section 2.5) and Lexis (Section 2.6) by considering more detailed changes to both texts at the lexicogrammatical level. These lexicogrammatical changes focus mainly on reducing experiential metaphor and grammatical intricacy by unpacking nominalizations. For grammatical intricacy, the two basic systems that determine how clauses relate to each other are Taxis relations and Logico-semantic relations (Halliday & Matthiessen 2004: 373). For Taxis, Halliday (1985) distinguishes:

(a) parataxis: logical interdependence between clauses of equal status such as in *There is a drought in many parts of England, and Wales has had its driest May ever.*
(b) hypotaxis: logical interdependence between clauses of different hierarchy such as in *This will put additional pressure on water resources, which are already stressed.*

(c) embedding: mechanism by which a clause functions as a constituent within the structure of a group, which is in turn part of a clause such as the clause-type grammatical subject of the verb *sees* in the clause *What was mild and equable British weather now sees the seasons reversed.*

The Taxis system combines with the Logico-semantic system, which distinguishes between different meanings. Martin (1992: 170) highlights the difficulties in developing a detailed classification for the Logico-semantic system, because, as Halliday (2006: 226) suggests, '[a] language is not an inventory of well-formed structures. On the contrary, it is a highly indeterminate, open-ended resource for making and exchanging meaning'. This paper will thus focus only on the two main Logico-semantic meanings of (a) expansion and (b) projection. In expansion, a secondary clause expands a primary clause mainly by restatement, clarification or addition (cf. Eggins 2004: 47), such as in *3.5 million farmers are on the brink of bankruptcy because they cannot feed their cattle or grow crops*. In projection, one clause anchors the complex by indicating who said or thought something (Eggins 2004, 47), such as in *Water scientists say that everyone may have to change to a vegetarian diet by 2050*.

In the following three sections, examples taken from the three versions of each text are compared in *ad hoc* tables which illustrate relevant instances of the simplifications made in selected clauses. The texts are analyzed using the clause as the unit of grammatical analysis (Halliday & Matthiessen 2004: 10). The expressions currently being discussed in each section are marked in bold in the corresponding tables.

2.4 Simplification criteria in Theme: Reducing experiential metaphors

The main changes in Theme involve unpacking complex nominal groups. In other words, there is a clear drift from intricate experiential metaphors that build up complex nominal groups to simpler, more congruent lexis and grammar. Table 2.1 shows an example from Text 1 which has been simplified by unpacking a nominalization (experiential metaphor) in Theme position.

The original text includes an instance of projection expressed metaphorically as a complex nominal group (Halliday & Matthiessen 2004: 467): *Dire warnings of water scarcity limiting food production*. In the simplified

Table 2.1 Simplification by unpacking a nominalization in Theme position

T1	Advanced Level	Intermediate Level	Elementary Level
5a	**Dire warnings of water scarcity limiting food production** come as Oxfam and the UN prepare for a possible second global food crisis in five years.	**Warnings that water scarcity could limit food production** come at the same time as Oxfam and the UN prepare for a possible second global food crisis in five years.	**There** are warnings that water shortages will limit food production.
5b			**At the same time, Oxfam and the UN** prepare for a possible second global food crisis in five years.

versions, this is unpacked as a finite clause and rewritten as *Warnings that water scarcity could limit food production* for intermediate level. At elementary level there is an even more significant change: the thematic nominal group in the advanced and intermediate texts becomes the cataphoric element *There*, which points towards what used to be Theme: *Warnings that water shortages will limit food production*. In other words, the existence of a warning is previously announced to the reader by the easily processed cataphoric element *There*. It is interesting to note that all versions preserve the use of the abstract entity *Warnings* for construing a metaphoric projection – a means often used in news articles to conceal the source of information (Halliday & Matthiessen 2004: 468).

Similarly, Table 2.2 provides an example from Text 2, again showing Theme simplification.

The grammatical Subject that functions as the unmarked Theme of this clause complex (*What was, until quite recently, predictable, temperate, mild and equable, British weather, guaranteed to be warm and wet*) has been unpacked at intermediate and elementary level into two different finite clauses. Moreover, at elementary level, the non-finite hypotactic clause *guaranteed to be warm and wet* is replaced by its finite counterpart *was always warm and wet*.

Table 2.3 provides an example from Text 1 where yet another nominalization (*With 70% of all available water being used in agriculture*) has been unpacked. It is the only marked Theme in the original version of Text 1.

Table 2.2 Simplification of a clause acting as Subject in Theme position

T2	Advanced Level	Intermediate Level	Elementary Level
6a	**What was, until quite recently, predictable, temperate, mild and equable, British weather, guaranteed to be warm and wet,** now sees the seasons reversed and temperature and rainfall records broken almost every year.	**British weather** was, until quite recently, predictable and mild.	**In the past,** the British weather was mild
6b		**It** was guaranteed to be warm and wet.	– **it** was always warm and wet –
6c		**Now** the seasons are reversed	**but now** the seasons are reversed
6d		**and temperature and rainfall records** are broken almost every year.	**and temperature and rainfall records** are broken almost every year.

Table 2.3 Simplification of nominalization in Theme by adding parataxis

T1	Advanced Level	Intermediate Level	Elementary Level
15a	**With 70% of all available water being used in agriculture,** growing more food to feed an additional two billion people by 2050 will place greater pressure on available water and land.	**Seventy per cent of all water** is used in agriculture,	**70% of all water** is used in farming
15b		**and growing more food to feed an extra two billion people by 2050** will place greater pressure on water and land.	**and growing more food to feed an extra two billion people by 2050** will put more pressure on water and land.

This marked Theme, a Circumstantial Adjunct, is a non-finite hypotactic clause. The circumstantial relation is signalled by means of the conjunctive preposition *with*. This structure is modified in the simplified versions by means of a paratactic relation between two finite clauses joined by the conjunction *and* (Halliday & Matthiessen 2004: 421).

Table 2.4 provides another interesting example of simplification taken from Text 2. It is an instance of a thematic equative, identified as a nominalization in Halliday & Mathiessen (2014: 94), which in fact fulfils two distinct functions: 'it identifies (specifies) what the Theme is; on the other hand, it identifies it (equates it) with the Rheme' (Halliday & Matthiessen 2004: 71). The intermediate text simplifies this complex structure to facilitate comprehension. At elementary level, the entire clause has been deleted.

Table 2.4 Simplification and deletion of thematic equative

T2	Advanced Level	Intermediate Level	Elementary Level
33	**But what concerns most climate scientists and observers** is that the extreme weather events are occurring more frequently, their intensity is growing and the trends all suggest long-term change as greenhouse gases steadily build in the atmosphere.	**But most climate scientists and observers** are worried because the extreme weather events are occurring more frequently, they are more extreme and the trends all suggest long-term change.	

In sum, the examples discussed above show that the main simplification criteria for Themes involve reducing experiential metaphor in three ways:

- by unpacking nominalizations in Unmarked Theme (i.e. the grammatical subjects) (cf. Table 2.1 and Table 2.2) or by omitting the nominalization altogether, especially at elementary level (cf. Table 2.4);
- by unpacking nominalizations in Marked Theme – in our example a hypotactic non-finite clause modified by means of a paratactic relation between finite clauses (cf. Table 2.3);

- by re-expressing complex structures, such as thematic equatives, as simpler nominal groups (cf. Table 2.4) or by omitting such clauses at elementary level.

In both texts, there are many further interesting examples of simplifications that involve reducing experiential metaphor in Theme position, such as anticipating the introduction of a new participant by means of the existential subject *there* or modifying the noun group in Theme to avoid complex processes in Rheme.

2.5 Simplification criteria in Rheme: Reducing grammatical intricacy

The adapted news articles include some interesting changes in Rheme to reduce grammatical intricacy by simplifying complex logical structures of expansion or projection. These simplifications involve two main procedures which we have already seen in the simplification of Theme: (a) changing hypotactic clauses (subordination) to paratactic clauses (coordination or, very often at elementary level, independent clauses) and (b) changing non-finite abstract clauses to finite clauses that anchor the proposition 'in the here and now'.

2.5.1 Simplifying hypotactic expansion

The non-finite expanding hypotactic clauses identified in the original version of Text 1 mostly indicate meanings of purpose. Most of them are preserved in the two simplified versions, albeit with modifications, particularly at elementary level. The grammatical structure involved is often known as 'infinitive of purpose' in the foreign language classroom. It is one of the most common kinds of clause of purpose (cf. Collins Cobuild English Grammar 1993: 353) and is taught at early stages. However, in the example presented in Table 2.5, taken from Text 1, the expanding non-finite clause *to avoid catastrophic shortages* is omitted at elementary level. This omission of a complex expression in addition shortens the clause complex, which has already been divided into two independent finite clauses at intermediate level.

Text 2 contains two such non-finite expanding hypotactic clauses (clause complexes 8 and 19), which function as Circumstantial Adjuncts in Rheme. Both of them are omitted at elementary level, clause complex 8 also at

Table 2.5 Simplification of non-finite hypotaxis in Text 1

T1	Advanced Level	Intermediate Level	Elementary Level
1	Leading water scientists have issued one of the sternest warnings yet about global food supplies, saying that the world's population may have to switch almost completely to a vegetarian diet by 2050 to avoid catastrophic shortages.	Water scientists have given one of the strongest warnings ever about global food supplies. They say that the world's population may have to change almost completely to a vegetarian diet by 2050 **to avoid catastrophic shortages**.	Water scientists have given a very strong warning about the world's food supplies. They say that everyone may have to change to a vegetarian diet by 2050.

Table 2.6 Simplification of non-finite hypotaxis in Text 2

T2	Advanced Level	Intermediate Level	Elementary Level
19	The government responded with a massive rain-making operation, **firing thousands of rockets to 'seed' clouds with silver iodide and other chemicals.**	The government responded by trying to 'make rain'. It fired thousands of rockets to provide the clouds with chemicals.	

intermediate level. Clause complex 19 is retained at intermediate level, but with extensive lexicogrammatical changes, as shown in Table 2.6. It is probably deemed difficult to process partly due to the non-finite expanding hypotactic clause of means (*firing thousands of rockets*), which is simplified at intermediate level and entirely omitted at the elementary level.

Finite expanding hypotactic clauses of time and condition, in contrast, have generally been preserved in the simplified versions of Text 1, albeit with lexicogrammatical changes and sometimes with omissions at elementary level. The example in Table 2.1 for simplifications in Theme also shows such changes in Rheme, where the hypotactic relation becomes a paratactic one. Table 2.1 shows how the expanding hypotactic finite clause *as Oxfam and the UN prepare for a possible second global food crisis in five years* is replaced by an independent clause at elementary level. Table 2.7 provides a further example where the clauses in bold are abbreviated or lexically simplified at intermediate level and deleted altogether at elementary level.

Table 2.7 Simplification of finite hypotaxis in Text 1

T2	*Advanced Level*	*Intermediate Level*	*Elementary Level*
19	'This will place additional pressure on our already stressed water resources, at a time **when we also need to allocate more water to satisfy global energy demand – which is expected to rise by 60% over the coming 30 years – and to generate electricity for the 1.3 billion people currently without it**,' said the report.	'This will put additional pressure on our water resources, which are already stressed, at a time **when we also need more water to satisfy global energy demand and to create electricity for the 1.3 billion people who are without it**,' said the report.	

Table 2.8 provides an example from Text 2. This is a finite expanding hypotactic clause expressing reason: *because they cannot feed their cattle or grow crops*. The hypotaxis has been deleted from both simplified versions, probably as a result of the need to delete the expression 'on the brink of bankruptcy', which is a metaphorical expression that elementary and intermediate learners of English may find difficult to process.

Table 2.8 Simplification of finite hypotaxis in Text 2

T2	*Advanced Level*	*Intermediate Level*	*Elementary Level*
26b	and the biggest farm union says that more than 3.5 million farmers are **on the brink of bankruptcy** because they cannot feed their cattle or grow crops.	and more than 3.5 million farmers cannot feed their cattle or grow crops.	and more than 3.5 million farmers cannot feed their animals or grow crops.

2.5.2 Simplifying embedded expansion

Most of the non-finite embedded expanding clauses in Text 1 are preserved in the simplified versions, with a few lexical changes. They all are what Halliday calls 'act clauses' in the sense that they represent the name of an action, event or other phenomenon (Halliday & Matthiessen 2004: 438). The embedded act clauses in our corpus serve as the core of a nominal group and constitute the nominalization of a process. Table 2.9 provides an example from Text 1 which contains two of these clauses (*eliminating waste*; *increasing trade*). They are preserved with some lexical changes at intermediate level, but the whole sentence is omitted at elementary level.

Table 2.9 Simplification of non-finite expansion

T1	Advanced Level	Intermediate Level	Elementary Level
13	Other options to feed people include **eliminating waste and increasing trade** between countries **in food surplus and those in deficit**.	Other options to feed people include **stopping waste and increasing trade** between countries that have a food surplus and countries that don't have enough food.	

Clauses of this type were also found in Text 2. The example in Table 2.2 above, showing simplifications in Theme, also shows simplifications in Rheme. In the original, the process *sees* is followed by two non-finite embedded clauses of expansion: *the seasons reversed* and *temperature and rainfall records broken almost every year*. These are replaced by paratactic finites in both simplified versions.

However, if the embedded expanding clause is finite, it tends to be retained. Table 2.10 provides such an example from Text 2 in which a finite embedded expanding clause is retained in both simplified versions. This type of defining relative clause appears early in general English teaching syllabi based on the Common European Framework of Reference for Languages (CEFRL) and would therefore probably not present major processing difficulty, especially as it defines the easy term *some of the largest wildfires*.

Table 2.10 Preservation of finite expansion

T2	Advanced Level	Intermediate Level	Elementary Level
23a	Arizonans were this week fighting some of the largest wildfires **they have known**,	Arizonans are fighting some of the largest wildfires **they have known**,	People in Arizona are fighting some of the largest wildfires **they have known**,

2.5.3 Simplifying hypotactic projection

The original texts include several cases of logical projections characterized by the introduction of witness and/or expert voices.

In Text 1, the instances of reporting with verbal processes are preserved at both intermediate and elementary level, albeit with omissions and the simplification of both lexis and grammar. Table 2.11 provides an example where the projection relation is preserved in the simplified versions although the projected clauses are shortened and subjected to major lexicogrammatical changes, particularly at elementary level.

In Text 2, on the other hand, the projection relation is retained less frequently than in Text 1. Of the eight instances of projection in Text 2, only one is retained at elementary level and three at intermediate level. Moreover, the instances that are retained are greatly reduced in length.

Both articles contain an instance of projection expressed experientially by means of an Angle circumstance. In Text 1, this instance of projection (*according to research by some of the world's leading water scientists*) is preserved at intermediate level but replaced at elementary level with a more straightforward logical expression which also involves a more frequently used verbal process (*say ... water scientists*). In Text 2, the projecting relation (*according to US meteorologist Jeff Masters, who co-founded leading climate tracker website Weather Underground*) is omitted in both simplified versions.

We have already noted that the voices of authority appear hyperthematically in the first clause complex of Text 1. In Text 2, on the other hand, the first voice of authority only appears in clause complex 8 and is therefore less central to its instantiation. Thus, omitting particularly complex projecting clauses altogether effectively simplifies Text 2 without affecting its coherence.

Table 2.11 Preservation of projection, with simplification

T1	Advanced Level	Intermediate Level	Elementary Level
10	**Adopting a vegetarian diet** is one option to increase the amount of water available to grow more food in an increasingly climate-erratic world, the scientists said.	**Changing to a vegetarian diet** is one way to increase the amount of water available to grow more food in a world where the climate is becoming increasingly erratic, the scientists said.	**Changing to a vegetarian diet** is one way to keep more water to grow food, the scientists said.

2.6 Omitting and simplifying Lexis

2.6.1 Lexical omission

Infrequently used words and expressions which may well exceed the vocabulary range of elementary and intermediate readers are omitted at both levels of simplification. Examples from Text 1 are *dire* in Table 2.1 and *leading* in Table 2.5. Examples from Text 2 are *equable* in Table 2.2 and *on the brink of bankruptcy* in Table 2.8.

2.6.2 Lexical change

Most lexical items that are simplified are words or expressions that are considered to be infrequently used according to dictionaries for learners of English. For instance, Longman's *Dictionary of Contemporary English* (2003) includes information on how frequently each lexical item is used. The codes S1 and W1 below indicate that a word is one of the 1,000 most commonly used words in spoken (S) or written (W) English, S2 and W2 indicate that it is one of the 2,000 most commonly used words, and S3 and W3 mean that it belongs to the 3,000 most frequently used words. Tables 2.12 and 2.13 illustrate some of these lexical changes, showing how the items selected for the simplified versions are systematically chosen from what are deemed to be more frequently used words or expressions.

26   *Analyzing the Media: A Systemic Functional Approach*

Table 2.12 Examples of lexical changes in Text 1

Advanced Level	*Intermediate Level*	*Elementary Level*
one of the sternest warnings yet	one of the strongest warnings ever	a very strong (S1 W1) warning
derive about 20%	get (S1 W1) about 20%	get (S1 W1) about 20%
option (S1 W2)	way (S1 W1)	way (S1 W1)

Table 2.12 above shows particularly interesting changes in Text 1 with the expression 'one of the sternest warnings yet' expressed as 'one of the strongest warnings ever' at intermediate level and 'a very strong warning' at elementary level. The change from *sternest* to *strongest* is due to the fact that *strong* is included among the most frequently used options (S1 W1). The whole superlative structure is simplified lexically at intermediate level not only by changing *sternest* to *strongest* but also by changing *yet* to *ever*. Finally, at elementary level, the superlative structure is changed to *a very strong warning*.

Table 2.13 Examples of lexical changes in Text 2

Advanced Level	*Intermediate Level*	*Elementary Level*
broke out	started (S2 W2)	started (S2 W2)
vast (S2 W2)	large (S1 W1)	large (S1 W1)
have been off the scale	have been much higher	have been much higher

Table 2.13 above shows relevant examples from Text 2, which include replacing the phrasal verb *broke out* by *started*, and changing the metaphorical expression *to be off the scale* to the more congruent expression *to be much higher*.

2.7 Conclusions

Our analysis shows that although simplifying articles involves making changes in grammar and lexis, the simplified versions preserve typical features of the news article genre, such as catchy headlines, the declarative mode for factual information and writer invisibility. The latter involves particularly the use of verbal processes attributed to participants who are the 'voices of authority'. In Text 1, these voices are kept in most instances, probably because the main voice of authority (leading water scientists) is identified in the first sentence of Text 1, making it part of the scaffolding of the whole text. Conversely, in Text 2, the first voice of authority is named only in clause complex 8, which may explain why voices of authority occur less frequently and are more often omitted.

Regarding the more detailed analysis of lexicogrammatical expressions in Theme position, simplification criteria mainly involve reducing experiential metaphor through unpacking or omitting nominalizations. This reduction in grammatical metaphor combines with a drift from hypotactic towards paratactic relations. For expressions in Rheme position, simplification criteria again involve a drift from hypotactic towards paratactic relations, combined with a drift from more abstract, non-finite clauses to more concrete, finite ones, thus reducing grammatical intricacy. Together with these changes in grammatical metaphor and grammatical intricacy, there are also changes in lexis. This involves going from more abstract metaphorical words and expressions to more concrete ones and replacing infrequently used words with more frequently used ones.

From a teaching perspective, the results illustrate a fundamental concept in Systemic Functional Linguistics: that of language as choice, both in grammar and in lexis. This can be exemplified in the classroom through a range of rewriting activities. Advanced students can be encouraged to select alternative linguistic expressions to express increasingly concrete or increasingly abstract meanings, as relevant, while at the same time respecting the fundamental genre characteristics of the news article.

About the authors

Ana María Coria teaches English Language and Reading Comprehension at the Universidad Nacional de La Plata, Facultad de Humanidades y Ciencias de la Educación. Her research interests are reading comprehension in second language, functional grammar, discourse analysis, genre studies and translation. She has taken part in several projects carried out in the frame of Systemic Functional Linguistics. As a Sworn Translator and Interpreter, she has worked in areas such as Law, Marketing and International Security.

María Cristina Spínola † taught English at advanced levels during many years at the Universidad Nacional de La Plata, Facultad de Humanidades y Ciencias de la Educación. She was an exceptional teacher and researcher, well loved by her students and her fellow colleagues. She unfortunately passed away in May 2016. She will always be remembered not only for her warmth, kindness and generosity but also for the excellence of her work in Systemic Functional Linguistics and literary stylistics.

Ann Montemayor-Borsinger has held professorial posts in several Argentinean universities in graduate and postgraduate programs in linguistics and discourse analysis. Her research interests focus on functional grammar, discourse analysis, genre studies, literary stylistics and translation. She has widely published, drawing on Systemic Functional Linguistics to investigate different types of discourse in English, Spanish and French. She has recently been appointed director of the research centre on Language and Literature Studies (LELLAE) at the National University of Rio Negro in Argentina.

References

Butt, D., Fahey, R., Feez, S., Spinks, S. & Yallop, C. (2003) *Using Functional Grammar. An Explorer's Guide.* Sydney: Macquarie University.

Christie, F. & Derewianka, B. (2008) *Learning to Write across the Years of Schooling.* London/New York: Continuum.

Christie, F. & Martin, J.R. (1997) *Genre and Institutions: Social Processes in the Workplace and School.* London/New York: Continuum.

Collins, Cobuild (1993) *Collins Cobuild English Grammar.* 5th edition. London/Glasgow: HarperCollins.

Eggins S. (2004) *An Introduction to Systemic Functional Linguistics.* London/New York: Continuum.

the Guardian (online) (2011-06-13) 'Warning: extreme weather ahead'. *the guardian.com*: https://www.theguardian.com/world/2011/jun/13/extreme-weather-flooding-droughts-fires

the Guardian (online) (2012-08-26) 'Food shortages could force world into vegetarianism, warn scientists'. *theguardian.com*: https://www.theguardian.com/global-development/2012/aug/26/food-shortages-world-vegetarianism

Halliday, M.A.K. (1985) *An Introduction to Functional Grammar.* London: Arnold.

Halliday, M.A.K. (1995 [2006]) 'Fuzzy grammatics'. In: Webster, J.J. (ed.) *Computational and Quantitative Studies. The Collected Works of M.A.K. Halliday.* Vol. 6. (2006) London/New York: Continuum, 213–238.

Halliday, M.A.K. & Matthiessen, C.M.I.M. (2004) *An Introduction to Functional Grammar.* 3rd edition. London: Arnold.

Halliday, M.A.K. & Matthiessen, C.M.I.M. (2014) *An Introduction to Functional Grammar.* 4th edition. London: Arnold.

Martin, J. (1992) *English Text: System and Structure.* Amsterdam/New York: John Benjamins.

Martin, J. & Rose, D. (2007) *Working with Discourse: Meaning beyond the Clause.* 2nd edition. London/New York: Continuum.

Martin, J. & Rose, D. (2008) *Genre Relations: Mapping Culture.* London/New York: Equinox.

Reah, D. (2002) *The Language of Newspapers.* London/New York: Routledge.

Rose, D. & Martin, J.R. (2012) *Learning to Write, Reading to Learn. Genre, Knowledge and Pedagogy in the Sydney School.* London/New York: Equinox.

van Dijk, T.A. (1983 [1996]) *La ciencia del texto.* Buenos Aires: Paidós.

3 Personalization as cultural practice: The interpersonal component of language in the opinion discourse of the British, German, and Italian quality press

Melanie Kerschner
Paris Lodron University Salzburg, Austria

3.1 Introduction

Michael Halliday views language from the perspective of three functions it has to serve: the ideational, the interpersonal and the textual metafunction. This chapter will expand on the second of these three metafunctions, the interpersonal, which helps us to enact and maintain our personal and social relationships and assigns different roles to participants in communication (cf. Feng & Liu 2010: 1). 'Through this function [...] social groups are delimited, and the individual is identified and reinforced, since by enabling him to interact with others language also serves in the expression and development of his own personality' (Halliday & Webster 2002: 175). Thus, apart from construing human experience, language is our main means of social interaction and it enables us to enact 'our personal and social relationships with the other people around us' (Halliday & Matthiessen 2014: 30). Interpersonal meaning can be expressed by the systems of mood and modality, but also, amongst other means, through particular use of the pronoun system (cf. Webster 2009: 7). In spoken or written discourse, people act in interpersonal exchanges in which they 'create meaning by exchanging symbols in shared contexts of situation' (Halliday 1984: 303). 'Systemic-functional grammar (SFG) [thus] seeks to identify the language-specific structures that contribute to the meaning of a text' (Webster 2009: 7). Among these language-specific structures that contribute to the interpersonal meaning of a text are the personal, the possessive and the reflexive pronouns.

The aim of this chapter is thus to explore exactly these 'patterns of interpersonal meaning-making' (Halliday & Matthiessen 2014: 42) in the form of pronouns in European editorial discourse. One linguistic tool in opinion discourse that has the potential to create 'a collective identity that includes the news site as well as the audience, thus aligning the site with the position of the reader' (Landert 2014: 199) is the use of the aforementioned personal, possessive and reflexive pronouns. After a brief introduction to personalization strategies in editorial discourse in general, this chapter will therefore focus on how personal pronouns are used strategically to convince the reader of the paper's point of view. It will then give an overview of the pronouns analyzed and their respective functions before discussing the detailed findings in each of the three news cultures to reveal the news-culture induced differences.

For the purpose of this analysis, 45 editorials from six national quality papers (i.e. the British *Guardian* and *Independent*, the German *Frankfurter Rundschau* and *Die Welt,* and the Italian *Corriere della Sera* and *La Stampa*) will be analyzed empirically for objectively measurable style differences in the linguistic realization of editorials dealing with the Snowden leaks, the ensuing NSA scandal and the more general debate about global surveillance.[1]

This thematic focus was chosen for three reasons: firstly, it is a hotly disputed and polarizing topic that has been dominating the European and the US media for quite some time; secondly, the related news events occurred outside the three countries in which the data were collected; and thirdly, each government in the three countries and each of the six newspapers analyzed have taken a different attitude towards the topic.

For several reasons, the genre of the editorial provides fertile ground for an empirical culture-contrastive analysis of interpersonal meaning making resources and personalization strategies in news discourse: firstly, editorials are opinion copy. This means they 'tend to state, often in an unvarnished form, what the paper claims to be the case at the present time; they also assert what should be the case, and they predict what will happen in the future'. (Morley 2004: 240)

In other words, opinions are explicitly stated, and ideally, the reader is supposed to be convinced by the text producer's reasoning. Secondly, what makes the genre of the editorial even more interesting is that the relationship between editorial writer and reader is often 'dual, and embodies a latent contradiction. On the one hand, the source [i.e. the author] claims the authority to explain an argument and to persuade the reader of its correctness. [...] Yet, on the other hand, the editorial claims solidarity by invoking consensus.' (Fowler 1991: 211–212)

Both the claiming of authority as well as the creation of a consensus between text producer and reader are achieved with the help of so-called 'personalization strategies' (see Section 2).

Two further complicating factors are the anonymity and the uni-directionality of mass media communication. In fact, newspaper editorials are directed at a large heterogeneous readership, and the main problem in identifying the actual audience is the lack of feedback from the recipients, which is generally a vital factor in communication. There are only two ways in which this feedback deficit can be overcome:

(a) through circulation figures and audience surveys (or, in case of online papers, the number of visitors to an online news site);
(b) through direct audience responses (i.e. online comments or letters to the editor). (cf. Landert & Jucker 2011: 1422–1423)

Since 'the audience exercise their main influence on the media just through being the audience – or by deciding to be someone else's audience' (Bell 1996: 87–88), and since news is a product that needs to be sold, identifying the actual audience and their political and social attitudes is of vital importance because readers will be more ready to accept an opinion if it corresponds with their own. It is thus the general aim of an editorial to give the reader the impression of a common consensus over the news event addressed (cf. Fowler 1991: 57).

In addition, the cultural dependency of editorials and their influence on public opinion make them the ideal object of research for a culture-contrastive analysis of personalization strategies in different news cultures. Indeed, editorials 'perhaps more than any other type of writing, reflect national styles regarding modes of styles […]. Good editorials are considered some of the best examples of persuasive writing in all countries; they set standards for written persuasion'. (Connor 1996: 143–144)

3.2 Personalization strategies in editorial discourse

While the personalizing potential of reader interaction is indisputable, personalization does not only play a key role with respect to the audience but is a general feature of news discourse to bridge the 'discursive gap' (Fowler 1991: 47) between text producers and readers. Landert (2014: 35) provides a concise overview of the dimensions and features of personalization. According to Landert, 'personalization' is

> the foregrounding of persons who are part of any of the three entities of mass media communication. If news actors – i.e. individuals appearing in the news, such as decision makers, witnesses and individuals who are directly affected by a news event – are given a high presence, this personalizes the news event. If readers are given a high presence, this means that the audience is personalized. Finally, if journalists, correspondents and news organizations are given a high presence in mass media publications, this amounts to the personalization of text producers. These three forms of personalization are not mutually exclusive; indeed, strong personalization of several entities can often be observed in the same text. (Landert 2014: 9)

Irrespective of which entity is given most prominence, the degree of abstraction or concreteness has to be determined. On the personal end of the scale, news actors, recipients and text producers can be portrayed on a highly personalized level, such as victims recounting their personal experiences, critical readers expressing their thoughts in online comments or letters to the editor, and columnists retelling their private experiences. On the abstract end of the scale, the three entities are portrayed as anonymous masses and abstract media organizations. (cf. Landert 2014: 10)

Apart from the three entities of mass media communication (i.e. text producers, news actors and readers) and the degree of personalization, the level on which personalization takes place is decisive. According to Landert (2014: 35), personalization can take place in the communicative setting, on the content level and on the level of the linguistic realization.

All features of personalization can be classified within these three dichotomies. In a culture-contrastive study of editorials, the genre of the editorial and its conventions constitute the framework of the communicative setting. On the content level, questions may be asked, such as whether the news event that is being addressed involves the reader in any sense. With respect to the linguistic realization of the news event, personal, possessive and reflexive pronouns are one linguistic tool to create a common consensus among the readership on the issue addressed. (cf. Landert 2014: 199)

The choice of pronoun (1st or 2nd person, singular or plural), the discourse participant(s) it refers to and its occurrence in or outside of direct speech determine the personalizing effect (cf. Landert 2014: 200). The 1st person singular unquestionably refers to the text producer, i.e. the editorial writer, whereas 1st person plural *we* may either be 'inclusive' (i.e. including the reader) or 'exclusive' (e.g. denoting the editorial board). In addition, the vague use of 1st and 2nd plural pronouns, i.e. *we* and *you*, can further be used in a collective sense. A typical example is the 'patriotic *we*' referring to the reader as part of a specific nation, e.g. *the British people*, *Europe*, etc. (cf. Landert 2014: 200–203)

Descriptions of the effects of these modes of address are manifold. In essence, three major effects of the 'inclusive *we*' are relevant for editorial discourse:

(a) the establishment of a pseudo-relationship between text producer(s) and reader(s), which is summed up by Fairclough (2001:195) as the concept of 'synthetic personalization', i.e. the simulation of solidarity with an anonymous mass audience by relating 'to members of [the] audience as individuals who share large areas of common ground' (Fairclough 2001:195);

(b) a shared perspective on the news event addressed, which falls under the concept of the 'ideology of consensus'. When describing the effect of personal pronouns in public discourse, Fowler (1991: 47–49) claims that '[c]onsensus assumes that, for a given grouping of people, it is a matter of fact that the interests of the whole population are undivided [...] [and they acknowledge] this "fact" by subscribing to a certain set of beliefs' (Fowler 1991: 49). The discursive gap can thus be bridged using personal or possessive pronouns (*we*, *our nation*, *our economy*) and positing ideas and values as matter-of-fact interests of the whole population;

(c) the creation of an ingroup and an outgroup through positive self-presentation and simultaneous negative other-presentation, which is achieved by creating dichotomies. Juxtaposed with the 3rd person pronouns *they/their*, the inclusive 1st person pronouns *we* and *our* effectively create a positive ingroup and a negatively connoted outgroup – a strategy which van Dijk (1998: 32–33) calls 'ideological squaring'. While the positive characteristics and social activities of the ingroup are being emphasized and the negative ones are de-emphasized, the author stresses the negative characteristics and actions of the outgroup and mitigates the positive ones at the same time. (cf. van Dijk 1998: 32–33; Richardson 2007: 47–54)

3.3 Empirical analysis

3.3.1 Research questions

Although the effects discussed in Section 2 can generally be observed in fact-based news discourse as well, opinion genres, such as columns and editorials, display a considerably higher frequency of unmediated 1st and 2nd person pronouns (i.e. pronouns that are put in the text by the journalist and are not quoted in direct speech). Evidently, the use of pronouns very much depends on the topic of the newspaper text and the genre. Landert's (2014: 213–214) findings on personalization strategies across different news genres suggest that the frequencies of unmediated pronouns in columns and in soft news are much more alike than in hard news articles. Her quantitative analysis revealed that 1st person singular pronouns occurred most often in soft news, while 1st person plural forms (i.e. 'inclusive' and 'exclusive *we*') were more frequent in columns than in soft news. 2nd person forms were found to be equally frequent in columns and soft news. Landert deduces from her empirical analysis that in columns the 1st person singular is primarily used for two reasons: firstly, to express the opinions of the text producers, and secondly, to recount their personal experiences and describe their feelings on the subject addressed (cf. Landert 2014: 237–239). In this context, the personal pronoun reinforces the argumentative strategy common to opinion-based news genres.

So far, it has been argued that 1st and 2nd person pronouns play a significant role in opinion-based news genres. In the following, it shall be shown what a cross-linguistic comparison of three different news cultures (i.e. the British, the German and the Italian) can reveal about the use of pronouns and their effect in editorials. In particular, there will be an exploration of the ways in which pronouns are predominantly used, as follows:

- for self-reference to the authors to express their opinion and describe personal experiences;
- as 'inclusive *we*' to show solidarity with the readership;
- as 'exclusive *we*' to stress the line of the editorial board and to explain their decision making;
- or for direct address of the audience to relate to the reader.

In addition, it shall be discussed which of the three news cultures exploits personal pronouns as a means to bridge the discursive gap the most and what effect this has on the general style of editorial writing.

3.3.2 Pronouns considered in the analysis

Table 3.1 gives an overview of all pronouns considered in the present analysis. These comprise 1st and 2nd person personal, possessive and reflexive pronouns in English, German and Italian. It has to be pointed out that due to the tendency of the Italian language to skip the personal pronoun if the pronoun is not being emphasized, Italian finite verbs in the 1st or 2nd person will also be taken into account. For the sake of simplicity, however, I will still use the term 'pronoun', which will subsume all personal, possessive and reflexive pronoun uses as well as Italian 1st and 2nd person finites. Furthermore, the marked forms of the Italian personal pronouns (e.g. *per me*, *per te*, etc.) are also included in the analysis.

3.3.3 Discussion of findings

Figure 3.1 and Table 3.2 show the frequencies of 1st and 2nd person pronouns per news culture. For the sake of comparability, the corpus length for each of the three news cultures was normalized to a text length of 15,000 words, i.e. 1,000 words per editorial. Therefore, a distinction has to be made between the normalized instances indicated in the figures and tables and the absolute instances, which are also included. The normalized frequencies in Figure 3.1 indicate that 46% of all 1st and 2nd person personal, possessive and reflexive pronouns (124 normalized instances) occur in the German editorials. Second in frequency are the pronouns in the Italian editorials with 37% (101 normalized instances). The British editorials contain only 17% of all pronouns (46 normalized instances). A closer look at the different kinds of pronouns, their distribution and their effects in the respective texts will give insight into their functions in the three corpora.

In essence, as argued above, the main function of 1st and 2nd person pronouns in the editorials appears to be to bridge the discursive gap and thus to demonstrate solidarity with the reader. This can be deduced from the fact that the 'inclusive we' makes up 76% of all pronoun instantiations and by far outnumbers the occurrences of the 1st person singular *I*, the 1st person plural 'exclusive *we*', and the 2nd person plural *you* (see Figure 3.2).

In comparison, the 1st person singular *I* (9%) and the 1st person plural 'exclusive *we*' (13%) are more similar in frequency. However, 'exclusive *we*' is restricted to the British and the Italian editorials of the corpus. In contrast, 2nd person plural *you* – intended as a direct address of the reader – turned out to be very rare (only 3%; i.e. 5 absolute instances).

38 *Analyzing the Media: A Systemic Functional Approach*

Table 3.1 1st and 2nd person personal, possessive and reflexive pronouns considered in the analysis

Person	*Personal pronoun (subject & object)*	*Possessive determiner Possessive pronoun*	*Reflexive pronoun*
	English		
1st sg.	*I, me*	*my, mine*	*myself*
1st pl.	*we, us*	*our, ours*	*ourselves*
2nd sg. & pl.	*you*	*you, yours*	*yourself/ yourselves*
	German		
1st sg.	*ich, mir, mich*	*mein*	*mir, mich*
1st pl.	*wir, uns*	*unser*	*uns*
2nd sg. & pl. (incl. polite form)	*du, dir, dich/Sie, Ihnen/ ihr, euch*	*dein/Ihr/euer*	*dir, dich/sich/ euch*
	Italian		
1st sg.	*io, mi, me*	*mio*	*mi*
1st pl.	*noi, ci*	*nostro*	*ci*
2nd sg. & pl. (incl. polite form)	*tu, ti, te/Lei, La, Le/ voi, vi*	*tuo/Suo/vostro, Vostro*	*ti/si/vi*

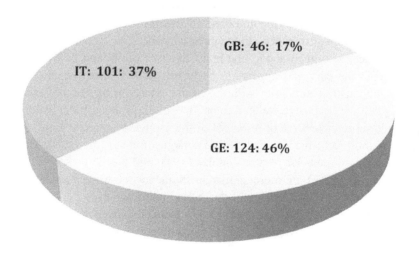

Figure 3.1 Overview of frequencies of 1st and 2nd person personal, possessive and reflexive pronouns per news culture (normalized to a text length of 1,000 words per editorial)

Table 3.2 Frequencies of 1st and 2nd person pronoun forms in all editorials, normalized and absolute

Form	GB norm.	GB abs.	GE norm.	GE abs.	IT norm.	IT abs.	TOTAL norm.	TOTAL abs.
1st p. sg. (*I, me, my, ...*)	0	0	13	11	10	8	23	19
1st p. plural (*inclusive we*)	22	13	111	93	73	56	206	162
1st p. plural (*exclusive we*)	24	14	0	0	10	8	34	22
2nd p. plural (*you, your, ...*)	0	0	0	0	7	5	7	5
TOTAL	46	27	124	104	100	77	270	**208**

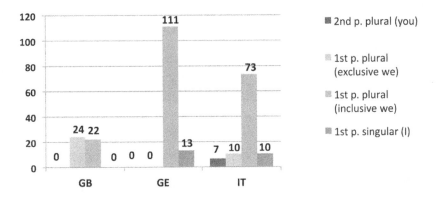

Figure 3.2 Detailed distribution of frequencies of 1st and 2nd person personal, possessive and reflexive pronouns ordered according to news culture (normalized to a text length of 1,000 words per editorial)

Furthermore, the 1st person singular pronoun *I* does not occur in the British editorials at all but only in the German and Italian ones. The majority of these occurrences, however, can be traced to two editorials which differ considerably from the rest of the data in terms of their content. In one of the two editorials, given in example 1, the journalist draws a comparison between the mass surveillance exercised by the NSA and his childhood experiences at a German boarding school, in which he uses ten absolute instances of self-reference in the form of 1st person singular pronouns:

(1) **Meine** Pubertät verbrachte **ich** in einem Internat. Ohne eigenes Zimmer. **Ich** ging mittags über die Felder, las und rezitierte, schrie hinaus, was **ich** dachte und zu denken erprobte. Sowie **ich** Leute sah, wurde **ich** ruhig, setzte **mich** irgendwohin, wo sie **mich** nicht sahen. Waren sie vorbeigezogen, legte **ich** wieder los. Leute sind heute immer dabei. Wir tragen sie mit uns. Sie hören uns zu, wenn wir lachen und wenn wir weinen. Sie belauschen unser Schweigen. Es gibt keinen unbeobachteten Raum mehr. Alles ist öffentlich. Das heißt auch: Nichts kann einfach mal ausprobiert werden. Alles ist ein möglicher Ernstfall. Da alles auch aufbewahrt wird, kann alles auch noch Jahrzehnte später gegen **mich** verwendet werden. So wird Freiheit vernichtet. So wird sie, schon bevor sie entstehen kann, erstickt. (G_FR_26.12.13)[2]

Translation: I spent **my** adolescence in a boarding school. Without a room of my own. At noon **I** wandered about the fields, read and recited, cried out what **I** was thinking or trying to think. As soon as **I** saw people passing by, **I** became silent, sat down somewhere where they could not see me. As soon as they had passed, **I** started again. People are always around nowadays. We are constantly accompanied by them. They keep listening to us, whether we are laughing or crying. They listen to our silence. There is no place to hide. Everything is public. This also implies that there is no room for experiments. Everything is a possible case of emergency. Since everything is being recorded, it can also be used against **me** decades later. In this way freedom is being destroyed. In this way, freedom is being suffocated long before it can develop.

In the second German editorial in which self-reference is employed it is used to point out which passage of one of Snowden's interviews was most relevant to the text producer. Again the personal dimension comes into play to relate more closely to the reader. This is in agreement with Landert's (2014: 237–239) observation that the 1st person singular pronoun takes on the function, amongst others, of describing personal experiences.

As shown in Figure 3.2, most personalization instantiations are expressed through the use of 'inclusive *we*', irrespective of the news culture. They account for 90% of all pronouns in the German corpus and 72% in the Italian corpus (see Figure 3.2). Especially in these two corpora, the 'inclusive *we*' is rather unevenly distributed, i.e. both corpora contain single editorials with an extremely high frequency rate (e.g. 31 absolute instances in one German editorial and 26 absolute instances in one Italian editorial). In the British corpus, singular 1st person pronouns and 2nd person pronouns do not occur at all. The British editorials also contain a considerably lower number of instances of the 'inclusive *we*' (i.e. only 22 normalized instances). Moreover, compared to the variety of functions this pronoun serves in the other two corpora, the British editorialists seem to use 'inclusive *we*' mainly, if not solely, in the sense of a 'patriotic *we*', i.e. as a vague reference with a collective meaning (e.g. '**our own** home secretary' (GB_GU_25.06.13), '**our own** security services' (GB_IN_21.08.13), '**our own** MPs and peers' (GB_GU_18.07.14)). This personalization strategy in matter-of-fact statements signals to the reader that as a proper British citizen one is expected to be of the same opinion as the text producer.

Apart from the function of a 'patriotic *we*', the direct address of the reader with 'inclusive *we*' serves a variety of different functions in the German and the Italian corpus. The function of ideological squaring is clearly visible in the nouns collocating with the possessive pronouns *unser* and *nostro* (i.e. 'our'). Both corpora tend to combine them with nouns denoting ethical values and legal concepts, such as *freedom*, *privacy*, *right*, *safety* and *life*, as shown in examples (2) to (5).

(2) **Unsere Freiheit** wird gefährdet durch die, die vorgeben, sie zu schützen – die Geheimdienste. (G_FR_10.12.13)
Translation: Our freedom is endangered by those who pretend to protect it – the secret services.

(3) **Unsere Sicherheit** wird gut verteidigt. (G_FR_18.01.15)
Translation: Our safety is well defended.

(4) È sacrosanto difendere fin dove è possibile **il nostro diritto alla riservatezza**: la privacy continua a far parte delle **nostre libertà essenziali**, anche nell'era del terrorismo, ma i limiti e i modi di proteggerla sono cambiati – e radicalmente – negli ultimi 15 anni. (I_COR_13.01.15)
Translation: The defence of **our right to privacy**, wherever possible, is sacrosanct: privacy continues to be part of **our essential liberties**, even in the age of terrorism, but the limits and modes to protect them have changed radically in the last 15 years.

(5) Mentre Assange ha rivelato segreti militari (una categoria che molti considerano legittima), Snowden dice al mondo che gli Stati Uniti entrano sistematicamente nelle **nostre case** e nella **nostra vita**. (I_COR_03.07.13)

Translation: While Assange has revealed military secrets (a category that most people consider legitimate), Snowden tells the world that the United States is systematically entering into **our houses** and **our lives**.

Quite frequently, these collocations are used as rhetorical devices to establish a positively connoted ingroup (*we*) and a negatively connoted outgroup (*them*). This so-called 'ideological square' (van Dijk 1998: 32–33) can be observed in example (6).

(6) Se **lo Stato** controlla la **nostra** vita. [...] Per questo è tanto più sorprendente che non ci sia nessuno che alza un sopracciglio, se invece è lo **Stato** a sapere tutto di **noi**: nello specifico, tutto sulle **nostre finanze**, e senza che **ci** abbia mai chiesto di acconsentire al trattamento dei dati. [...] Già oggi lo **Stato** può facilmente **farci** i conti in tasca: consumi, investimenti, debiti. (I_STA_26.03.15)
Translation: If **the government** controls **our life**. [...] It is thus all the more surprising that nobody raises an eyebrow if it is the government, in contrast, which knows everything about **us**: in particular everything about **our finances**, and this without having ever asked **us** for our consent for processing our personal data. [...] Nowadays the government can easily meddle in **our affairs**: purchases, investments, debts.

A less invasive way of persuading the reader of the paper's point of view is to use the 'inclusive *we*' to express directives. In example (7), the author expresses solidarity with the reader by stating necessities that need not only be fulfilled by the reader but, supposedly, also by the author:

(7) Ma **dovremmo** piuttosto **chiederci** se non sia giusto, nell'interesse dell'Europa e dei rapporti con gli Stati Uniti, che qualcuno manifesti finalmente il suo disappunto. (I_COR_11.07.14)
Translation: But **we rather need to ask ourselves** if it is not in the interest of Europe and of the relationship with the US that somebody finally shows his disappointment.

A similar use of the 'inclusive *we*' with a slight difference in tone and meaning can be observed in the German editorials. By pointing out popular misconceptions seemingly shared by the author and the reader, the author indirectly tells the reader what to believe and what to doubt. Consider example (8):

(8) Schließlich glauben **wir** ja, dass diese Überwachung **uns** nicht gefährdet, **wir** können ja frei reisen und konsumieren, wie es **uns** gefällt. (G_FR_24.10.13)
Translation: After all, **we** believe that this surveillance does not put **us** in any danger. **We** can still travel and consume without restrictions, as **we** like.

Looking at the overall distribution of 1st and 2nd person pronouns across the three news cultures, it becomes apparent that the 'inclusive *we*' is not only the most frequently used pronoun but that it is also the only pronoun that occurs in each of the three corpora. Use of the 'exclusive *we*' is restricted to the British and the Italian editorials. Its omission in the German editorials can perhaps be explained with the high prevalence of 'inclusive *we*'. A high frequency of both 'inclusive' and 'exclusive *we*' in the same journalistic text would be counter-productive, given the fact that 'inclusive *we*' tries to form a bond between the reader and the writer, whereas 'exclusive *we*' stresses the differences between the two or refers to the editorial board specifically without including the reader.

In the British corpus, the exclusive *we* is the most frequently used pronoun (52% of all British pronouns; see Figure 3.2). A look at the overall distribution of this pronoun across the news cultures shows that 71% of all (normalized) instances occur in the British editorials. In order to interpret these findings, the main functions of 'exclusive *we*' in the British corpus need to be investigated more closely. Quite often it is employed to refer to articles published earlier in the same newspaper, as example (9) illustrates:

(9) In print and online on Saturday, **we** [i.e. the editorial board of the *Guardian*] publish the fruits of more than seven hours of interviews with the former NSA contractor, a technical expert who has worked on the inside of the biggest intelligence agencies in the western world. (GB_GU_18.07.14)

3.4 Conclusion

In summary, the corpus analysis of editorials from three different news cultures has revealed that German editorial writers use *I* and 'inclusive *we*' most frequently to show solidarity with their readers, followed by Italian editorial writers. The British seem to keep more personal distance by abstracting the individual reader to the whole nation through the use of the 'patriotic *we*'. More often, however, they describe the beliefs, actions and work ethics of their own journal using the 'exclusive *we*'.

The findings confirm that 1st and 2nd person pronouns do play a significant role in personalizing editorials by creating a collective identity and a shared perspective on the news event. There are undoubtedly additional relevant 'patterns of interpersonal meaning-making' (Halliday & Matthiessen 2014: 42) which provide the genre of the editorial with a distinctive voice and a persuasive tone and which call for a closer investigation. Furthermore, the analysis of news-culture induced style differences needs to be taken a step further, e.g. by examining opinion discourse across cultures from different angles (e.g. from the perspective of the text producers, the readers, and the news actors). These differences would need to be systematically classified and contextualized in a model of editorial discourse which makes the stylistic differences between news cultures measurable and comparable. This aim of uniting a theoretical framework with a series of analytical tools to determine the role of news culture in the writer-reader relationship has been taken on in Kerschner (2017) *Fifty Shades of Opinion: Culturally Induced Style Differences in the Opinion Discourse of British, Italian and German Quality Papers*.

About the author

Melanie Kerschner has been a lecturer in the Department of English and American Studies of the University of Salzburg, where she also studied English and Italian. After finishing her PhD (on the role of news culture in the opinion discourse of British, German and Italian quality papers), she started teaching at the Pädagogische Hochschule Oberösterreich (Linz, Austria) and at the Zentrum für Fachsprachen und Interkulturelle Kommunikation at the Johannes Kepler University of Linz (Austria). Her research interests lie primarily in corpus linguistics and media linguistics, particularly in the contrastive analysis of newspaper articles in diverging linguistic and sociocultural contexts. Further areas of interest include sociolinguistics, linguistic diversity among speakers with differing cultural backgrounds, language change in contact languages, and pidgin and creole studies. Her publications include the monographs *Laik vs. Klostu – Current and historical changes in Tok Pisin's time-mood-aspect system: the increasing complexity of Tok Pisin's TMA markers* (2012) and *Fifty Shades of Opinion: Culturally Induced Style Differences in the Opinion Discourse of British, Italian and German Quality Papers* (2017) as well as several articles on culture-induced style differences in press coverage and on personalization strategies in the news.

Notes

1. For the editorials analyzed, see Section 5.2.
2. Whenever one of the texts analyzed is quoted, only the abbreviation is indicated. All abbreviations follow the pattern XX_YY_DD.MM.YY, where XX stands for the country, YY for the newspaper, and the rest for the date of publication. All texts are listed with their abbreviations in the References section.

References

Bell, A. (1996) *The Language of News Media.* Oxford/Cambridge, MA: Blackwell.

Connor, U. (1996) *Contrastive Rhetoric.* Cambridge/New York: Cambridge University Press.

Fairclough, N. (2001) *Language and Power.* Harlow: Longman.

Feng, H. & Liu, Y. (2010) 'Analysis of interpersonal meaning in public speeches: A case study of Obama's speech'. *Journal of Language Teaching and Research* 6(1), 825–829.

Fowler, R. (1991) *Language in the News.* London/New York: Routledge.

Halliday, M.A.K. (1984) 'On the ineffability of grammatical categories'. In: Webster, J.J. (ed.) *On grammar. The collected works of M.A.K. Halliday.* Vol. 1. London/New York: Continuum, 291–322.

Halliday, M.A.K. & Matthiessen, C.M.I.M. (2014) *Halliday's Introduction to Functional Grammar.* London/New York: Routledge.

Halliday, M.A.K. & Webster, J.J. (2002) *On Grammar.* London: Continuum.

Halliday, M.A.K. & Webster, J.J. (eds.) (2009) *Continuum Companion to Systemic Functional Linguistics.* London/New York: Continuum.

Kerschner, M.A. (2011) *Laik vs. Klostu: Current and Historical Changes in Tok Pisin's Time-Mood-Aspect System: The Increasing Complexity of Tok Pisin's TMA Markers.* Oakland: University of Papua New Guinea Press/Masalai Press.

Kerschner, M.A. (2014) 'One story – three languages – a hundred opinions: Culturally induced style differences in the opinion discourse of British, Italian and German quality papers'. *Moderne Sprachen* 58, 69–94.

Kerschner, M.A. (2017) '"Let us hope that it is": Personalisierungsstrategien in deutschen, britischen und italienischen Leitartikeln'. In: Bilut-Homplewicz, Z., Hanus, A., Lüger,H.-H. & Mac, A. (eds.) *Medienlinguistik und interdisziplinäre Forschung II: Kontrastive Ansätze im medial geprägten Kontext: Studien zur Text- und Diskursforschung.* Frankfurt: Peter Lang, 171–188.

Kerschner, M.A. (2017) 'Zum Einfluss der Medienkultur in europäischen Zeitungen: Vorschlag eines Modells zur kultur-kontrastiven Analyse von Leitartikeln'. In: Lenk, H. & Giessen, H.W. (eds.) *Persuasionsstile in Europa III: Linguistische Methoden zur vergleichenden Analyse von Kommentartexten in Tageszeitungen europäischer Länder.* Hildesheim: Georg Olms, 205–223.

Kerschner, M.A. (2017) *Fifty Shades of Opinion: Culturally Induced Style Differences in the Opinion Discourse of British, Italian and German Quality Papers.* Vienna: Praesens.

Landert, D. (2014) *Personalisation in Mass Media Communication: British Online News between Public and Private.* Amsterdam: John Benjamins.

Landert, D. & Jucker, A.H. (2011) 'Private and public in mass media communication: From letters to the editor to online commentaries'. *Journal of Pragmatics* 43(5), 1422–1434.

Morley, J. (2004) 'The Sting in the tail'. In: Partington, A., Morley, J. & Haarman, L. (eds.) *Corpora and Discourse.* Bern/New York: Peter Lang, 239–255.

Richardson, J.E. (2007) *Analysing Newspapers.* Basingstoke/New York: Palgrave Macmillan.

van Dijk, T.A. (1998) 'Opinions and ideologies in the press'. In: Bell, A. & Garrett, P. (eds.) *Approaches to Media Discourse.* Oxford/Malden: Blackwell, 21–63.

Webster, J.J. (2009). 'An introduction to continuum companion to systemic functional linguistics'. In: Halliday, M.A.K. & Webster, J.J. (eds.) *Continuum Companion to Systemic Functional Linguistics.* London/New York: Continuum, 1–11.

News texts analyzed

Funk, V. (2013, Oct. 24) 'Danke dafür, NSA!: Eine nützliche Affäre'. *Frankfurter Rundschau.* http://www.fr-online.de/datenschutz/ leitartikel-abhoeraffaere-danke-dafuer – nsa – eine-nuetzliche-affaere,1472644,24771070.html [05.05.2015] (G_FR_24.10.13)

Funk, V. (2013, Nov. 11) 'Gefährliche Beschützer'. *Frankfurter Rundschau.* http://www.fr-online.de/datenschutz/leitartikel-zur-nsa-affaere-gefaehrliche-beschuetzer,1472644,25583896.html [05.05.2015] (G_FR_10.12.13)

Gaggi, M. (2015, Jan. 13) 'Il confine tra diritti e sicurezza'. *Corriere della Sera*. http://www.corriere.it/editoriali/15_gennaio_13/confine-diritti-sicurezza-cd3707bc-9ae8-11e4-bf95-3f0a8339dd35.shtml [05.05.2015] (I_COR_13.01.15)

Guardian Media Group (2013, Jun. 25) 'Edward Snowden: in defence of whistleblowers'. *The Guardian*. https://www.theguardian.com/commentisfree/2013/jun/25/editorial-edward-snowden-history [05.05.2015] (GB_GU_25.06.13)

Guardian Media Group (2014, Jul. 18) 'The Guardian view on Edward Snowden's challenges for society'. *The Guardian*. https://www.theguardian.com/commentisfree/2014/jul/18/guardian-view-edward-snowden-challenges-society [05.05.2015] (GB_GU_18.07.14)

Haufler, D. (2015, Jan. 18) 'Im Reich der Paranoia'. *Frankfurter Rundschau*. http://www.fr-online.de/leitartikel/vorratsdatenspeicherung-im-reich-der-paranoia,29607566,29601686.html [05.05.2015] (G_FR_18.01.15)

Independent Voices (2013, Aug. 21) 'Whether or not you support the Snowden leaks, what has happened since is disquieting'. *Independent*. http://www.independent.co.uk/voices/editorials/whether-or-not-you-support-the-snowden-leaks-what-has-happened-since-is-disquieting-8778399.html [05.05.2015] (GB_IN_21.08.13)

Mingardi, A. (2015, Mar. 26) 'Se lo Stato controlla la nostra vita'. *La Stampa*. http://www.lastampa.it/2015/03/26/cultura/opinioni/editoriali/se-lo-stato-controlla-la-nostra-vita-nMvbatDLiSyh3AklchltxO/pagina.html [05.05.2015] (I_STA_26.03.15)

Romano, S. (2014, Jul. 11) 'Una candida arroganza'. *Corriere della Sera*. http://www.corriere.it/editoriali/14_luglio_11/candida-arroganza-d688464e-08b9-11e4-89ec-c067e3a232ce.shtml [05.05.2015] (I_COR_11.07.14)

Widmann, A. (2013, Dec. 26) 'Edward Snowden hat Recht'. *Frankfurter Rundschau*. http://www.fr-online.de/datenschutz/leitartikel-zur-abhoeraffaere – edward-snowden-hat-recht,1472644,25732588.html [05.05.2015] (G_FR_26.12.13)

4 Generic structures, rhetorical relations and thematic patterns in English and Spanish journalistic texts: A comparative study

Julia Lavid-López and Lara Moratón Gutiérrez
Instituto Universitario de Lenguas Modernas y Traductores (UCM) at Universidad Complutense de Madrid, Spain

4.1 Introduction

In spite of the increasing interest in discourse features, such as generic, rhetorical and thematic structures in different language domains, and the consolidated strand of research on media discourse, in general, and journalistic discourse, in particular, much work remains to be done on the cross-generic and cross-linguistic characterization of different newspaper genres in terms of these discourse features. In fact, although there are a number of studies contrasting different newspaper genres across languages and cultures (e.g. Van Dijk 1988; Wang 2007; Hauser 2012; Ansary & Babaii 2009; Lee 2011) and although some previous studies have also demonstrated the role of thematic choices as signals of the generic organization of texts (see Lavid et al. 2010a, 2013; Lavid et al. 2010b: Chapter 5), there are, to our knowledge, no studies which examine the correlations between genre, thematic progression and rhetorical relations in different newspaper genres.

The aim of this chapter is to advance knowledge in this area by focusing on the generic organization, the thematic progression and the rhetorical structures which characterize three well-known newspaper genres – News Reports, Editorials and Letters to the editor – in two different discourse communities: the British and the European Spanish. In particular, we will answer these three research questions:

1 Is it possible to characterize journalistic texts (i.e. News Reports, Editorials, and Letters to the editor) in generic terms? What types of generic structures or 'moves' characterize these three genres in English and Spanish?
2 In what ways are rhetorical and thematic patterns distributed in these texts?
3 Are there any correlations between generic structures, rhetorical relations and thematic patterns in these genres?

In so doing, we hope to contribute to the consolidated strand of research on journalistic discourse, in general, and from a systemic-functional perspective, in particular.

The chapter is organized as follows: Section 4.1 presents the main research questions underlying our work; Sections 4.2 and 4.3 describe the data, the methodology applied in our analysis and the main theoretical concepts used in the study; Section 4.4 discusses the results of the qualitative and the quantitative analyses. Finally, Section 4.5 provides a summary and some concluding remarks.

4.2 Data

The data for analysis consists of a bilingual comparable corpus of a total of fifty-two texts, comprising sixteen News Reports, sixteen Editorials and twenty Letters to the editor, evenly divided into English and Spanish. White (1998: 243) defines News Reports as 'grounded in communicative events such as speeches, interviews and press releases', which 'act primarily to represent, not activity sequences, but the points of view of various external sources'. In contrast, Editorials belong to a class of argumentative texts where views are expressed by either an editorial team or by a journalist. Their communicative function within the larger context of newspaper coverage is similar to that of commentaries, i.e. 'to offer newspaper readers a distinctive and sometimes authoritative voice that speaks to the public directly about matters of public importance' (Wang 2008: 170). Letters to the editor represent a more personal type of argumentation, often written in first person, and they are usually subjective and passionate. All the texts were randomly collected from British and Spanish high-circulation newspapers between 2009 and 2013. The English texts were extracted from the three British online newspapers *Times online,* the *Independent* and the *Telegraph,* while the Spanish texts were gathered at random from the online versions of the three high-circulation Spanish newspapers *El País, El Mundo* and *La Vanguardia*.

4.3 Methodology for analysis

We used several analytical tools for the study. For the analysis of the generic (global) structures, we relied on Halliday and Hasan's concept of 'Generic Structure Potential' (Halliday & Hasan 1989; Yu 2001), and Martin and colleagues' definition of genre as a reflection of the goal-oriented aspect of the text (Martin 1984; Martin et al. 1987; Eggins & Martin 1997) and its characterization into 'generic stages' or 'moves' (Swales 1990, 2004; Nwogu 1997: 123–124; Skelton 1994: 455–456). According to the latter scholars, 'moves' are defined as 'discoursal or rhetorical units that perform a coherent communicative function in a written or spoken discourse' (Swales 2004: 228) and are identified by 'text segment[s] made up of a bundle of linguistic features (lexical meaning, propositional meanings, illocutionary force, etc.) which give the segment a uniform orientation and signal the content of discourse in it' (Nwogu 1997:122).

The generic structure analysis of the texts was carried out following some of the steps proposed by Eggins & Slade (1997), namely:

(a) defining the social purpose of the genre,
(b) identifying and defining the stages or 'moves' within a genre,
(c) specifying the obligatory and optional stages/moves, and
(d) devising a structural formula to describe the genre.

For the identification and definition of the stages or 'moves' in each genre, the characteristic distribution of the rhetorical relations and some of the thematic patterns were used as linguistic signals or evidence for the generic structure. This was done on the basis of previous studies which have either hypothesized (Fries 1995: 319) or empirically demonstrated the functional role of Themes in discourse, i.e. the signalling of new phases in the discourse (Martin & Rose 2003:179; Lavid et al. 2010a: Chapter 5).

For the rhetorical structure analysis, we used the original version of Rhetorical Structure Theory, henceforth RST (Mann & Thompson 1988), as well as White's notion of rhetorical potential, which he analyzed in News Reports (White 1998: 265).

In addition, the three newspaper genres were examined in terms of the notion of Thematic Progression (TP), originally developed by Daneš (1974), and extensions and reformulations thereof (e.g. Dubois 1987; Eggins 2004). Some of the revisions made to these four types of TP patters is that made by Dubois, who reduced Daneš' four types to two, one themic the other rhemic, each of which may be simple or multiple, contiguous or gapped. In the Rhemic TP pattern (including the Simple Linear Progression and the Split Rheme Progression), the Themes of subsequent clauses derive from the Rhemes of the previous ones. In the Themic TP pattern (including the Constant Progression and the Derived Hyperthematic Progression), the Themes of subsequent clauses derive either from previous Themes or from a more general 'Hypertheme'. The TP patterns used in our analysis are schematically presented in Figure 4.1 to Figure 4.4 below.

Simple linear progression (Figure 4.1): Elements introduced as New information in the Rheme of the first clause are retrieved as the Theme of the second clause. This can be represented schematically as follows:

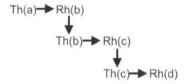

Figure 4.1 Simple linear progression

Split Rheme progression (Figure 4.2): Here the large Rheme of the first clause, consisting of two smaller Rhemes, is picked up again in the two Themes of the second clause:

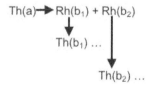

Figure 4.2 Split Rheme progression

Constant progression (Figure 4.3): In this pattern, the same Theme is maintained in the following clauses, creating a continuous reference chain:

Figure 4.3 Constant progression

Derived Hyperthematic Progression (Figure 4.4): The different Themes of a number of Theme–Rheme structures are all related to a 'Hypertheme' or 'Global Topic':

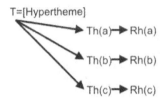

Figure 4.4 Derived Hyperthematic Progression

For our analysis, we first segmented all texts into clause complexes which we used as the basic units of analysis for quantitative purposes. We then carried out a thematic analysis in order to identify the Thematic and the Rhematic fields, following the model of thematization for English and Spanish proposed by Lavid (Lavid et al. 2010: Chapter 5). The Thematic field in this model includes the clause-initial material from the beginning of the clause complex up to and including the first nuclear experiential constituent in the main clause. The identification of the Thematic field in each clause complex formed the basis for the analysis of the TP patterns in the subsequent step. The characteristic distribution of Themes and TP patterns helped identify the different generic stages or moves in each text since in many cases they acted as signals of transition between moves. Generic stages or moves were considered 'common' if they appeared in over half of the texts in each newspaper genre; this value is in line with that used by Nwogu (1997: 124) and was chosen for comparative purposes. An RST analysis of each text ensued, and the distribution of the different patterns was subjected to a statistical analysis in order to compare the results across the three genres and the two languages.

54   *Analyzing the Media: A Systemic Functional Approach*

4.4 Results

In this section we will present the results of the generic structure, rhetorical relations and thematic progression analysis of each of the three newspaper genres in English and Spanish. Section 4.4.1 will begin with the analysis of the News Reports, followed by the analysis of Editorials in Section 4.4.2. Finally, Section 4.4.3 will focus on Letters to the editor. An overall contrastive discussion will be given in the final Section 4.5.

4.4.1 News Reports

The generic structure of News Reports (Figure 4.5) consists of three Moves. Move 0 corresponds to the Headline, as illustrated in examples (1) and (2) below:

(1) OPEC hawks want to cut oil production to keep up price
(2) Barclays recibe 9.200 millones de fondos soberanos para evitar acudir al fondo de Brown
    [translation: Barclays receives 9200 millions of state funds to avoid calling Browns' funds]

The rhetorical structure of News Reports is characterized by an orbital structure (White 1998) where satellites refer back to the points in the nucleus (Headline and Lead) in the form of 'elaboration'. As example (3)

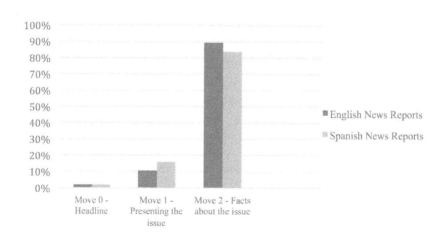

Figure 4.5 Generic structure of News Reports (English and Spanish)

Generic structures, rhetorical relations and thematic patterns 55

shows, the Headline (3a) is elaborated by different satellites that clarify and give more information on it (3b and 3c):

(3)
    a) Dominique Strauss-Kahn, head of the IMF, escapes dismissal over affair
    b) Dominique Strauss-Kam, the French head of the International Monetary Fund, escaped dismissal for a one-night stand with a subordinate today, but was denounced by board members for a 'serious error of judgment'.
    c) But his reputation took a battering in the statement by the IMF board, which said the relationship 'was regrettable and reflected a serious error of judgment on the part of the managing director'.

This genre also contains a high number of 'attribution relations' (signalled through quotes, dashes and verbal processes). This is demonstrated in example (4):

(4)
    a) Shakour Shaalan, the fund's executive director, said IMF staff, and notably female staff, 'are not at all happy' with Mr Strauss-Kahn, whose amorous adventures in France have earned him the epithet le grand seducteur.
    b) 'The managing director has expressed his regrets. I don't think that we can ask him to do more at this time,' said Mr Shaalan. 'We will continue to work with him.'

Figure 4.6 displays the RST structure graphically:

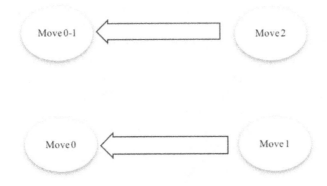

Figure 4.6 Rhetorical structure of News Reports (English and Spanish)

Finally, in terms of the Thematic organization, Headlines (Move 0) in News Reports are explicative and encapsulate the thematic and rhematic information of the report, thereby acting as 'Hyperthemes'. In Move 1, the typical progression is a Constant Themic pattern, whereas in Move 2, the typical thematic pattern is formed by Gapped Themes (where a theme is picked from another theme that does not immediately preceed it) or New Themes, plus some Linear Themes in Spanish. This thematic organization is displayed in Figure 4.7:

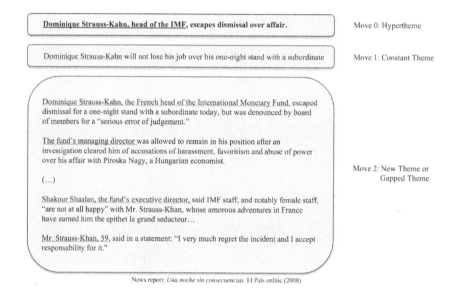

Figure 4.7 TP patterns and Moves in a Spanish News Report

The English text and the Spanish text in Figure 4.8 illustrate how the Headlines encapsulate and summarize the thematic and rhematic information of the report and act as Hyperthemes for the rest of the Themes in the texts. In both the English and the Spanish text, Move 1 (Lead) uses the Constant Themic pattern. The same pattern is also used in Move 2 in the English texts, whereas the Spanish texts combine both the Constant and the Linear pattern.

A summary of the generic structures (i.e. moves), rhetorical structures and TP patterns is displayed in Figure 4.9.

Generic structures, rhetorical relations and thematic patterns 57

Barclays rejects government funding, secures £5.8b from Qatar and Abu Dhabi	Move 0: Hypertheme
Barclays is to raise £7.3 billion from investors after securing a £5.8 billion cash injection...	Move 1: Constant Theme
The bank announced this morning that …(…) It will raise Barclays is to raise £7.3 billion from …(…)	Move 2: Constant Theme

News report: *Barclays rejects government funding (…).* Times online (2008)

Barclays recibe 9.200 millones de fondos soberanos para evitar acudir al fondo de Brown [Barclays receives 9.2 billion sovereign funds to avoid going to Brown's fund]	Move 0: Hypertheme
La entidad pasará a estar controlada en un 30% por los inversores del Golfo [The entity will be controlled in 30% by Gulf investors]	Move 1: Constant Theme
El Barclays recurrirá en su mayor parte a inversores del Golfo Pérsico para llevar a cabo una ampliación de capital de hasta 7.300 millones de libras…(…) [Barclays will resort mostly to investors from the Persian Gulf to carry out a capital increase of up to 7.3 billion pounds ... (…)] La entidad emitirá 3.000 millones de libras…(…) [The entity will issue 3,000 million pounds ... (…)] De esta segunda cantidad 2.800 millones de libras (3.567 millones de euros) irán a esos fondos del Golfo Pérsico y otros 1.500 millones de libras (1.910 millones de euros) a actuales accionistas e inversores institucionales. [Of this second amount 2,800 million pounds (3,567 million euros) will go to those funds of the Persian Gulf and another 1,500 million pounds (1,910 million euros) to current shareholders and institutional investors.]	Move 2: Constant and Linear Theme

News report: *Barclays recibe 9.200 millones de fondos soberanos (…).* El País online (2008)

Figure 4.8 TP patterns and Moves in an English and a Spanish News Report

GENERIC STRUCTURE	RHETORICAL STRUCTURE	TP PATTERNS
Move 0: Headline (explicative)	Nucleus	Hypertheme
Move 1: Presenting the issue	Nucleus (Restatement)	Constant Theme
Move 2: Facts about the issue	Elaboration	Gapped Themes, New Theme (Linear Themes in Spanish)

Figure 4.9 Summary of textual structures in News Reports

4.4.2 Editorials

In comparison to News Reports, the generic structure of Editorials tends to be longer and consists of four different Moves: Move 0 corresponds to the Headline, which tends to be short and metaphorical, usually with the aim of catching the reader's attention without disclosing the full content of the Editorial (i.e. The Vanishing Bomb). Move 1 develops and clarifies the topic of the Editorial and addresses the main issues to be dealt with in the rest of the Editorial. It is usually short in the English texts (5.40%) but considerably longer in the Spanish ones (16.51%).

Move 2 makes up the core of the Editorial where the author outlines the arguments. It is the longest move both in English (51.26%) and in Spanish (58.71%). It usually contains several sub-moves in which the editorialist presents and evaluates the arguments. These are not discussed one after the other but rather in a leapfrogging fashion with an exposition sub-move followed by an evaluation and then back again to exposing more arguments and evaluating them.

Move 3, finally, articulates the position of the author after finishing the exposition and the evaluation of facts. It takes up 43.32% of the total number of clause complexes in English Editorials and 24.77% of the total number of clause complexes in the Spanish ones. This distribution is graphically displayed in Figure 4.10.

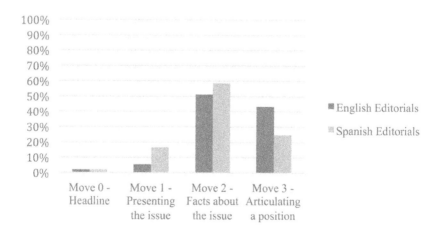

Figure 4.10 Generic structure of Editorials (English and Spanish)

Generic structures, rhetorical relations and thematic patterns 59

The standard rhetorical pattern in the analyzed Editorials in our bilingual sample consists of a nuclear schema (conveyed by the Headline) and two satellite spans: one satellite provides an *Elaboration*, i.e. the writer adds further detail and additional information relating to the Hypertheme, and the other provides a *Restatement*, i.e. in the last two units of the texts, the writer repeats the first part of the title and implies the second part.

As to the TP patterns occurring in this newspaper genre, Move 1 (Introducing the issue) usually acts as a Hypertheme, which is further elaborated on in the subsequent paragraphs. Move 2 (Outlining the arguments) is characterized by the use of Split and Derived Themes. Finally, Move 3 (Closing evaluation) wraps up the Editorial through Derived Themes. This distribution is illustrated by the English and Spanish examples displayed in Figures 4.11 and 4.12.

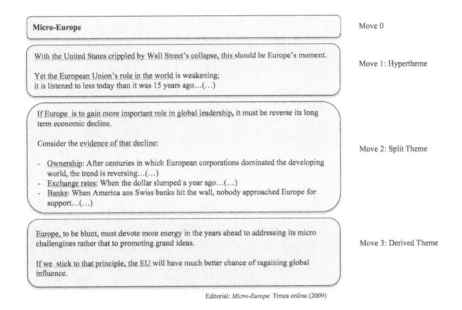

Figure 4.11 TP patterns and Moves in an English Editorial

> Outlining the argument: Move 2
>
> History could be profitably subdivided into eras defined by the prevailing prime movers.
>
> The longest span (from the first hominids to the domestications of draft animals) is made up of the age when human muscles were the only prime mover.
>
> Then came the addition of draft animals and gradual supplementation of animal prime movers by mechanical prime movers, such as sails and wheels, that capture natural energy flows.
>
> A fundamental break with this millenia-long pattern came only with... (...)
>
> During the 1830's, the first water turbines marked the beginning of the end of the waterwheel era.
>
> The next two key milestones came during the 1880's, ...(...)

Hypertheme: Derived Theme

Editorial: *The Limits of Energy Innovation*. Project syndicate (2009)

> La Ley de Partidos es una norma excepcional motivada por una situación que también lo es.
>
> [The Law of Parties is an exceptional rule motivated by a situation that is also.]
>
> Esa excepcionalidad implica dos riesgos principales: que se relativicen, en nombre de las razones de Estado, las exigencias propias del Estado...(...)
>
> [This exceptionality implies two main risks: that, in the name of State reasons, the State's own demands are relativized ... (...)]

Linear Theme

Editorial: *Equilibrio de poderes*. El País online (2009)

Figure 4.12 TP patterns and Moves in an English and a Spanish Editorial

4.4.3 Letters to the editor

The generic structure of Letters to the editor consists of four different Moves: Move 0 corresponds to the Headline, which is compact and metaphorical, often with no direct TP relation to the rest of the text (e.g. BBC inspires all classes); Move 1 introduces the issues, Move 2 outlines the arguments, and Move 3 contains the closing. Also, the generic structure of Letters to the editor is less stable and includes more sub-functions in the Spanish data (e.g. Making an appeal in the closing move).

This generic structure is shown in column 3 of Figure 4.13, which displays a contrastive illustration of the generic structures of the three newspaper genres analyzed in this chapter.

As for the rhetorical structures, Move 1 (Introducing the issue) functions as the Nucleus, while Move 2 provides Evaluations, and Move 3 consists of Restatements or Recommendations.

Generic structures, rhetorical relations and thematic patterns 61

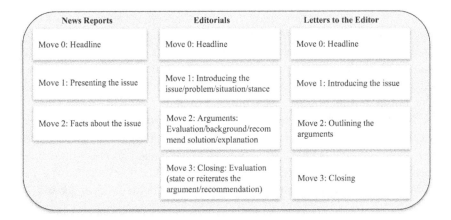

Figure 4.13 Comparison of generic structures in the three newspaper genres

GENERIC STRUCTURE	RHETORICAL STRUCTURE	TP PATTERNS
Move 0: Headline	-	-
Move 1: Introducing the issue / Pointing out the problem	Nucleus	New Theme
Move 2: Argument	Evaluation	New Theme
Move 3: Closing	Summing up arguments and/or making/restating recommendation/making an appeal	Constant Theme (English) Linear Themes (Spanish)

Figure 4.14 Summary of textual structures in Letters to the editor

In terms of TP patterns, Move 1 (Introducing the issue) is characterized by the presence of New Themes; in Move 2 (Outlining the arguments), New Themes introduce evaluations, and in Move 3 the typical pattern in the English texts is the Constant Thematic Progression, while the Spanish texts consist of Simple Linear Progression. These textual structures are displayed in Figure 4.14.

4.5 Discussion and concluding remarks

The analysis of the bilingual corpus of newspaper genres undertaken in this chapter has shown that it is possible to characterize these journalistic texts (i.e. News Reports, Editorials, and Letters to the editor) in generic terms.

Each genre exhibits characteristic generic structures consisting of different Moves which are usually similar in English and Spanish although some language-specific differences apply. Thus, for example, the last Move in the English Editorials (Articulating a position) is not always present in the Spanish data. As for the TP patterns, the Simple Linear progression pattern is more frequent in the Spanish data.

In addition to these findings, the thematic and rhetorical structures revealed in the contrastive analysis indicate that their distribution in these genres is not random but can be interpreted functionally as indicative of the genre under study and correlating with generic moves. The contrastive analysis showed that the patterns differ for each genre in the following ways:

- In News reports, the Headline encapsulates the information and acts as the text's Hypertheme. The Lead restates the Headline and, together with the Headline, conveys the nuclear schema of the RST structure. The rest of the text elaborates on this Nucleus.
- In Editorials, the Headline conveys the nuclear schema of the text, with two satellite spans: an Elaboration span functioning as the text's Hypertheme, and a Restatement span occurring in the last two units of the text.
- In Letters to the editor, the authors place their opinions in the Headline, expressing them in a subjective way as in: *A Disappointing Day for Democracy* or *Dangerous Ways to Raise Money*. Nuclear information is presented in Move 1, and Move 2 evaluates the information presented in the Nucleus. Move 3 usually restates information or makes an appeal.

We hope that the cross-linguistic and cross-generic analysis carried out in this chapter paves the way for further discourse studies on journalistic texts using some of the useful tools proposed in Systemic Functional Linguistics. As shown in the chapter, the combined use of generic structure analysis, thematic progression analysis and rhetorical structure analysis has proved to be illuminating in the investigation of these three newspaper genres in English and Spanish. It would be interesting to explore whether similar patterns occur in other genres and other discourse communities. In our future work, we will provide more detailed rhetorical analyses of such texts, and we will develop reliable annotation guidelines for the large-scale annotation of English and Spanish newspaper texts.

About the authors

Julia Lavid-López has been Full Professor of English Linguistics at Universidad Complutense de Madrid (UCM) since 2006, where she has developed an outstanding academic career as researcher, instructor, faculty member and as Chair of the department of English Philology I (2010–2014). She has recently been elected Director of the Research Institute for Modern Languages and Translation (IULMYT) at UCM. She has also developed an international career in the USA as invited visiting scholar at the ISI (Information Sciences Institute, USC) and in Europe through her research stays and collaboration in multiple projects and research-networks funded by the European Commission and other European funding bodies. Her research covers a wide range of topics related to the functional analysis of English (often in comparison with Spanish and other European languages) and frequently applies computational and corpus-based methodologies. She has an extensive list of high-impact publications including eight books and more than one hundred articles published in international journals or as book chapters in international collective volumes. She has also been the principal investigator in multiple research projects funded by national and international institutions and is currently the Research Director of the FUNCAP research group at Universidad Complutense with external collaborations with research groups in Europe, Canada and the USA. She also functioned as co-editor-in-chief of the *Complutense Journal of English Studies* (Estudios Ingleses de la Universidad Complutense) between 2005 and 2015, and she has been member of the editorial boards of numerous international journals.

Lara Moratón Gutiérrez studied English and Linguistics at Universidad Complutense de Madrid and completed her PhD on Thematic Patterning in English and Spanish: Contrastive Annotation of a Bilingual Newspaper Corpus for Linguistics and Computational Applications in 2015 under Julia Lavid's supervision. She has published widely on SFL and Spanish and on computational linguistics and has worked as a linguistic consultant for several electronics companies.

References

Ansary, H. & Babaii, E. (2009) 'A cross-cultural analysis of English newspaper editorials: A systemic-functional view of text for contrastive rhetoric research'. *RELC Journal* 40(2), 211–249.

Daneš, F. (1974) 'Functional sentence perspective and the organization of the text'. In: Daneš, F. (ed.) *Papers on Functional Sentence Perspective.* The Hague/Paris: Mouton, 106–128.

Dubois, B. L. (1987) 'A reformulation of thematic progression typology'. *Text* 7(2), 89–116.

Eggins, S. (2004) *Introduction to Systemic Functional Linguistics.* London: Continuum.

Eggins, S. & Martin, J.R. (1997) 'Genres and registers of discourse'. In: van Dijk, T.A. (ed.) *Discourse as Structure and Process. Discourse Studies: A Multidisciplinary Introduction.* London: Sage, 23–256.

Eggins, S. & Slade, D. (1997) *Analysing Casual Conversation.* London: Cassell.

Fowler, R. (1991) *Language in the News: Language and Ideology in the Press.* London: Routledge.

Fries, P.H. (1995) 'Themes, methods of development and texts'. In: Hasan, R. & Fries, P.H. (eds.) *On Subject and Theme: A Discourse Functional Perspective. Current Issues in Linguistic Theory* 118. Amsterdam: John Benjamins, 317–359.

Halliday, M.A.K. & Hasan, R. (1989) *Language, Context, and Text: Aspects of Language in a Social-Semiotic Perspective.* Oxford: Oxford University Press.

Hauser, S. (2012) 'Genre matters: Theoretical and methodological issues of a genre-based approach to contrastive media analysis'. In: Hauser, S. & Luginbühl, M. (eds.) *Contrastive Media Analysis: Approaches to Linguistic and Cultural Aspects of Mass Media Communication.* Amsterdam: John Benjamins, 219–244.

Lavid, J., Arús, J. & Moratón, L. (2010a) 'Signalling genre through Theme: The case of news reports and commentaries'. *Discourse. Special Issue on Multidisciplinary Approaches to Signalling Text Organisation.* (Proceedings of MAD10), 82–89.

Lavid, J., Arús, J. & Zamorano-Mansilla, J.R. (2010b) *Systemic Functional Grammar of Spanish: A Contrastive Study with English.* 1st edition. London: Bloomsbury Academic.

Lavid, J., Arús, J. & Moratón, L. (2013) 'Thematic variation in English and Spanish newspaper genres: A contrastive corpus-based study'. In: Aijmer, K. & Altenberg, B. (eds.) *Advances in Corpus-based Contrastive Linguistics. Studies in honor of Stig Johansson.* Amsterdam: John Benjamins, 261–286.

Lee, N.I. (2011) 'Academic and journalistic writing in English and Japanese: A contrastive study on stance and engagement expressions'. *Journal of Modern Languages* 21(1), 59–71.

Mann, W.C. & Thompson, S.A. (1988) 'Rhetorical structure theory: Toward a functional theory of text organization'. *Text-Interdisciplinary Journal for the Study of Discourse* 8(3), 243–281.

Martin, J.R. (1984) 'Language, register and genre'. In: Christie, F. (ed.) *Children Writing: reader.* Greelong, Australia: Deakin University Press, 21–30.

Martin, J.R. & Rose, D. (2003) *Working with Discourse: Meaning beyond the Clause.* London: Bloomsbury Publishing.

Martin, J.R., Christie, F. & Rothery, J. (1987). 'Social processes in education: A reply to Sawyer and Watson (and others)'. In: Reid, I. (ed.) *The Place of Genre in Learning: Current Debates.* Greelong, Australia: Deakin University Press, 35–45.

Nwogu, K.N. (1997) 'The medical research paper: Structure and functions'. *English for Specific Purposes* 16(2), 119–138.

Skelton, J. (1994) 'Analysis of the structure of original research papers: An aid to writing original papers for publication'. *British Journal of General Practice* 44, 455–459.

Swales, J. (1990) *Genre Analysis: English in Academic and Research Settings.* Cambridge: Cambridge University Press.

Swales, J. (2004) *Research Genres: Explorations and Applications.* Stuttgart: Ernst Klett Sprachen.

Van Dijk, T.A. (1988) *News Analysis. Case Studies of International and National News in the Press.* Hillsdale, NJ: Erlbaum.

Wang, W. (2007) 'The notions of genre and micro-genre in contrastive rhetoric research: Newspapers commentaries on the events of September 11th'. *University of Sydney papers in TESOL* 2(1), 83–117.

Wang, W. (2008) 'Newspaper commentaries on terrorism in China and Australia: A contrastive genre study'. In: Connor, U., Nagelhout, E. & Rozycki, W. (eds.) *Contrastive Rhetoric: Reaching to Intercultural Rhetoric.* Amsterdam/Philadelphia: John Benjamins, 169–191.

White, P.R. (1998) *Telling Media Tales: The News Story as Rhetoric.* Doctoral Dissertation. Sydney: University of Sydney.

Yu, H. (2001) 'On the Notion of Generic Structure Potential and Its Application'. *Journal of Pla University of Foreign Languages* 1.

5 Popular science articles in broadsheet newspapers, consumer magazines, and specialized magazines: Engagement resources from a translation perspective

Marina Manfredi
University of Bologna, Italy

5.1 Introduction

Science permeates our lives. As many aspects of modern society are impacted by scientific knowledge and technological expertise, we are increasingly called upon to make decisions about rapidly changing science-related affairs. As a major source of information about science and technology, most people rely on the mass media, ranging from the press to the radio, from TV to the web.

While scientists and academics tend to use English as a global *lingua franca* to spread scientific knowledge, non-specialized readerships interested in science findings commonly depend on translations. Popular science *in and for* the mass media is thus an area of significant importance for research on linguistic aspects and translation. However, the field is as yet largely under-explored within translation studies (henceforth TS), with a few exceptions (Liao 2011, 2013; Kranich et al. 2012; Olohan 2016). From a linguistic perspective, most existing research examines popular science within the broad field of scientific discourse and mainly offers contrastive studies of scientific texts and popularized ones (Myers 2003; Hyland 2010). Even though it is widely acknowledged that popular science encompasses a wide range of discourses, its role as a journalistic practice has not received much attention in linguistic studies so far, apart from sparse contributions (Macdonald 2005; Hewings 2010). As communication scholar Nelkin (1987: x) argues, popular science shares features of both science and journalism and so can also be viewed as science journalism. Systemic Functional Linguistics (henceforth SFL) has largely explored journalistic discourse[1], although its major concern has been on newspaper journalism and on the language of the so-called 'hard news'. Most research into popular science from an SFL perspective deals with either popularized science books (Fuller 1998) or academic vs. popular science journals (Minelli de Oliveira & Pagano 2006), while there has been less interest in popular science writing as science journalism.

This chapter offers a contribution to the field of popular science journalism from a linguistic and translational perspective. There is a specific focus on the feature article, translated from a wide range of written media, from broadsheet newspapers to consumer magazines and specialized science magazines. In feature articles, writers have some freedom to experiment with style and introduce their own voice. Moreover, as rhetoric of science scholar Tinker Perrault points out, popular science articles not only present facts, i.e. 'the truth', but they also give readers information in a way that lets them take a critical stance, inviting them 'to engage with science-related issues not as spectators but as members of civil society' (Tinker Perrault 2013: 138).

What happens when such issues cross cultural and linguistic borders through a process of interlingual transfer? What is the role of the translator's intervention in dealing with the writer's intersubjective stance in the process of translating a source text (henceforth ST) into a target text (henceforth TT)? In order to answer these questions, this chapter will be concerned with the translation of the interpersonal metafunction (Halliday 1994; Halliday & Matthiessen 2014), which, as Munday (2015: 407) contends, has still largely been underexplored in translation research informed by SFL. In particular, a systematic approach will be offered by applying Appraisal Theory (Martin & White 2005) and, more specifically, by applying the resources of the 'attendant' system of Engagement, 'by which speakers/writers adopt a stance towards the value positions being referenced by the text and with respect to those they address' (Martin & White 2005: 92). While Appraisal Theory has been amply exploited in linguistic studies on newspaper discourse both from a monolingual (Bednarek 2006) and a plurilingual perspective (Thomson & White 2008), it has rarely been applied to journalistic translation (Zhang 2011) and, at least to my knowledge, it has not yet been applied to science journalism translation. As regards the Engagement System in particular, it has so far been relatively overlooked in TS, apart from a small number of studies (e.g. Vandepitte et al. 2011; Munday 2012, 2015; Quian 2012).

The aim of this contribution is to explore the issues of subjectivity and dialogism in popular science texts as conveyed by evaluative linguistic choices. This will be done through the illustration of a case study dealing with translations from English to Italian. More specifically, the study focuses on a small corpus of texts published in different written media (both print and online) and translated for a printed journalistic medium. The purpose of the chapter is to give account of any 'shifts' in the translation of Engagement resources and to see (1) whether these shifts can be linked to different degrees of popularization in the STs, (2) whether they can be related to different communicative preferences in the two 'linguacultures' (English/American and Italian), and (3) to what extent they may affect the cultural process of 'democratization of knowledge', which has been taking place in the UK and the US in the past 20 years (Kranich et al. 2012: 332) and which has more recently also affected Italy. But before turning to the details of the case study, a brief description of the theoretical framework on which this chapter is based, an overview of the field of investigation, and an account of the materials analyzed and the methods applied will be given.

5.2 Theoretical framework

This chapter draws on SFL (and therein on Appraisal Theory) and on TS, with some insights from journalism, media studies and science communication studies. SFL offers the analytical toolkit to examine the instantiation of intersubjective stance in popular science texts translated from one language into another. TS give the conceptual framework to explore issues of translation theory, both traditional and SFL-informed. Science communication studies provide a critical context for interpreting linguistic and translational choices in the light of the role of science in society.

5.2.1 Appraisal Theory: The Engagement System

The SFL-framework this study is based upon is Appraisal Theory (Martin & White 2005),[2] which offers a systematic account of evaluation, and more specifically the system of Engagement, which 'is concerned with the ways in which resources [...] position the speaker/writer with respect to the value position being advanced and with respect to potential responses to that value position'. (Martin & White 2005: 36)

Engagement is informed by Bakhtin's notions of dialogism and heteroglossia in that it recognizes the diversity of alternative voices associated with all alternative positions. However, it acknowledges different viewpoints to a degree which can vary from dialogic 'contraction' to 'expansion', according to whether it makes space or, conversely, denies space to alternative points of view. It can be instantiated through a large variety of lexicogrammatical resources and is dependent on co-text.

The resources of Engagement include Disclaim, Proclaim, Entertain and Attribute. Disclaim and Proclaim encompass those meanings which 'act to contract the dialogic space', while Entertain and Attribute work 'to open it up'

(Martin & White 2005: 117). In particular, whereas with Disclaim the textual voice excludes some alternative position, with Proclaim it limits its scope. Martin & White (2005: 121–133) identify three sub-categories of Proclaim: Concur, Endorse and Pronounce, which involve formulations by which the speaker is in agreement with a dialogic partner, considers the external voice as correct or explicitly intervenes into the text to state the validity of a proposition. Entertain (Martin & White 2005: 104–111) and Attribute (Martin & White 2005: 111–117) are instantiated when a speaker presents a proposition as but one of a range of possible positions and grounded either in one's individual subjectivity or in that of an external voice. The category of Attribute entails two sub-types: Acknowledge and Distance (Martin & White 2005: 112–114), the former including those formulations in which there is no overt indication as to where the authorial voice stands with respect to the attributed proposition, the latter where it explicitly expresses a distance between the two.

For the purpose of this chapter, only the categories of Proclaim, Entertain and Attribute will be considered as they are particularly relevant in the translation process from English into Italian. Indeed, because of structural characteristics of the source language (henceforth SL) and the target language (henceforth TL), instantiations of these resources can be either easily transferred or skilfully conveyed through establishing 'functional equivalence'. When shifts occur, they seem fundamentally the result of the translator's (or editor's) intervention.

5.2.2 Translation 'shifts' and functional equivalence

Some traditional issues of translation theory, such as the notions of 'shift' (Catford 1965) and 'equivalence',[3] shall be revisited here in the light of an SFL perspective. I argue that the common notion of 'translation shifts', defined as 'departures from formal correspondence in the process of going from the SL to the TL' (Catford 1965: 73), can be re-interpreted in terms of 'functional shifts'. Those shifts that are more relevant for a scholar working within an SFL perspective are usually not the ones opted for by a translator because of structural differences between two languages, but they are rather optional shifts that are chosen by the translator for stylistic, ideological or cultural reasons.

The concept of 'shifts' thus needs to be considered with respect to the postulated concept of 'equivalence'. Equivalence has always been a thorny issue central to any linguistic approach to translation. Broadly speaking, translation theories have identified two main types of translation equivalence, one more 'formal', i.e. more adherent to the lexicogrammatical choices of the SL, and one more 'communicative' or 'functional', i.e. aimed at conveying the meaning rather than the structures of the SL. For scholars working within an SFL paradigm, equivalence cannot simply have to do with formal similarities between linguistic structures but needs to be underpinned by the idea of 'function' and must thus be pursued at different levels. House (1997), who proposes a Hallidayan model of translation quality assessment, adopts the concept of 'functional equivalence'. Halliday himself (2001: 15) puts forth a categorization of equivalence according to three parameters: stratification (between ordered strata: phonetic, phonological, lexicogrammatical and semantic), metafunction (with respect to the different types of meaning: ideational, interpersonal and textual) and rank (which deals with formal strata). In this chapter, we shall apply the distinction between 'direct equivalence' and 'functional equivalence', the former referring to a term that is translated into its most direct one-to-one equivalent (e.g. the English 'perhaps' translated into the Italian *forse*), and the latter encompassing all those cases where the translator reproduces the functional meaning of the ST through different lexicogrammatical structures. By way of example, consider the segment 'Animals **might** be capable of learning' (de Waal 2013) translated into *Forse sono capaci di imparare* (**Perhaps** they are capable of learning). In this case, the modal operator 'might', construing possibility, thus entertaining, has been rendered through a functionally equivalent modal adjunct ('perhaps'), while its direct equivalent would have been *Gli animali potrebbero essere capaci di imparare*.

5.3 Popular science writing

Popular science writing, according to Tinker Perrault (2013: xiii), 'refers to all written forms of science popularization'. Thus it refers to books, newspaper and magazine articles and essays, as well as to online forums, like blogs. It can be defined as 'science-related writing that is aimed at non-specialist audiences', which includes both lay audiences and scientists, but in different fields of expertise (Tinker Perrault 2013: 5). Studies on science communication, as Gualdo and Telve (2011: 183) remark, reveal different attitudes of critics with respect to popular science writing, varying over time and different contexts of culture.

5.3.1 From PAST to CUSP models

In the twentieth century, science writing was seen in the light of basically two different models: PUS (Public Understanding of Science) and PEST (Public Engagement with Science and Technology) (Gualdo and Telve 2011: 183). Tinker Perrault (2013: 6) prefers talking about science writing in terms of

PAST (Public Appreciation of Science and Technology) rather than PUS and adds a third dimension named CUSP (Critical Understanding of Science in Public), which seems to characterize today's view of popular science writing.

Especially in Anglo-Saxon societies, the 1990s saw a dominance of the PUS (or PAST) model, which was promoted by London's Royal Society and aimed at spreading scientific literacy among the general public (Gualdo & Telve 2011: 183). In other words, science popularization had the purpose of informing and educating the general readers, engendering their curiosity. As Myers (2003: 266) observes, this was a 'deficit model' since it encompassed a one-way form of communication, from the expert to the lay reader, with the public being viewed as being in a 'blank state of ignorance on which scientists write knowledge'. After the 1990s, the PEST model gained pace, changing the idea of 'popularization' into 'communication', which entailed a two-way dialogue between specialists and non-specialists (Gualdo & Telve 2011: 184).

In this regard, Tinker Perrault (2013: 15–16) calls for a more democratic model named CUSP, which allows science to play an interactive role in civil society and which encourages critical evaluation on the part of the public. In other words, within this perspective, popular science texts are not only supposed to inform the readers but let them take a critical stance. This is reflected in the dialogic perspective displayed in most journalistic texts, at least in the Anglo-American context of culture, where the so-called goal of objectivism has been replaced by a more dialogic Engagement (White 2012). This is in line with the changing role of the science journalist, who is not merely seen as a mediator and a popularizer of a specialized source but as an active participant who, drawing on more sources, offers information and opinion.

5.3.2 Popular science in broadsheet newspapers, consumer and specialized magazines: The feature article

Today, print and online journalism are paying increasing attention to science and technology in different sectors of the publishing industry. Popular science articles can be found in local and national newspapers, in popular magazines, in trade and science journals and on the web, dealing with a wide range of topics spanning from life sciences to physical and environmental sciences. Articles frequently address more than one field of expertise at the same time. For example, articles dealing with economic and business affairs often interface with technological issues. Quality newspapers regularly include science columns or offer special weekly supplements, while consumer magazines of a general interest frequently host special science sections. As we saw, the audiences at whom popular science articles are directed are diverse, even though they are primarily non-specialists in the field. The so-called 'broadsheet' (or 'quality') newspapers essentially cater for a university-educated, typically middle-class readership. Consumer magazines, i.e. those periodicals that provide their readers with information and entertainment, aim at a larger audience particularly interested in the topics. More specialized science magazines, which offer more in-depth articles, are geared towards interested lay readers who, albeit not experts, are already informed and engaged with the topics under discussion.

Scientific and technological issues are debated both in news and feature articles. In journalism studies, '[f]eatures are as often defined by reference to what they [are] *not* – hard news – as to what they *are*' (Harcup 2005: 140, emphases in the original). A feature article can be distinguished from a hard news story because it 'tends to be longer, carry more background information, colour, [a] wider range of sources and [the] journalist's opinion can be prominent' (Keeble 2005: xiv). Far from being a purely objective text type, the feature article often embodies subjectivity intruding into the text. Even in popular science feature articles, despite the widely held belief that science has to be purely objective, the writers' stance emerges when they foster a dialogic relationship with their readers.

5.4 Materials and methods

The study is based on the analysis of a small corpus of popular science feature articles that appeared in the 'Science' and 'Technology' sections of the Italian weekly news magazine *Internazionale* in the 11 issues from March to May 2013 (N° 990–1000). *Internazionale* has a strong international and translational focus: it publishes a weekly selection of in-depth articles almost exclusively translated from the foreign press.[4] It is published in print and digital formats, both available on subscription. In the Italian context, it can be considered a high-quality news magazine. Translators working for *Internazionale* are freelance professional translators regularly collaborating with the magazine; only editors and copy editors are staff members (Momigliano 2012).

The corpus consists of 25 Italian TTs translated from different English sources, both British and American. Out of 28 articles taken from the relevant issues, 27 were translations from English. One article was translated from a different language (German) and was therefore excluded.[5] Two of the translations from English were not included in the study as they represented either a different medium (CNN) or a different text type (interview). In the latter, the quantity and quality of interpersonal meanings and, most importantly, their communicative function were not comparable to the other texts. Therefore, findings would not have been consistent with other results.

Within the final 25 articles, 17 address the field of science, while eight focus on technology. They were taken either from print or digital editions. Ten articles had been translated from broadsheet national newspapers: the *Guardian* (5), the *New York Times* (3) and the *Wall Street Journal* (2). Nine articles had been translated from consumer magazines: *The Economist* (5), the *New York Times Magazine* (1), the *New Yorker* (1), the *Atlantic* (1) and the online-only magazine *Slate* (1). Finally, six articles had been translated from specialized science magazines: the weekly *New Scientist* (5) and the *Stanford Medicine Magazine* (1). Seven articles included in the print issue of *Internazionale* had been translated from online sources, either online newspapers and magazines or blogs.

From a methodological point of view, the study is descriptive and empirical. It fundamentally employs a bottom-up procedure in that lexicogrammatical features in both STs and TTs are analyzed and discussed with respect to the realization of the interpersonal metafunction. Particular analytical focus is given to the Appraisal system of Engagement.

Feature articles have been classified and sub-divided into categories on the basis of the *Revised Field of Science and Technology (FOS) Classification* (OECD 2007), which encompasses a taxonomy spanning from the so-called 'hard sciences' (like physics and astronomy) to 'softer' ones (like biology) and 'very soft ones' (like psychology and sociology). The five main fields are 1. Natural Sciences, 2. Engineering and Technology, 3. Medical and Health Sciences, 4. Agricultural Sciences and 5. Social Sciences, all sub-divided into more specific sub-fields.

I have carried out an empirical analysis of the 25 original articles and their Italian translations. Manual analysis has been chosen since Engagement can be instantiated through many different lexicogrammatical resources and invariably depends on context and co-text. I analyzed the translation of instances of Engagement in the TTs, grouping them into four different categories: Engagement conveyed through direct equivalence; Engagement conveyed through functional equivalence; Engagement not completely conveyed since subjected to minor shifts; and Engagement not conveyed because of major shifts, omissions or monogloss. Within an SFL perspective, I did not consider 'shifts' at the level of language but only 'shifts' at the level of metafunction. Translations where the function of Engagement was conveyed, albeit with the use of different linguistic items, were not considered 'shifts' but rather instances of 'functional equivalence'. By way of illustration, let us consider the following example (1):

(1) News isn't entirely a commodity, but it almost is. What's the core, though? The point of view? Presentation? The analysis and

discussion (including comments) around articles? **You can argue for each.** (Arthur 2013, emphasis added)

In the extract above, the function of Entertaining is instantiated by the clause in bold construing probability, which allows space for alternative points of view. In the TT, it has not been rendered through direct equivalence but through a structurally different clause with a functionally equivalent effect: *Ognuna di queste risposte può avere senso* (each of these answers **can** make sense).

Portions of STs which are clearly omitted in the translations have been ignored since they are not deemed part of the translation: indeed, in this area of professional translation, translators are commissioned to work on STs that have already been abridged. Likewise, I have not taken into account paratextual elements such as the headline and the standfirst, given that these elements are largely manipulated by editors who are responsible for editing the translations and for writing headlines and captions. Neither have projected locutions, i.e. reported speech, been taken into account. Even though they might be subject to the writer's manipulation, they are presented as quotes and so, for the purpose of our investigation, do not openly disclose the writer's intervention. Let us now turn to the main findings of this study and discuss a selection of illustrative examples.

5.5 Analysis and discussion of findings

Most of the SFL-oriented literature on journalistic discourse where the Engagement System is exploited as an analytical toolkit mainly focuses on the category of Attribution (e.g. White 2012). This is not surprising, given that the relevant research has mostly dealt with the analysis of news, where the goal of 'objectivity' is largely pursued through attribution resources. However, since the focus of this chapter is on the register of the popular science feature article, the analysis will also deal with other categories of Engagement and their sub-categories.

5.5.1 The study

The 25 articles included in the corpus can be classified into three main fields according to the OECD (2007) taxonomy: Natural Sciences (4), Medical and Health Sciences (7), and Social Sciences (14). The articles can be grouped as shown in Table 5.1.

Table 5.1 The corpus of feature articles on the basis of the *Revised Field of Science and Technology (FOS) Classification* (OECD 2007)

Field	Sub-field	# of articles
1. Natural Sciences (4)	1.3 Physical Sciences – Astronomy	1
	1.6 Biological Sciences – Behavioural Sciences Biology; Marine Biology	2
	1.7 Other Natural Sciences	1
3. Medical and Health Sciences (7)	3.1. Basic Medicine – Neurosciences (including Psychophysiology)	3
	3.2 Clinical Medicine – Psychiatry	1
	3.3 Health Sciences – Public and Environmental Health; Infectious Diseases; Epidemiology	2
	3.4 Medical Biotechnology	1
5. Social Sciences (14)	5.1 Psychology	2
	5.4 Sociology	1
	5.7 Social and Economic Geography – Environmental Sciences (social aspects)	2
	5.8 Media and Communications – Information Science (social aspects)	9

Out of the four articles on natural sciences, only one concerns the so-called 'hard' sciences and is taken from *The Economist* blog, a consumer magazine. It relates to the natural sciences field of Astronomy. The other three concern what are commonly considered 'softer' sciences, i.e. biological sciences, and herein, in particular, the behavioural sciences of Biology and Marine Biology.

Within the broadsheet newspapers, nine out of ten articles are representative of very 'soft' sciences, i.e. social sciences. Interestingly, fields that both in the common view and in the literature are not even considered 'sciences' represent the largest group, with 14 feature articles contained in the papers' Science or Technology sections. Six of them (two appeared on blogs) are on technology and can be classified under the OECD's label of 'Media and Communications: Information Science (social aspects)'. Seven articles concern the major area of Medical and Health Sciences and herein three the sub-field of Basic Medicine: Neurosciences (including Psychophysiology). One of these three was published in *The Economist* and two appeared in the *New Scientist*.

The results from the analysis of STs and their respective TTs in terms of the Engagement resources exploited in the texts are presented in Table 5.2.

Table 5.2 Instances of Engagement in STs and TTs

Medium	Category of Engagement	Sub-category of Engagement	Conveyed: Direct Equivalence	Conveyed: Functional Equivalence	Not completely conveyed: Minor Shifts	Not conveyed: Major Shifts Omissions Monogloss
Broadsheet papers	Entertain: 65		26	15	6	18
	Attribute: 40	Acknowledge: 38	8	17	7	6
		Distance: 2	–	2	–	–
	Proclaim: 30	Concur: 10	1	4	–	5
		Endorse: 11	3	4	–	4
		Pronounce: 9	1	2	1	5
Consumer magazines	Entertain: 112		50	28	8	26
	Attribute: 79	Acknowledge: 78	11	51	7	9
		Distance: 1	–	–	1	–
	Proclaim: 34	Concur: 6	1	1	–	4
		Endorse: 19	7	7	2	3
		Pronounce: 9	4	4	1	–
Science magazines	Entertain: 79		35	13	5	26
	Attribute: 70	Acknowledge: 70	12	42	6	10
		Concur: 5	–	4	–	1
	Proclaim: 47	Endorse: 33	12	13	–	8
		Pronounce: 9	–	1	1	7
Total		556		379		177

As Table 5.2 shows, while a more traditional contrastive analysis based on the search for equivalent units would have revealed a higher number of 'shifts', an SFL approach limits 'shifts' to those cases where the instantiations of Engagement are either not completely rendered in the TTs through minor shifts or not conveyed at all because of major shifts, omissions or monoglossic solutions. When shifts occurred within the same category of Engagement, they were considered minor shifts.

There were 556 explicit instances of Engagement identified in the 25 STs under scrutiny. Of these, 379 were conveyed in the TTs, either through 'direct equivalence' (31%) or through 'functional equivalence' (37%). The remaining 177 instances were 'not conveyed' or 'not completely conveyed' in the TTs, and this will be given the main focus of attention in the following sections.

5.5.1.1 Shifts in Proclaim

Proclaim is the engagement resource where the subjectivity of the writer is most prominent: 'by representing the proposition as highly warrantable [...], the textual voice sets itself against, suppresses or rules out alternative positions' (Martin & White 2005: 98).

The corpus features 111 instances of Proclaim, subdivided into the three categories of Concur (21), Endorse (63) and Pronounce (27). Considering the three different types of media, there were 30 instances of Proclaim in broadsheet newspapers, 34 in consumer magazines and 47 in science magazines. In broadsheet newspapers, 50% of the instances of Proclaim:Concur were not conveyed, neither were 66% in consumer magazines. This contrasts markedly with science magazines, where 80% were conveyed through functional equivalence. Within the sub-category Endorse, 63% of instances contained in broadsheet newspapers were conveyed, as well as more than 70% of instances in consumer magazines and 75% in science magazines, either through direct or through functional equivalence. As far as the sub-category Pronounce is concerned, findings are strikingly different: only 33% of the instances in articles in broadsheet newspapers were conveyed into Italian, while 90% were conveyed in consumer magazines. Significantly, in science magazines 90% were not conveyed.

Functional equivalence was achieved when different solutions were sought that eschewed direct equivalence, such as 'certainly'>*di sicuro* (surely) rather than *certamente*, an instance of Concur, 'unsurprisingly'>*ovviamente* (obviously) or 'obviously'>*palesemente* (patently). Likewise, the translators opted for functionally equivalent solutions for conveying Endorse, like 'shows'>*dimostra* (demonstrates), 'has shown'>*ha scoperto* (has discovered), 'proved'>*si è rivelato* (revealed), 'A recent study found'>*Da un recente studio è emerso...* (From a recent study ... emerged). Pronounce was conveyed, e.g. in 'in fact'>*davvero* or *proprio* (really, indeed).

In contrast, Engagement resources in the ST were not rendered in the Italian TT when a minor or major shift or an omission was applied. Minor shifts occurred when the sub-category of an instantiation was changed from one to another, e.g. within Proclaim from Pronounce to Endorse, as in 'There is plenty of evidence that'>*Diversi studi dimostrano* (Various studies demonstrate). Here the translation in the TT conveys a weaker position. Cases of shift from a main category of Engagement to another were considered major shifts, as in 'points out'>*dice* (says), or 'found'>*dicono* (they say), which reveal shifts from Proclaim:Endorse to the Engagement category Attribute. Here the TT solutions are deemed more neutral. It also happened that an instantiation of Proclaim:Concur was converted into another system of Appraisal, i.e. Graduation, as in 'certainly influenced'>*molto influenzata* (very influenced), where the modal adverb 'certainly' was translated into the intensifier *molto* (very) to the effect that the dialogism in the TT was invariably reduced. Major shifts also occurred when instances of Proclaim:Concur were translated with modal adverbs of usuality, as in the following extract from the *Wall Street Journal*:

(2) That, after all, is how we gain the space to make decisions – many of them **undoubtedly** wrongheaded. (Morozov 2013, emphasis added)

The translation of the adverb 'undoubtedly' into Italian as *spesso* (often) weakened the writer positioning.

Furthermore, the analysis revealed various instances of omissions which transformed the TT segments into monoglossic assertions, as in the following example, taken from the beginning of an article translated from the online edition of the *New York Times*:

(3) Bosses, **as it turns out, really** do matter. (Lohr 2013, emphasis added)

This sentence was translated into the monoglossic *I dirigenti [0] sono [0] importanti* (Management [0] is [0] important), where both instantiations of Proclaim (Endorse and Pronounce) were omitted and the TT simply became a categorical assertion without any attempt at engaging the reader.

However, there are also exceptions with respect to the predominant patterns of reduction of Engagement resources which emerged. For example, in an article translated from *The Economist*, the sentence 'This **really is** Seldon country' was translated as *Sembra davvero il paese di Seldon* (It **really seems** Seldon country). Here, the instance of Proclaim:Pronounce (really) in the ST was literally rendered in the TT (*davvero*). Yet, the TT adds the category Entertain through the translation of 'is' into the appearance-based *sembra* (seems), adding space for more negotiation.

A similar instance was found in a text translated from the *New Scientist*:

(4) **There is** also **evidence that** political and business leaders who get angry rather than sad in response to a scandal are granted higher status. (Young 2013, emphases added)

The instantiation of Proclaim:Pronounce construed by 'There is also evidence that' was translated into *Sembra inoltre* (It **seems** moreover that), a typical case of Entertain, which gives the target reader more dialogic power.

This section has shown how, from a translational point of view, resources of Proclaim were treated differently with respect to both the three sub-categories and the three different media.

5.5.1.2 Shifts in Attribute

Attribute occurs when 'by representing the proposition as grounded in the subjectivity of an external voice, the textual voice represents the proposition as but one of a range of possible positions – it thereby entertains or invokes these dialogic alternatives' (Martin & White 2005: 98). It is most typically instantiated through projection, i.e by reporting verbs that introduce projected locutions or thoughts in verbal or mental processes.[6] In order to examine instances of equivalence or shift along with considering the rendering or not rendering of Attribution, I also took into account 'the attitudinal value connoted by the reporting verbs themselves, which are covert indicators of the stance of the authorial voice' (Munday 2015: 410, referring to Martin & White 2015: 112).

Many examples of functional equivalence concern the translation of the English present tense of certain reporting verbs into the Italian past tense. While in English journalistic style the present tense conveys immediacy, Italian newspapers and magazines tend to prefer a more formal style and privilege the typical tense of narration, i.e. the past tense. Most instances of Attribute concern the translation of the common English reporting verb 'says' into *spiega* (explains), *dichiara* (declares), *aggiunge* (adds), *osserva* (observes), *risponde* (answers), etc., all of which function as synonyms.

In the specific case of 'says' translated as *conclude* (concludes), I did not consider it the reinforcement 'of a proposition against possible alternatives via the use of some evidence or supporting argumentation,' as posited by White (2012: 65). With respect to the TL and taking into account the co-text of the examples at issue, I simply analyzed this as an instance of functional equivalence that offers stylistic variation.

Only two substitutions of reporting verbs were not considered functionally equivalent, i.e. the translation of 'says' into *afferma* (affirms) and *sostiene* (claims, asserts), which have been analyzed as minor shifts. In the case of *affermare* (to affirm), which, according to a bilingual dictionary, could be translated as 'to declare, to state, to affirm' or as 'to maintain, to claim, to assert' (Ragazzini 2017), I agree with Munday (2015: 413) that the Italian verb, like the Spanish equivalent *afirmar*, is not strictly a synonym of the more neutral 'say' but generally conveys a more positive value, thus more assertiveness on the part of the writer. On the same lines, the Italian *sostiene* conveys a sense of determination which the English 'say' does not entail.

Let us now focus on the typical instance of Attribute:Distance construed by 'claim', through which the writer takes distance from the attributed proposition. Whenever the verbal group was rendered as *sostiene* (claims, asserts), it was analyzed as a direct equivalent. This is not the case in the following extract from the *New Yorker*:

(5) The Culturelle ad **claims** that its active ingredient, Lactobacillus GG, has been shown to 'survive those good-bacteria-gobbling stomach acids and successfully stick to the intestinal walls where it's needed most'. (Specter 2012, emphasis added)

The verbal group 'claims', typically conveying Attribution:Distance, was translated into the prepositional construction *Secondo la pubblicità di Culturelle...* (According to the Culturelle ad...), which is more neutral.

5.5.1.3 Shifts in Entertain

Among the resources of Engagement, Entertain is the most dialogic one since 'the authorial voice indicates that its position is but one of a number of possible positions and thereby, to greater or lesser degrees, makes dialogic space for those possibilities' (Martin & White 2005: 104). In Appraisal Theory, it encompasses modals of probability (both verbal and adjuncts), reality phase and certain types of interpersonal metaphor.

It should be pointed out that even though Italian lexicogrammatical resources conveying Entertain are similar to English ones – and this seems confirmed by the fact that translated texts display a high number of instances of direct equivalence (26) – other linguistic resources that are apt to convey the same function were employed. For example, the modal operator 'might' was rendered into the functionally equivalent modal adjunct *forse* (maybe), the modal operator 'could', construing, in SFL terms, implicit modality, was translated into the objective explicit *è possibile* (it is possible), the adverb 'apparently' was rendered with a prepositional construction, e.g. *a quanto sembra* (as it seems), etc. In addition, future tense was frequently used by Italian translators to convey instances of 'may'.

The STs contained in consumer magazines featured the highest number of instances of Entertain (112). Interestingly, even in TTs which were condensed onto one page, most instantiations were rendered (70%). Indeed, the translated texts contain a high number of instances of direct equivalence, but also functional equivalence was amply employed, e.g. with the translation of 'may' into *magari* (if only) or the rendering of the verbal group in the clause 'X is **thinking**' with the nominal group *possibilità* (possibility).

In terms of non-rendering of Engagement resources under the label of minor shifts, I considered instances where the TT displayed a slightly different level of Engagement, e.g. when the modal operator 'might', instantiating lower probability, was turned into a more assertative *può* (can), or vice versa, when 'may' was translated as *forse* (perhaps) or with the conditional *potrebbe* (might), which both construe lower probability.

In addition, the corpus offered many examples of major shifts from Entertain to other categories of Engagement, such as Proclaim, as the extract below, taken from the *New Scientist*, shows:

(6) They are **perhaps** best recognised as a measure of abstract reasoning, says psychologist Richard Nisbett at the University of Michigan in Ann Arbor. (Adee 2013)

In the TT, the entertaining 'perhaps' was shifted into *in realtà* (actually), which reduces the space for alternative viewpoints.

Two further illustrative cases of major shifts are provided by the following two examples:

(7) More intriguingly, the latest research **may suggest** ways to evade a condition that can plague us all. (Adee 2013)

(8) An analysis by [...] found that 689 other human genes contain 15-base-pair strings found in BRCA1, **suggesting** Myriad's patents technically cover those unrelated genes, too. (*The Economist* 2013)

In (7), the instantiation of Entertain through both the modal operator 'may' and the verb 'suggest' was shifted into Proclaim:Endorse, construed in the TT as *dalle ultime ricerche emergono* (from the latest research ... **have emerged**), which reduces the space for negotiation. In (8), an example from *The Economist*, the entertaining 'suggesting' was shifted in the TT into *quindi tecnicamente i brevetti della Myriad coprono anche geni non direttamente collegati* (**so** technically the patents of Myriad also cover not directly related genes), where *quindi* (so) is a conjunction which construes a paratactic enhancing clause with a monoglossic value.

Finally, there are also sparse cases of omissions which can be explained with stylistic reasons. For example, consider the following extract, which was included in the pay-off of a feature article published in the *Guardian* online:

(9) **Perhaps** I will wait until FairPhone manufactures a handset. Or **perhaps** I won't bother. I **might** resign myself to less immediacy, less accessibility and a little more space in which to think. (Monbiot 2013, emphases added)

In this case, the TT features the omission of the second 'perhaps', maybe due to the textual function of avoiding repetition, a cohesive device which is not always appreciated in Italian journalistic style. After all, as journalism studies expert Harcup (2016: 145) remarks, the pay-off is a crucial segment of feature articles since it 'rewards the reader for sticking with you', and this is also valid for a translated text, which is read by the target readers as if written for them. What is more, omissions can also contribute to transform heteroglossic statements into monoglossic ones, but limited space precludes further exemplification here.

As a conclusion of this section, consider the analysis of an example where all resources of Engagement are represented in the ST:

(10) I asked Paul Carr, a former MediaGuardian writer (and, disclosure, friend) [...] for his view. **He thinks** porous paywalls are stupid: they 'reward casual readers and punish enthusiastic ones, which is the precise opposite of logical'. **(I have to say I agree with him there.)** [...] 'The Guardian will **absolutely** go paywall'. Though **arguably**, that's the wrong way to do it. (Arthur 2013, emphases added)

The extract above from the *Guardian* Media Blog displays the attributing 'he thinks', the proclaiming (Concur) 'absolutely', as well as the entertaining 'arguably'. Furthermore, through the segment in parentheses, the writer intrudes into the text with an overtly subjective comment. The TT preserved Attribution through direct equivalence (*Carr pensa*>'Carr thinks') and conveyed Proclaim:Concur through functional equivalence (*di sicuro*>'surely'). In addition, it transformed the comment '(I have to say I agree with him there)' into Attribute: *Secondo Paul Carr*>'According to Paul Carr', and it omitted the entertaining value construed by 'arguably'. Ultimately, the dialogistic nature of the ST was reduced in the TT.

5.5.2 Discussion

The findings show that, in general, English STs tend to be more addressee-oriented leaving more room for alternative views. Italian TTs, in contrast, despite their integrating a large number of instantiations of functional equivalence, in some cases opt for reducing some explicit indicators of Engagement either through shifts towards a higher degree of certainty or through omissions.

The analyses of the case study lead us to the conclusion that English STs are representative of the CUSP model (see Section 5.3.1), since they frequently engage the reader through different instantiations of Engagement, while Italian TTs sometimes seem closer to the PUS-PAST model.

In terms of translation strategies, the effective use of functional equivalence seems to confirm the high quality of the magazine *Internazionale* and of the professional translators working for it, who are capable of dealing with the SL and the TL in a creative way and of moving beyond literal translation.

Let us now give an answer to the initial research questions.

The first issue concerned the question whether shifts seem to be linked to the different degrees of popularization of the STs. Indeed, we do find differences in the instantiation of Engagement resources both in the STs and in their translations. For example, instances of Entertain and Attribute are less frequent in the feature articles published in broadsheet newspapers, as if they pursued the so-called 'objectivism' of news discourse. In terms of translation choices, 35–37% of Entertain, Attribute and Proclaim:Endorse resources were not conveyed. But the most striking finding is that about 66% of the instances of Proclaim:Pronounce were not rendered. Obviously, Italian translators (or their editors) undervalue heteroglossia in the TTs.

On the other hand, consumer magazines are the medium where 'equivalence' at the level of Engagement (excluding the sub-category of

Proclaim:Concur) is higher. This might be explained with the authority of the STs. Five articles were translated from the authoritative *Economist*. In addition, the two longest articles in the corpus were published in the Sunday *New York Times Magazine* and in the *New Yorker*. The former represents a combination of information and entertainment, the latter is 'not bought because readers want to read reportage or opinions expressed in a corporate monotone: [it is] bought precisely for the variety and literary quality of voices [it] offer[s]' (McKay 2013: 79). In other words, the texts published in these magazines may have been seen as more similar to literary texts and therefore may have entailed more respect for their stylistic features.

Finally, the analysis of articles included in specialized science magazines has revealed that subjectivity abounds in the STs, which contain the highest number of instances of Proclaim. In the categories Concur and Endorse, the Engagement resources are mainly conveyed in the TTs, which may reflect a search for a higher degree of equivalence in more specialized media. It seems that translators have been closer to the rhetorical style of academic and scientific discourse using language in a more tentative and non-assertive way. On the other hand, the fact that most instances of Proclaim:Pronounce are not conveyed in the TTs might be interpreted as evidence of the typical attitude on the part of translators to reduce risk (cf. Munday 2015: 415).

When looking at the scientific field the texts address, it is interesting that the only article that represents the category of 'hard sciences' contains no instances of Proclaim, only one instance of Attribute – conveyed through functional equivalence – and seven instances of Entertain, five of which were rendered through direct equivalence. Even though one article cannot be said to be representative of a register family and larger corpora are obviously needed for more consistent conclusions, we may observe that, even in a science blog, 'hard sciences' are treated with more respect both on the part of the (anonymous) science writer and of the translator, who conveyed almost all the Engagement resources at work.

The second research question was whether shifts can be related to different communicative preferences in the two linguacultures. Even though it is undoubted that 'forms of interpersonal realization and interaction can vary enormously between languages' (Munday 2012: 35), there is not sufficient work available on the comparison of popular science discourse across Anglo-American and Italian journalistic cultures. Nevertheless, the fact that our analysis revealed sparse evidence of more dialogism added in the TTs (see ex. 4) seems to discourage the hypothesis that patterns of shifts or omissions are due to the target context of culture. The only shifts that might be due to different conventions of textual organization in the Italian journalistic context could be those cases where omissions seem to aim at avoiding repetition in the TT.

We also tend to dismiss the assumption that 'TT variation may be indicative of speaker idiolect' (Munday 2015: 68) for two reasons: first, the small corpus contains articles translated by seven different translators; second, all the TTs – albeit translated from different sources – were published in the same target magazine, *Internazionale*, which follows a strong editorial policy: any article translated for this magazine is revised and edited by at least five people, including editors and copy editors (Momigliano 2012).

To account for shifts, practical constraints also have to be taken into account: the corpus includes 17 instances of longer source features condensed into one-page articles, and thus certain omissions may occur because of a higher degree of manipulation and abridgement. Yet it is surprising that certain omissions concern interpersonal rather than ideational meanings.

The third research question asked to what extent translation shifts may affect the process of 'democratization' of science. Hewings (2010: 17) asserts that '[t]here is a broad consensus that it is important for citizens and their leaders to be scientifically literate so that they can both appreciate the role of science in society and be part of an informed debate about its applications, benefits and limitations'.

Also Tinker Perrault (2013: 113) points out that, depending on the way popular science texts 'pose problems, they may invite readers to be passive recipients of knowledge, or to be engaged coparticipants in figuring out what the knowledge means'. Since in Italy popular science articles reach larger audiences especially through translation and since a journalistic TT is read as 'original writing', the reduction or elimination of a certain number of dialogistic resources may have an impact on the final receptors. In other words, the Italian public may perceive fewer heteroglossic texts as expressions of the previous PAST model (see Section 5.3.1). But what readers ultimately think of this conscious or unconscious manipulation occurring in the TTs has to be left to reception studies.

5.6 Concluding remarks

Investigating interpersonal meanings is fundamental for investigating the positioning of the writer, of the reader and, as Munday (2015: 407) suggests, 'by extension, of the translator'. In this chapter, focussing on the process of translation of popular science feature articles in the written media, I have sought to offer a small contribution to the research based on the Engagement System and to show its potential for analytical purposes from a linguistic and translational perspective. The small size of the case study does not clearly permit any definitive conclusions about properties of translated popular science texts in different media, so further research is required. In particular, more studies of larger parallel corpora are needed in order to see whether my findings can be validated as typical of the register and its translation.

Although one of the limits of the study is that it is exclusively centred on the language pair English>Italian, I nonetheless argue that a similar approach could be extended to other languages. Furthermore, given that shifts occurring in the process of translation may have a significant impact on the reception of the texts, additional research could look into the perception of interested lay-readers with respect to their engagement in the reading experience and could delve into the area of reception studies, which might offer fruitful insights. Last but not least, even though this chapter is primarily intended as a contribution to SFL and TS, it can transcend the borders of these disciplines and engage science communication studies. Hence, a concerted effort by scholars from different fields would ultimately make a contribution to civil society, helping the public to develop a critical understanding of science journalism.

About the author

Marina Manfredi is a Lecturer in English Language and Translation at the University of Bologna, Italy. She teaches English Language and Linguistics to undergraduate students and English Translation to postgraduates. Her main research interests lie in the fields of Systemic Functional Linguistics and Translation Studies and include Teaching Translation, Postcolonial Translation Studies, Translation and World Englishes (especially Indian English), Audiovisual Translation (in particular of multicultural television programmes for younger audiences) and Metaphor Translation. She has contributed to national and international conferences on these topics and has published various articles and two books (*Translating Text and Context: Translation Studies and Systemic Functional Linguistics, Volume 1: Translation Theory*, Bologna: Dupress, 2008; *Translating Text and Context: Translation Studies and Systemic Functional Linguistics, Volume 2: From Theory to Practice*, Bologna: Asterisco, 2014). Her current research mainly concerns translation for the media, in particular, translation of popular science for press magazines and for the web, and news translation.

Notes

1 For an overview, see White (2012).
2 Space restrictions preclude illustration of the theory. For a detailed account, see Martin & White (2005).
3 For an overview of the notion of 'equivalence' in TS, see Manfredi (2008: 65–71).
4 Similar magazines are the *Courrier International* in France and the *Courrier Internacional* in Portugal.
5 The article was translated from *Die Tageszeitung* (*Internazionale* 990, 8 March 2013).
6 Verbal groups introducing a quotation or a reported locution were not included in the analysis since they are not relevant to translation aspects.

References

Bednarek, M. (2006) *Evaluation in Media Discourse. Analysis of a Newspaper Corpus*. London/New York: Continuum.

Fuller, G. (1998) 'Cultivating science: Negotiating discourse in the popular texts of Stephen Jay Gould'. In: Martin, J.R. & Veel, R (eds.) *Reading Science*. London/New York: Routledge, 35–62.

Gualdo, R. & Telve, S. (2011) *Linguaggi specialistici dell'italiano*. Rome: Carocci.

Halliday, M.A.K. (1994) *An Introduction to Functional Grammar*. 2nd edition. London: Arnold.

Halliday, M.A.K. (2001) 'Towards a theory of good translation'. In: Steiner, E. & Yallop, C. (eds.) *Exploring Translation and Multilingual Text Production: Beyond Content*. Berlin/New York: Mouton de Gruyter, 13–18.

Halliday, M.A.K. & Matthiessen, C.M.I.M. (2014) *Halliday's Introduction to Functional Grammar*. 4th edition. London/New York: Routledge.

Harcup, T. (2005) 'Doing it in style: Feature writing'. In: Keeble, R. (ed.) *Print Journalism*. London/New York: Routledge, 140–148.

Hewings, M. (2010) '"Boffins create 'Supermouse'": The role of popular science press in creating the public image of scientists and their work'. In: Gea-Valor, M.-L., García-Izquierdo, I. & Esteve, M.-J. (eds.) *Linguistic and Translation Studies in Scientific Communication*. Bern: Peter Lang, 15–36.

House, J. (1997) *Translation Quality Assessment: A Model Revisited*. Tübingen: Gunter Narr.

Keeble, R. 'Introduction'. In: Keeble, R. (ed.) *Print Journalism*. London/New York: Routledge, xiii–xiv.

Kranich, S., House, J. & Becher, V. (2012) 'Changing conventions in English-German translations of popular scientific texts'. In: Braunmüller, K. & Gabriel, C. (eds.) *Multilingual Individuals and Multilingual Societies*. Amsterdam/Philadelphia: John Benjamins, 315–334.

Liao, M.-H. (2011) 'Interaction in the genre of popular science: Writer, Translator and Reader'. *The Translator* 17(2), 349–368.

Liao, M.-H. (2013) 'Popularization and Translation'. In: Gambier, Y. & van Doorslaer, L. (eds.) *Handbook of Translation Studies*. Vol. 4. Amsterdam/Philadelphia: John Benjamins, 130–133.

Macdonald, S.P. (2005) 'The language of journalism in treatments of hormone replacement news'. *Written Communication* 22, 275–297.

Manfredi, M. (2008) *Translating Text and Context: Translation Studies and Systemic Functional Linguistics*. Vol. I. *Translation Theory*. Bologna: Dupress.

Martin, J.R. & White, P.R.R. (2005) *The Language of Evaluation: Appraisal in English*. Basingstoke/New York: Palgrave.

Minelli de Oliveira, J. & Pagano, A.S. (2006) 'The research article and the science popularization article: A probabilistic functional grammar perspective on direct discourse representation'. *Discourse Studies* 8(5), 627–646.

Momigliano, A. (2012) 'Dentro Internazionale'. *Studio* Vol. 8 (http://www.rivistastudio.com/standard/nella-fabbrica-di-internazionale/)

Munday, J. (2012) *Evaluation in Translation*. London/New York: Routledge.

Munday, J. (2015) 'Engagement and graduation resources as markers of translator/interpreter positioning'. *Target* 27(3), 406–421.

Myers, G. (2003) 'Discourse studies of scientific popularization: questioning the boundaries'. *Discourse Studies* 5(2), 265–279.

Nelkin, D. (1987) *Selling Science: How the Press Covers Science and Technology*. New York: Freeman.

OECD (2007) *Revised Field of Science and Technology (FOS) Classification in the Frascati Manual*. (http://www.oecd.org/science/inno/38235147.pdf)

Olohan, M. (2016) *Scientific and Technical Translation*. London/New York: Routledge.

Qian, H. (2012) 'Investigating Translators' Positioning via the Appraisal Theory: A Case Study of the Q&A Part of a Speech Delivered by the U.S. Vice President Cheney'. *Sino-US English Teaching* 9(12), 1775–1787.

Ragazzini, G. (2016) *Dizionario Inglese-Italiano/Italiano-Inglese*. Bologna: Zanichelli.

Thomson, E. & White, P.R.R. (eds.) (2008) *Communicating Conflict: Multilingual Case Studies of the News Media*. London/New York: Continuum.

Tinker Perrault, S. (2013) *Communicating Popular Science: From Deficit to Democracy*. Basingstoke/New York: Palgrave Macmillan.

Vandepitte, S., Vandenbussche, L. & Algoet, B. (2011) 'Travelling certainties: Darwin's doubts and their Dutch translations'. *The Translator* 17(2), 275–299.

White, P.R.R. (2012) 'Exploring the axiological workings of "reporter voice" news stories – Attribution and attitudinal positioning'. *Discourse, Context & Media* 1, 57–67.

Zhang, M. (2011) 'The language of Appraisal and the translator's attitudinal positioning'. In: Zhang, J.Y. (ed.) *Functional Linguistics and Translation Studies*. Beijing: Foreign Language Teaching and Research Press, 180–190.

News texts analyzed

Adee, S. (2013) 'Stupid is as stupid does'. *New Scientist*, 30 March, 2013.

Arthur, C. (2013) 'Paywalls for all or not? The real issue is what's the core offering'. *Guardian*, 31 March, 2013. (https://www.theguardian.com/media/media-blog/2013/mar/31/paywalls-news-commodity-core-product) [31.07.2017]

De Waal, F. (2013) 'The brains of the animal kingdom'. *Wall Street Journal*, 23 March, 2013.

Lohr, S. (2013) 'Big data, trying to build better workers'. *New York Times*, 21 April, 2013.

Monbiot, G. (2013) 'My search for a smartphone that is not soaked in blood'. *Guardian*, 11 March, 2013. (https://www.theguardian.com/commentisfree/2013/mar/11/search-smartphone-soaked-blood) [31.07.2017]

Morozov, E. (2013) 'Is smart making us dumb?' *Wall Street Journal* (online), 23 February, 2013.

N.A. 'Natural justice'. *The Economist*, 20 April, 2013.

Specter, M. (2013) 'Germs are us'. *New Yorker*, 22 October, 2012.

Young, E. (2013) 'Do get mad'. *New Scientist*, 9 February, 2013.

6 The interpersonal metafunction of *and*-parenthetical clauses in English journalism

Carlos Prado-Alonso
University of Oviedo, Spain

6.1 Introduction

'Parenthetical constructions', also called 'supplementals' (cf. Huddleston & Pullum 2002: 1350), are detached structures (often clauses) which are inserted but not fully integrated in the middle of another structure so that they can be omitted without affecting the rest of the structure. Consider the example given in (1):[1]

(1) Thus, an act of reconstruction, of encampment, is an articulation of one's religious 'identity', and it is, <u>I believe</u>, an utterly necessary activity.[2]

Over the last decade, several types of parenthetical constructions, as illustrated in (2) to (6) below, have been the subject of extensive research from a functional perspective (for example, Burton-Roberts 1999, 2006; Blakemore 2005, 2007; Dehé 2014; Dehé & Kavalova 2006, 2007; Potts 2002, 2005; Prado-Alonso 2015). This study is a further contribution to this line of research and offers a corpus-based analysis of one type of parentheticals, namely the so-called '*and*-parenthetical' construction, as shown in (6). The analysis seeks to cast light on the frequency, distribution and metafunction (cf. Halliday & Matthiessen 2004) of this construction in Present-day English journalism, particularly in reportage, editorials and reviews.

(2) One might even arrive at the position, *as is the case in commercial lettings*, where a farm let to a good tenant is worth as much as it would be if in hand. (*as*-parenthetical)

(3) We will proceed towards this amalgamated trade union by way of a purely 'economic thoroughfare' (*or garden path*) with the political ramifications kept neatly in the background. (*or*-parenthetical)

(4) Robert Protherough suggests that there is a spectrum between what is objectively correct – *that is, something which all speakers of a language will agree on as being 'there' in the text* – and things which are subjective. (*that is*-parenthetical)
(5) I've been dreaming of winning a gold medal for *what* 20 years now. (*what*-parenthetical; taken from Dehé & Kavalova 2006: 289.)
(6) Any glossary of the Russo-American political vocabulary (*and I am thinking of everyday speech as well as official statements*) must include these entries. (*and*-parenthetical)

The data for the study are taken from six digitized corpora of British and American Present-day English: (1) the *Lancaster-Oslo-Bergen Corpus of British English* (LOB; compilation date: 1961), (2) the *Brown Corpus of American English* (Brown; compilation date: 1961), (3) the *Freiburg-Lancaster-Oslo-Bergen Corpus of British English* (FLOB; compilation date: 1991), (4) the *Freiburg-Brown Corpus of American English* (FROWN; compilation date: 1992), (5) the *British English 2006 Corpus* (BE06) and (6) the *American English 2006 Corpus* (AmE06) (for details see Hofland et al. 1999 and Baker 2009). Each corpus comprises around 1,000,000 words and is divided into fifteen textual categories, of which the following have been selected for the present analysis: *Press Reportage, Press Editorial* and *Press Review*, as illustrated in Table 6.1. A total sample of 1,056,000 words has been analyzed. Since the three press categories differ in size, frequencies have been normalized per 100,000 words in line with Biber's (1988: 14) proposal for a 'normalized frequency of a feature'.

Table 6.1 Sources and distribution of the corpus texts from LOB, Brown, FLOB and FROWN, BE06, AmE06

Textual categories	*Subcategories*	*Samples*	*Words*
Press Reportage	Political newspapers Society newspapers Sport newspapers Financial newspapers Spot news newspapers Cultural newspapers	264	528,000
Press Editorial	Institutional texts Personal texts Letters to the editor	162	324,000
Press Review	Reviews	102	204,000
TOTAL		528	1,056,000

The paper is organized as follows: Section 6.2 offers some preliminary observations on the structural patterns of the *and*-parenthetical construction and its syntactic differences with *and*-coordination. Section 6.3 analyzes the overall distribution of the construction in different journalistic genres. This distribution will be the basis for the functional and textual analysis provided in Section 6.4. Finally a summary of the main conclusions is offered in Section 6.5.

6.2 '*And*-parenthetical' and '*and*-coordinated' constructions

In terms of syntax, *and*-parenthetical constructions are 'and-conjuncts' that normally occur in an interpolated position, as illustrated in (7). 'Interpolations' take place when, as in (8), the *and*-parenthetical construction is located at a position between the beginning and end of a main clause and represents an interruption in the flow of the clause (cf. Huddleston & Pullum 2002: 1350). Alternatively, *and*-parentheticals may occur as 'appendages' and be loosely attached to the beginning or end of a clause, as in (9). However, as shown in Dehé & Kavalova (2007:149) and further demonstrated in the present corpus-based analysis (cf. Section 6.3), *and*-parentheticals functioning as appendages are rare.

(7) No previous Byron biographer that I fancy *(and they have been many)* has had access at the same time to so many important manuscripts.

(8) If Indian agriculture continues to modernize rapidly – *and one should not be excessively optimistic here* – then the presence of a large rural service sector will provide something of a surplus labour pool.

(9) One almost expected to see Ayman Al Zawahiri sitting cross-legged beside him (and, in fact, a recently released GOP ad actually does show Bin Laden making his threats.)

(10) Can any warrant or sanction for them be found in existing Anglican formularies, or in the main stream of the Anglican theological tradition? If not, *and we think that the answer is no,* then they can have no rightful place in Catechism for the Church of England.

And-parentheticals have been considered discontinuous constituents, not only because they interrupt the syntactic string and often the prosodic flow of a host structure but also because they do not have a syntactically specified function in that host structure: they do not function as heads, specifiers, complements or adjuncts (cf. Haegeman 1988, Espinal 1991, Peterson 1999). This discontinuity is also phonologically marked since *and*-parentheticals tend to be intonationally separate from the rest of the sentence ('comma intonation', cf. Emonds 1979). The intonation break is realized in writing by punctuation marks: parentheses, colons, dashes, or commas, as shown in (8) to (10). According to Burton-Roberts (2006: 180), this is a feature that most parentheticals share in that 'they are marked off from their hosts by some form of punctuation in writing and special intonation contour in speech.'[3]

Formally, *and*-parentheticals resemble canonical *and*-coordination in that they make use of the connector *and*. However, there are syntactic criteria to distinguish the two constructions. *And*-parentheticals, for instance, are omissible in discourse: that is, the host sentence can exist freely and be grammatical regardless of the parenthetical that is interpolated, as shown in (11). By contrast, the omission of constituents in *and*-coordination constructions is not normally allowed. This is illustrated in (12), where the omission of the coordinator and the second constituent renders the sentence ungrammatical. As Kavalova (2007: 153) notes, coordinated conjoins 'usually form a constituent together which influences or is influenced as a whole by the syntactic structure of the clause'. In other words, in *and*-coordination both conjoins share the same thematic function. This is not the case in *and*-parentheticals since the construction exists independently and does not share its thematic role and form with its adjacent constituents.

(11) (a) There is a prima facie connection between a person's sex and gender – *and I use this latter term simply because it serves to distinguish between psychological and physical sex and has recently gained some currency* – but the connection is not invariable or insoluble in Gaskell.

(b) There is a prima facie connection between a person's sex and gender but the connection is not invariable or insoluble in Gaskell.

(12) (a) In terms of size and scale, only Glasgow and Edinburgh are comparable to the English core cities, if we are to offer a market of a similar range.

(b) *In terms of size and scale, only Glasgow are comparable to the English core cities, if we are to offer a market of a similar range.

(13) (a) She came back the other day to reassure me that she studied *and observed, and is convinced* that her young man is going to be endlessly enchanting.
  (b) She came back the other day to reassure me that she studied and *[she]* observed, and *[she]* is convinced that her young man is going to be endlessly enchanting.
(14) (a) Einstein sometimes invoked the name of God *(and he is not the only atheistic scientist to do so)* inviting misunderstanding by supernaturalists eager to misunderstand and claim so illustrious a thinker as their own.
  (b) *Einstein sometimes invoked the name of God *(and is not the only atheistic scientist to do so)* inviting misunderstanding by supernaturalists eager to misunderstand and claim so illustrious a thinker as their own.

Another syntactic difference between the two constructions is that canonical coordination allows the ellipsis of elements in the structure, while this is not so with *and*-parentheticals. Coordinated structures allow the omission of a constituent when that constituent is shared by both conjoins in the structure. This is illustrated in (13) above, where the subject *she* is shared in the three conjoins and is therefore factored out in the second and third of these (cf. 13b). *And*-parentheticals, by contrast, do not allow such omission, as shown in (14a), where the *and*-parenthetical construction and the host utterance share the same subject-referent *Einstein*, yet it is not possible to omit the subject in either of the clauses (cf. 14b). This has led some scholars (cf. Safir 1986) to argue that *and*-parentheticals are syntactically independent of the host utterance in which they occur. Kaltenböck and Heine (2014: 358), for instance, consider *and*-clauses, such as those illustrated in (11a) and (14a), to be a type of 'constructional thetical'. Such a claim, to which I will return in Section 6.4, regards parentheticals – and *and*-parentheticals in particular – as a separate domain of grammar referred to as 'thetical grammar', which competes with and complements the domain of 'sentence grammar'. Formally speaking, *and*-parentheticals are therefore considered to be syntactically independent of their environment: they do not have any syntagmatic link (paratactic or hypotactic) to their host clause, and they convey a non-restrictive meaning (cf. Huddleston & Pullum, 2002: 1350–62). This is so because the meaning of *and*-parentheticals is not restricted to or determined by the syntax of the host utterance. Rather, according to Kaltenböck and Heine

96   *Analyzing the Media: A Systemic Functional Approach*

(2014: 353), it relates to the situation of discourse. In (11a), for instance, the meaning of the *and*-parenthetical construction is not semantically part of the sentence *There is a prima facie connection between a person's sex and gender but the connection is not invariable or insoluble in Gaskell*. Instead, the meaning has scope over the situation of discourse: the addressor-addressee interaction.

The following section provides a corpus-based analysis of *and*-parentheticals in three text-types that are typical of English journalism: reportage, editorials and reviews. It will be shown that there are differences in the distribution of these constructions in these genres and that these differences are based on the metafunction that the structures serve in discourse.

6.3 A corpus-based analysis of *and*-parentheticals in English journalism

To date, the analysis of *and*-parentheticals has received very little attention in corpus linguistics. Biber et al. (1999: 1067), for example, is a highly regarded grammar with a focus on corpus data, yet it does not provide any corpus-based or register-based analysis of the distribution of *and*-parentheticals. In general, most of the literature on *and*-parentheticals has neglected studying them in real data. The only exception appears to be Kavalova (2007), whose analysis is restricted to unplanned spoken language on the grounds that parenthetical constructions have been said to be less frequently attested in writing (cf. Wichmann 2001: 189). Kavalova's analysis is based on a sample of 70 instances drawn from the *International Corpus of English* (ICE-GB) and the *Diachronic Corpus of Present-day Spoken English* (DCPSE). The size of the sample makes it possible to exemplify pragmatic claims but does not allow for reliable statistical claims regarding the distribution and use of the construction in real language.

The analysis of data from the LOB, FLOB, Brown, FROWN, BE06 and AmE06 corpora provides a total of 603 instances of *and*-parenthetical constructions, distributed as illustrated in Figure 6.1. The data show that *and*-parenthetical constructions do occur in journalistic writing and demonstrate that the analysis of these constructions should not be restricted to unplanned spoken discourse only.

As Figure 6.1 shows, *and*-parenthetical constructions occur more frequently in editorials (64.19) than in reviews (56.86), and even less often in reportage (52.46). A preliminary explanation for this distribution across

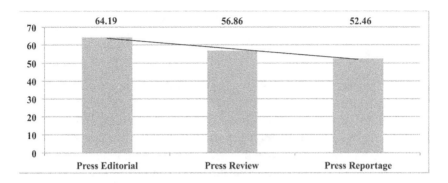

Figure 6.1 Normalized distribution of *and*-parenthetical clauses in Press Reportage, Press Editorial and Press Review

the three genres can be found in Biber (1988:127), who shows that the categories of *Press Editorial* and *Press Review* typically contain discourse including interactional, affective or involved purposes, whereas *Press Reportage* is typically more objective and presents a straightforward packaging of information which serves stronger informational purposes – carefully crafted and edited – with fewer rhetorical effects. In this latter context, parenthetical constructions, with their potentially digressive structure, would indeed be expected to be less frequent. However, in order to look at specific reasons for this difference in distribution, a more comprehensive analysis of the construction is given in Section 6.4. Based on Biber's (1988, 1995) analyses of the textual categories of the LOB and the Brown corpus, this analysis applies a stable and previously tested set of six dimensions of linguistic variation: (1) Involved versus Informational Production, (2) Narrative versus Non-narrative Concerns, (3) Explicit versus Situation-Dependent Reference, (4) Overt Expression of Persuasion, (5) Abstract versus Non-abstract Information, and (6) On-line Informational Elaboration. The results of the distribution of *and*-parenthetical structures in the three journalistic categories of the six corpora analyzed here will be compared to Biber's analysis. Since the structure of LOB and Brown matches that of FLOB, FROWN, BrE06 and AmE06 (for details see Hofland et al. 1999, Mair 2002), the present analysis will show whether the distribution of *and*-parenthetical constructions across the three genres is sensitive to Dimension 1 of linguistic variation.

6.4 *And*-parentheticals in English journalism

6.4.1 A multidimensional analysis

As stated above, Biber (1988, 1995) analyzes linguistic variation in the textual categories of the LOB and the Brown corpora in terms of six dimensions. Dimension 1, which he labels 'Involved versus Informational Production', makes a distinction between two types of discourse: (a) discourse that serves interactional, affective or involved purposes and that is controlled by strict real-time production and comprehension constraints, and (b) discourse that serves highly informational purposes. Dimension 2, 'Narrative versus Non-narrative Concerns', distinguishes discourse pursuing primarily narrative purposes from discourse pursuing non-narrative purposes, hence dealing with the difference between active, event-oriented discourse and more static descriptive or expository types of discourse. Dimension 3, 'Explicit versus Situation-Dependent Reference', distinguishes between discourse that identifies referents fully and explicitly, and discourse that relies on non-specific deictics and references to external situations for identification purposes. This dimension thus corresponds closely to the distinction between 'endophoric' and 'exophoric' reference (cf. Halliday & Hasan 1976). Dimension 4, 'Overt Expression of Persuasion', refers to those features associated with the speaker's expression of point of view or with argumentative styles which have clearly persuasive aims. Dimension 5, labelled 'Abstract versus Non-abstract Information', distinguishes between texts with a highly abstract and technical informational focus and those with a non-abstract focus. Finally, Dimension 6, 'On-line Informational Elaboration', distinguishes between informational discourse produced under highly constrained conditions in which the information is presented in a relatively loose, fragmented manner, and other types of discourse, be it informational discourse that is highly integrated or discourse that is non-informational in nature.

Biber's work, in fact, confirms that pure text types are rare and that texts should be seen by default as multidimensional. As an example, fictional texts cannot simply be considered similar to, or different from, non-fictional texts. Rather they are more, or less similar with respect to each dimension of linguistic variation. In addition to multidimensionality, variation is treated as continuously scalar in Biber's analysis. The six parameters, then, define continua of variation rather than discrete poles. For example, although it is possible to describe a text as simply abstract or non-abstract, it seems more accurate to describe it as more or less abstract. The similarities and differences among textual categories can therefore be considered with regard to all six dimensions; thus, the same genres can be similar with respect to some dimensions but quite different with respect to others.

6.4.2 The *and*-parenthetical construction and the degree of addressor's involvement

For Dimension 1, 'Involved versus Informational Production', Biber (1988:142) shows that the texts in the category *Press Reportage* have very low mean scores (cf. Figure 6.2 below). This means they exhibit a high degree of informational content and are frequently characterized as the most information-based texts in a newspaper (cf. Lüger 1983: 66). In contrast, texts from the categories *Press Review* and *Press Editorial* typically showcase higher mean scores in Dimension 1. Editorials, or authorial comments (cf. Jones 1983: 87), are primarily argumentative by nature (cf. Wikberg 1992: 248) and belong to the class of persuasive text types within the taxonomies of journalistic writing (cf. Lüger 1983: 82). These types typically contain addressor-based prominence features and incorporate a stronger presence of the interpersonal function of language (cf. Halliday & Matthiessen 2004). Reviews in newspapers tend to deal with art, music, films, radio programs, books, TV, etc. and, at first sight, appear to have a lot in common with editorials. They have also been characterized as primarily argumentative (cf. Wikberg 1992: 48) or persuasive (cf. Lüger 1983: 87). However, it has also been shown that reviews have a stronger representative component than editorials (cf. Biber 1989) and that a typical review consists of both informational and persuasive parts.

The comparison of Biber's findings for the 'Involved or Informational' nature of texts (cf. Figure 6.2) with the distribution of *and*-parentheticals in the three journalistic categories analyzed here (cf. Figure 6.3) confirms that the *and*-parenthetical construction is favoured in text categories with a higher degree of addressor involvement (cf. Biber 1995: 156), and disfavoured in those with a lower degree. What is more, the more information-based a journalistic text is, the fewer *and*-parentheticals are to be expected.

As shown in Table 6.2, this tendency is seen even more clearly if we measure the correlation between Biber's (1988) mean scores on Dimension 1 and the normalized frequencies of *and*-parenthetical constructions by calculating a Pearson correlation coefficient.[4] The result, which is highly significant at the $p \leq 0.001$ level, is *–0.9534* and confirms that the more

```
              +   INVOLVED  /  – INFORMATIONAL
                  |
                  | telephone conversations
                  |
        35-       | face-to-face conversations
                  |
        30-       |
                  |
        25-       |
                  |
        20-       | personal letters
                  | spontaneous speeches
                  | interviews
        15-       |
                  |
        10-       |
                  |
         5-       |
                  | romantic fiction
                  | prepared speeches
         0-       | mystery and adventure fiction
                  | general fiction
                  | professional letters
                  | broadcasts
        -5-       |
                  | science fiction
                  | religion
                  | humor
       -10-       | popular lore; press editorials; hobbies
                  |
                  | press reviews
                  | biographies
       -15-       | academic prose; press reportage
                  |
                  | official documents
       -20-
              –   INVOLVED  /  + INFORMATIONAL
```

Figure 6.2 Mean scores of Dimension 1: Involved vs. Informational Production (cf. Biber 1988: 128, emphases added)

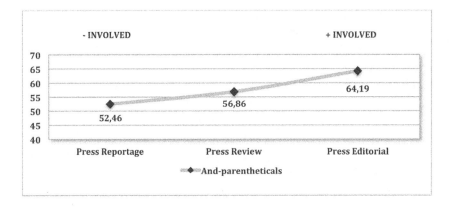

Figure 6.3 Distribution of the *and*-parenthetical construction in the journalistic textual categories of the corpora

Table 6.2 Pearson correlation coefficient for the distribution of *and*-parenthetical clauses and Biber's (1988: 122–124) mean scores on Dimension 1

	Mean scores of selected categories on Dimension 1	*Normalized frequencies for and-parentheticals*
Press Reportage	−10.0	52.46
Press Review	−13.9	58.86
Press Editorial	−15.1	63.19
CORRELATION COEFFICIENT	−0.9534	

information-oriented a text is, the fewer *and*-parenthetical constructions are to be expected.[5] In journalistic writing, the frequency of *and*-parenthicals therefore seems to be dependent on the involved nature of the text in which these constructions occur.

6.4.3 The interpersonal metafunction of *and*-parentheticals in English journalism writing

In recent decades, parentheticals have received extensive attention from a range of pragmatic perspectives (cf. Potts 2002, 2005; Dehé & Kavalova 2007; Dehé 2014; Lee-Goldman 2012; Kaltenböck & Heine 2014, among others). They have been described as 'mitigators' (cf. Schneider 2007), 'hedges' (cf. Hand 1993), 'turn-taking devices' (cf. Mazeland 2007), 'implicatures' (cf. Potts 2005), and 'partitions' (cf. Ziv 2002). In the case of *and*-parentheticals, they have been seen as constructions that an addressor can use to achieve 'optimal relevance' (cf. Blakemore 2006). Optimal relevance is the core principle of Relevance Theory and states that 'every act of overt communication communicates a presumption of its own optimal relevance' (Sperber & Wilson 1995: 158). Optimal relevance is therefore defined in terms of cognitive effects and processing effort (cf. Sperber & Wilson 1995) so that it increases with the number of effects and decreases with the amount of processing required. Blakemore (2005: 1167) maintains that *and*-parentheticals 'are the result of a deliberate stylistic choice' and are used in the pursuit of optimal relevance, as illustrated in (15). She argues that, since the addressor always aims at optimal relevance, he makes assumptions about the addressee's contextual resources and processing ability and, based on these assumptions, chooses a style thought to be relevant. In (15), for instance, the addressor, in his desire to be relevant, does the following: (a) he introduces the *and*-parenthetical construction in mid-clause position (to explain who Emmanuel Shinwell is); (b) at the same time, he disambiguates the sentence (not any Emmanuel Shinwell but the previous Defence Minister, whose opinion is valid in the context); and (c) he enriches the utterance from an informational point of view. In other words, the addressor achieves the three sub-tasks involved in the identification of a propositional form: disambiguation, reference assignment and enrichment (cf. Sperber & Wilson 1995: 185).

(15) Emmanuel Shinwell thought *and he is after all the previous Defence Minister* that you can't have informed opinion on this vital matter. (taken from Kavalova 2007: 158)

According to Blakemore (2005), the achievement of optimal relevance justifies the addressor's motivation for interrupting the natural pace of the utterance with an *and*-parenthetical clause and, in what seems to be an inconvenience for the process of interpretation, allows the expression of certain kinds of information and the creation of cognitive effects which would otherwise be less accessible to the addressee. In other words, by interrupting the main string with the parenthetical, the addressor achieves optimal relevance at a minimal processing cost.

In the present analysis, the data seem to corroborate Blakemore's claim in that the *and*-parenthetical constructions from the corpora also aim at achieving optimal relevance. However, my data also show that many of these constructions are not only used for this purpose but they also serve to express the author's commitment to the proposition in the main utterance.

In other words, they allow the involvement of the addressor and contain interpersonal or affective content.

Biber's (1988: 105) study shows that categories that score moderately low on Dimension 1 contain features that can be associated in one way or another with an involved, non-informational focus, due to a primarily interactive or affective purpose towards the information to be conveyed. The use of private verbs (e.g. *think, feel, reckon, believe*, etc.) is among the features with the largest weight on the degree of involvement, indicating a verbal style, as opposed to a nominal style, in which an overt expression of private attitudes, thoughts and emotions is present. Biber also demonstrates that first and second person pronouns also weigh heavily on the degree of involvement. They refer directly to the addressor and addressee and are thus used frequently in highly involved discourse.

My data show that *and*-parenthetical constructions are not only at home in those textual categories with a higher degree of addressor's involvement (i.e. 'Press Editorial' and 'Press Review') but they also serve an interpersonal function. Many of the *and*-parenthetical clauses retrieved from the corpora contain first person pronouns and private verbs, which are used to convey involvement in the texts in which they occur, as shown in the examples (16) to (21) below.

(16) If the money is there – *and we believe it is* – it should be spent equitably.
(17) I'm starting to believe – *and this, I suppose, is the weird part* – that maybe this day was the most important day of my entire life.
(18) If not *(and we think that the answer to all three questions is no)*, then they can have no rightful place in a Catechist.
(19) If the New Testament is a time-conditioned document – *and I agree that it is* – one can do no more with a quotation from Paul on this matter than point it out.
(20) A production that does not respond to such contrasts *(and we think this is only one example)* whatever its other merits, offers only an incomplete view of Mozart's play.
(21) At the end, Hood didn't even find Gepetto: she just melted into the darkness, still cloning fiendishly away. Certainly, this is a novel idea which – *and I suppose it might catch on* – has a sleuth who never apprehends anyone.

Biber (1988: 106) shows that subordination constructions such as causative subordination, sentence relatives, *wh*-clauses and conditional subordination may be used to express involvement in discourse. Causative subordination (e.g. *because*) can be considered to mark affect or stance, i.e. providing justification for actions or beliefs, while conditional subordination (e.g. *if, unless*) introduces conditions for actions or beliefs. Similarly, on the basis of the present corpus-analysis, the *and*-parenthetical construction in journalistic discourse can also be considered to serve such an interpersonal function (cf. Halliday & Matthiessen 2004: 117 ff.) as it is used to insert personal attitudes or feelings towards the information presented in the main clause. In (16), for instance, the inserted parenthetical gives rise to certain contextual assumptions, and the readers are prompted to include these in their processing of the utterance. They can draw conclusions about the addressor's emotional state and level of commitment to the information conveyed. This seems to be in line with Kavalova (2007: 169), who notes that in her oral corpus of 70 *and*-parentheticals some of the constructions are used to intensify the addressor's attitude towards the proposition in the main utterance through the reduplication (within the *and*-parenthetical construction) of a word which is already used in the main utterance. This is illustrated in (22), where the addressor's degree of commitment to the information expressed in the main utterance is reflected by his emphasis on *could*, which is repeated in the parenthetical construction.

> (22) Madam will the Minister confirm that come the single uh Common Market that three hundred million EEC nationals *could, and I emphasise could*, seek employment in this country without the need to obtain a work permit.
> (taken from Kavalova 2007: 150, emphases added)
> (23) There are thousands and thousands of flowers.

This type of *and*-parenthetical construction resembles 'coordinator-marked reduplication' (cf. Huddleston & Pullum 2002: 1304), as shown in (23), and may be restricted to oral communication as no example of reduplication has been attested in *and*-parentheticals retrieved from the written corpora. In writing, however, *and*-parentheticals may also perform an interpersonal function. They can be considered 'constructional theticals', that is 'recurrent syntactic patterns having a schematic format and function' (cf. Kaltenböck & Heine 2014: 358). They belong to a separate domain of grammar known as 'thetical grammar', which complements the domain of sentence grammar. Both the sentence and the thetical domain operate on their own principles: while the sentence is constrained by a syntactic hierarchy, the thetical domain is not syntactically constrained and is suitably used for immediate communication needs. In order to communicate successfully, addressors have the option of choosing between the two domains during the production of their texts. While the domain of sentence grammar has been claimed to be used to present ideational information (cf. Halliday & Matthiessen 2004: 75ff.), the thetical domain lends itself particularly well to the expression of interpersonal information. This certainly seems to be the case with *and*-parentheticals: they are part of the thetical domain, and, as the data analyzed here show, in journalistic discourse they are commonly related to expressing a writer's involvement and attitude. Since the thetical domain is syntactically more independent, it allows the insertion of the parenthecial construction almost anywhere in an utterance. As Kaltenböck and Heine (2014: 352) note, the use of the *and*-parenthetical in the thetical domain comes at a lower processing cost for the addressee than would be required for packaging the same information in the sentence grammar domain.

6.5 Summary and conclusions

As discussed in this chapter, *and*-parenthetical clauses have previously received very little attention from a corpus-based perspective. The *Longman Grammar of Spoken and Written Discourse* (Biber et al. 1999), for example, is a highly regarded grammar with a focus on corpus data, yet it provides no corpus-based or cross-register comparison of the distribution of *and*-parentheticals. The present corpus-based analysis has sought to begin the process of bridging this gap in the literature and has attempted to shed light on the distribution and function of *and*-parenthetical structures in Present-day written English.

It has traditionally been claimed that *and*-parentheticals are the result of a deliberate stylistic choice and are used to achieve optimal relevance in discourse (cf. Blakemore 2005). The achievement of such optimal relevance has been considered the main reason for the addressor's interruption of the natural pace of an utterance with an *and*-parenthetical construction. In other words, the use of *and*-parentheticals allows the writer to create certain informative and cognitive effects that would not be accessible to the recipients if he used a linear structure in an utterance. Beyond that, however, the present analysis has also demonstrated that the use of *and*-parentheticals is related to the degree of involvement of the texts in which they occur. The construction has been less commonly attested in press reportage, where texts are typically more objective, than in editorials and reviews, which represent discourse with interactional, affective or involved purposes. The comparison of Biber's (1988) findings for the involved or informational nature of texts with the distribution of the *and*-parenthetical construction in the corpora analyzed here has shown that the construction is less favoured in those journalistic texts which are less involved and where the presence of the writer is less commonly felt. Similarly, the results have shown that the more informational a text is, the fewer *and*-parentheticals are to be expected. It has also been shown that the construction itself frequently serves the interpersonal metafunction in journalistic writing. Many of the *and*-parenthetical clauses retrieved from the corpora contain first person pronouns and private verbs and are associated with the elaboration of personal attitudes or feelings towards the information presented in the main clause. Hence, it has been shown that the *and*-parenthetical construction can be considered a discourse marker used to express involvement in journalistic discourse. The construction serves the interpersonal metafunction, and the higher the degree of a writer's involvement in a journalistic text, the higher the number of *and*-parenthetical clauses that can be expected.

Acknowledgements

For generous financial support, I am grateful to the Spanish Ministry of Economy, Industry and Competitiveness (grant FFI2017-86884-P).

About the author

Carlos Prado-Alonso works as a full time lecturer in *English Language and Linguistics* at the University of Oviedo (Spain) and is a member of the Research Group *Variation Linguistic Change and Grammaticalization*, based at the University of Santiago de Compostela. He studied *English Language and Literature* at the University of Santiago de Compostela, from where he received his PhD in 2008. From 2009 to 2012 he worked at this university as a postdoctoral research fellow. He also stayed as a Visiting Fellow at the University of Manchester (2006), the Complutense University of Madrid (2009–2010) and the University of Edinburgh (2011–2012). Most of his published work has been on the systemic functional, corpus-based analysis of English syntax, e.g. on inverted constructions, verbal anaphoric structures and parenthetical clauses. His monograph *Full-verb Inversion in Written and Spoken English* (2011, Bern: Peter Lang) received the prestigious *ESSE 2012 Book Award* in 2012, awarded by the *European Society for the Study of English* in the category of English Language and Linguistics.

Notes

1   However, it is important to note that not all parenthetical constructions are semantically and syntactically detached from their hosts to the same degree (cf. Wichmann, 2001). Perhaps not surprisingly, more integrated or anchored parentheticals tend to coincide with the kind of parenthetical phenomena that have interested scholars hitherto.
2   Unless otherwise stated, the examples used in this study are taken from the LOB, Brown, FLOB, FROWN, BrE06 and AmE06 corpora.
3   However, as Kaltenböck and Heine (2014: 352) point out, a number of studies have shown that comma-intonation is not a reliable criterion for the identification of parentheticals (cf. Reinhart 1983: 178-179; Espinal 1991: 734; Wichmann 2001: 186; or Kaltenböck 2007: 3, among others). Some parentheticals lack a prosodic cue, and hence whereas the presence of a separate intonation is indicative of the presence of a parenthetical, its absence does not mean that the unit is not a parenthetical.
4   The Pearson Correlation measures the way in which two variables correlate. Its value indicates both the direction (positive or negative) and the strength of the correlation between two variables. The value +1 indicates a perfect positive correlation and the value −1 a perfect negative correlation, whereas a value of 0 indicates no correlation at all (cf. Butler 1985, Baayen 2008, and Johnson 2008, among others).
5   In statistics, the p-value or 'statistical significance' of a result is the probability that the observed relationship between variables in a sample occurred by pure chance. Results that are significant at the $p <= .01$ level are commonly considered statistically significant, at a $p <= .005$ level they are very significant, and at a $p <= .001$ level they are usually referred to as 'highly' significant.

References

Baayen, R.H. (2008) *Analyzing Linguistic Data: A Practical Introduction to Statistics Using R*. Cambridge: Cambridge University Press.

Baker, P. (2009) *Contemporary Corpus Linguistics*. London: Continuum.

Blakemore, D. (2005) '*And*-parentheticals'. *Journal of Pragmatics* 37, 1165–1181.

Blakemore, D. (2006) 'Divisions of labour. The analysis of parentheticals'. *Lingua* 116, 1670–1687.

Blakemore, D. (2007) '"Or"-parentheticals, "that is"-parentheticals and the pragmatics of reformulation'. *Journal of Linguistics* 43.2, 311–339.

Biber, D. (1988) *Variation across Speech and Writing*. Cambridge: Cambridge University Press.

Biber, D. (1989) 'A typology of texts'. *Linguistics* 27 (1), 3–43.

Biber, D. (1995) *Dimensions of Linguistic Variation. A Cross-linguistic Comparison*. Cambridge: Cambridge University Press.

Biber, D., Johansson, S., Leech, G., Conrad, S. & Finegan, E. (1999) *The Longman Grammar of Spoken and Written English*. London: Longman.

Burton-Roberts, N. (1999) 'Language, linear precedence and parentheticals'. In: Collins, P. & Lee, D. (eds.) *The Clause in English*. Amsterdam/Philadelphia: John Benjamins, 33–52.

Burton-Roberts, N. (2006) 'Parentheticals'. In: Brown, K. (ed.) *Encyclopaedia of Language and Linguistics*. 2nd edition. Boston: Elsevier Science, Vol. 9, 179–182.

Butler, C. S. 1985. *Statistics in Linguistics*. Oxford: Blackwell.

Dehé, N. & Kavalova, Y. (2006) 'The syntax, pragmatics and prosody of parenthetical what'. *English Language and Linguistics* 10.2, 289–320.

Dehé, N. & Kavalova, Y. (eds.) (2007) *Parentheticals* (Linguistik Aktuell/Linguistics Today 106). Amsterdam/Philadelphia: John Benjamins.

Dehé, N. (2014) *Parentheticals in Spoken English: The Syntax-Prosody Relation*. Studies in English Language. Cambridge: Cambridge University Press.

Emonds, J. (1979) 'Appositive relatives have no properties'. *Linguistic Inquiry* 10, 211–243.

Espinal, T.M. (1991) 'The representation of disjunct constituents'. *Language* 67, 726–762.

Haegeman, L. (1988) 'Parenthetical adverbials: the radical orphanage approach'. In: Chiba, S. Ogawa, A., Fuiwara, Y., Yamada, N., Koma, O. & Yagi, T. (eds.) *Aspects of Modern Linguistics. Papers presented to Masatomo Ukaji on his 60th Birthday.* Tokyo: Kaitakushi, 232–254.

Halliday, M.A.K. & Matthiessen, C.M.I.M. (2004) *Introduction to Functional Grammar*. 3rd edition. London: Edward Arnold.

Halliday, M.A.K. & Hasan, R. (1976) *Cohesion in English*. London: Longman.

Hand, M. (1993) 'Parataxis and parentheticals'. *Linguistics and Philosophy* 16, 495–507.

Hofland, K., Lindebjerg, A. & Thunestvedt, J. (1999) *ICAME Collection of English Language Corpora*. 2nd edition. CD-ROM version. Bergen: The HIT Centre.

Huddleston, R. & Pullum, G.K. (2002) *The Cambridge Grammar of the English Language*. Cambridge: Cambridge University Press.

Johnson, K. (2008) *Quantitative Methods in Linguistics*. Oxford: Blackwell.

Jones, L. B. (1983) *Pragmatic Aspects of English Text Structure*. A Publication of The Summer Institute of Linguistics and The University of Texas at Arlington. Publication 67.

Kaltenböck, G. (2007) 'Spoken parenthetical clauses in English'. In: Dehé, N. & Kavalova, Y. (eds.) *Parentheticals* (Linguistik Aktuell/Linguistics Today 106). Amsterdam/Philadelphia: John Benjamins, 25–52.

Kaltenböck, G. & Heine, B. (2014) 'Sentence grammar vs. thetical grammar: Two competing domains?' In: MacWhinney, B., Malchukov, A. & Moravscik, E. (eds.) *Competing Motivations in Grammar and Usage*. Oxford: Oxford University Press, 348–363.

Kavalova, Y. (2007) '*And*-parenthetical Clauses' In: Dehé, N. & Kavalova, Y. (eds.) *Parentheticals* (Linguistik Aktuell/Linguistics Today 106). Amsterdam/Philadelphia: John Benjamins, 145–172.

Lee-Goldman, R. (2012) 'Supplemental relative clauses: Internal and external syntax'. *Journal of Linguistics* 48.3, 573–608.

Lüger, H.-H. (1983) *Pressesprache*. Tübingen: Niemeyer

Mair, C. (2002) 'Three changing patterns of verb complementation in Late Modern English a real time study based on matching corpora'. *English Language and Linguistics* 6.1, 105–131.

Mazeland, H. (2007). 'Parenthetical sequences'. *Journal of Pragmatics* 39, 1816–1869.

Peterson, P. (1999). 'On the boundaries of syntax: Non-syntagmatic relations'. In: Collins, P., Lee, D. (eds.) *The Clause in English*. Amsterdam: John Benjamins, 229–250.

Potts, C. (2002a) 'The lexical semantics of parenthetical-as and appositive-which'. *Syntax* 5.1, 55–88.

Potts, C. (2002b) 'The syntax and semantics of *as*-parentheticals'. *Natural Language and Linguistic Theory* 20.3, 623–689.

Potts, C. (2005) *The Logic of Conventional Implicature*. Oxford: Oxford University Press.

Prado-Alonso, C. (2015) 'The *as be the case* construction'. *English Studies* 96/6, 690–709.

Reinhart, T. (1983) *Anaphora and Semantic Interpretation*. London: Croom Helm.

Safir, K. (1986) 'Relative clauses in a theory of binding and levels'. *Linguistic Inquiry* 17 (4), 663–689.

Schneider, S. (2007) *Reduced Parenthetical Clauses as Mitigators: A Corpus Study of Spoken French, Italian and Spanish*. Amsterdam/Philadelphia: John Benjamins.

Sperber, D. & Wilson, D. (1995) *Relevance, Communication and Cognition.* Oxford: Blackwell.

Wichmann, A. (2001) 'Spoken parentheticals'. In: Aijmer, K. (ed.) *A Wealth of English. Studies in Honour of Göran Kjellmer*. Göteborg: Acta Universitatis Gothoburgensis, 177–193.

Wikberg, K. (1992) 'Discourse category and text type classification: procedural discourse in the Brown and LOB corpora'. In: Leitner, G. (ed.) *New Directions in English Language Corpora: Methodology, Results, Software Development*. Berlin: Mouton de Gruyter, 247–262.

Ziv, Y. (2002) 'This, I believe, is a processing instruction: Discourse linking via parentheticals'. In: Falk, Y.N. (ed.) *Proceedings of Israel Association for Theoretical Linguistics* 18. Bar Ilan University.

7 Packaging voices in the British press: Aspects of the logogenesis of science dissemination

Miriam Pérez-Veneros
University of Salamanca, Spain

7.1 Introduction

In the last two decades, there has been growing concern over scientific developments and the influence these developments can have on people's lives. As a result, there has also been a growing interest in how scientific knowledge is disseminated to non-expert people who are interested in science and in its impact on their lives. Numerous scholars (Calsamiglia 2003; Calsamiglia & Van Dijk 2004; Gil-Salom 2000–2001; Gotti 2014) have turned their attention to the study of science popularization articles as one of the main vehicles for science dissemination. Some studies describe popularization articles as a genre that is hybrid (Elorza 2011) and polyphonic in nature (Calsamiglia & López Ferrero 2003; de Oliveira & Pagano 2006; de Oliveira 2007; García Riaza 2012; Pérez-Veneros 2017). Polyphony implies a multiplicity of voices that can be heard (including the journalist's voice) and through which the journalist integrates scientific knowledge, builds up the text and establishes a relationship with the readership.

This chapter explores how scientific meaning is construed in popularization articles and how the system of projection is exploited in the dissemination of science in the British press. Previous studies have focused on modes of meaning projection other than hypotaxis and parataxis (Elorza & Pérez-Veneros 2014; Semino & Short 2004), on types of reporting verbs which frame and introduce these structures (Thompson 1994b; Thompson & Ye 1991) and on the participants that are given voice (Hawes 2014; Hawes & Thomas 2012). Thompson (1994a) suggests that there are two ways in which the construal of meanings in text can be studied: by tracking meaning within a text to see whether it is construed as Proposition, Fact or Thing (nominalization) or by analyzing the distribution and function of a single meaning and the ways it is projected throughout the text. He posits that meanings ideally develop along a cline of projection from their first appearance in text as Propositions (by means of direct speech) until they evolve into fully packaged nominalizations which, in turn, can function as participants of new projections (cf. also Klein & Unsworth 2014; Moyano 2015).

In a study of how scientific knowledge is disseminated in the press, we are interested not only in the frequency with which that knowledge appears as projected meaning but also in the implications of the different modes of projection that are distributed throughout the text. Typically, in an article written for a non-expert audience, we would expect the new information to be presented as partially mediated or interpreted data in order for the audience to more easily understand the narrated key concepts. As the text unfolds, this semi-packaged meaning can be fully developed into propositions, allowing the writers to justify why they interpreted the data the way they did. Finally, we would expect fully-packaged meanings at the end of the text, where the journalists can present the matters previously reported and interpreted as already established, shared and accepted knowledge. According to Halliday and Matthiessen (2004: 625), such fully-packaged projections are considered the most mediated type of meaning since the writer has already carried out a 'full' interpretation of previously presented matters. Therefore, these projections are expected to appear towards the end of texts when scientific knowledge has already been accepted and validated by the lay audience.

It can be claimed that in popularization articles, the logogenetic projection of scientific meaning also depends on the journalist's alignment with or detachment from the information integrated. Hence, this chapter's main purpose is to explore how scientific meanings are construed logogenetically in text in order to see how such meanings develop in popularizations and to what extent the modes of projection are linked to the journalist's epistemological positioning in the text. This will be done by analyzing the types of projection used in science popularization articles and by investigating the different degrees of 'packaging' of scientific knowledge. Furthermore, I will explore which participant types are related to the projections and how they are developed throughout the text. Special attention will be given to cases of material entities (e.g. *the study, the findings*) to see whether they are the result of the 'packaging' of a previously projected meaning and whether they can still act as participants of a new projection (cf. Klein & Unsworth 2014). The use of nominalizations in popularization articles has been studied before (Sušinskienė 2012; Unsworth 1998), and it has been suggested that nominalization contributes to 'the condensing of information and the dynamism [it] adds to the structure of a sentence' (Sušinskienė 2012: 141). However, these studies investigated nominalizations which would be congruently construed as material processes. The study of nominalizations which are the result of the packaging of previous representations of the world or of nominalizations congruently construed as verbal or mental processes has so far been neglected for this genre. Therefore, I will explore the lexicogrammatical cline in terms of the grammatical resources (modes of projection) as well as the lexical resources (nominalizations) with which journalists choose to either act as mediators of the information by attributing it to external sources of expertise or, conversely, as narrators of events by averring them using their own voice (cf. Hunston 2000). To this effect, a corpus consisting of 115 cases of projection (henceforth the *Proj_Sci* corpus) has been compiled and manually analyzed. The results show that projection is mainly realized through Propositions and Facts in popularization articles although there are also cases in which the words of others are projected as Things, sometimes taking the role of participants of a new projection. These fully-packaged projections tend to appear at the beginning of a text (cataphoric position) to evolve later into either projected Propositions or Facts. These findings contrast greatly with results from previous research (cf. Thompson 1994a).

7.2 Projection and the unfolding of scientific meaning

Halliday and Matthiessen describe projection as the representation of a previous (linguistic) representation (2004: 441). When meaning is projected, there is no direct reference to the real world but to the reproduction of a previous representation of that world. This phenomenon encompasses a logico-semantic relationship between the projecting clause (normally consisting of a verbal or mental process and its associated participant(s)) and the projected clause in which the represented meaning is projected. Halliday and Matthiessen state that there are three different systems through which we can distinguish different types of projection:

1. The level of projection: This system deals with the type of content a projected clause can integrate. When the projected clause integrates the content of a mental clause, the projections are 'ideas'. Conversely, if the projected clause integrates the content of a verbal clause, the projections are 'locutions'.
2. The mode of projection: The interdependency relations established between projecting and projected clauses are those of parataxis and hypotaxis. Meanings projected paratactically are 'quotes', whereas those projected hypotactically are 'reports'. Additionally, we can also find the constituency relation of 'embedding', as in: *the witness' claim* **that she saw one young man open fire** *seems plausible*

(from Halliday & Matthiessen 2004: 443). While hypotaxis and parataxis are relations between clauses, embedding is 'a semogenic mechanism whereby a clause or phrase comes to function as a constituent of a clause' (Halliday & Matthiessen 2004: 426). Hence, the relationship between the main clause and the embedded clause is an indirect one where the embedded clause typically functions as post-modifier or head in a nominal group or as post-modifier in an adverbial group.
3. The speech function: We can project two different types of speech function. The projection of a statement is a projected 'proposition', while the projection of an offer, a command or a request is a projected 'proposal' (Halliday & Matthiessen 2004: 444).

Studies on projection have mainly addressed the mode of projection, focusing either on the projecting or the projected clauses or on the interdependency relations established between them. Hence, previous studies have mainly focused on the range of structural options available to project meaning, i.e. the projected clause (Elorza & Pérez-Veneros 2014; Semino & Short 2004; Semino, Short & Culpeper 1997). Some studies have also focused on the projecting clause, paying attention to the mental and verbal processes and the meaning they encode (Thompson 1994b; Thompson & Ye 1991) or to the participants typically associated with these processes (Hawes 2014; Hawes & Thomas 2012; Pérez-Veneros 2017).

Projection can also be realized by means of nominalization, whereby a congruent verbal or mental process is realized as an entity (Sušinskienė 2012). Some studies have delved into the exploration of nominalizations as a way to project meaning (Halliday & Matthiessen 2004; Hood 2010; Moyano 2015; Thompson 1994a). These nominalizations can sometimes act as participants of new projections. Halliday and Matthiessen (2004) outline different possibilities of nominalizations as packaged projected meaning. They distinguish between 'nouns of projection' and 'nouns of projection with embedded fact', and between 'nouns of fact' and 'nouns of fact with embedded fact'. Nouns of projection are considered nominalizations of verbal processes (Hood 2010) in which a process that would be congruently construed as a verb is construed as a noun. This is seen as an instance of grammatical metaphor (Halliday 2004: 172–176; Klein & Unsworth 2014: 2), where 'a semantic element that would be construed congruently through one grammatical choice is reconstrued through a different grammatical choice' (Klein & Unsworth 2014: 2; cf. Halliday 2004; Liardét 2016). Nominalizations realized as grammatical metaphors are typically of the ideational type since they derive from a congruent clause nexus. On the other hand, nouns of projection with embedded fact are nominalizations that can integrate more information by encoding it in the form of embedded clauses, e.g. *Boyle's tentative **suggestion that heat was simply motion** was apparently not accepted by Stahl* (Halliday & Matthiessen 2004: 468). Contrary to nouns of projection and nouns of projection with embedded fact, 'nouns of fact', e.g. *fact, issue, problem, chance, possibility* (see classification by Halliday & Matthiessen 2004: 469), and 'nouns of fact with embedded fact', e.g. *The **fact that Lear never ever alluded to that at the end** is a sign that he didn't learn very much through the course of the play* (Halliday & Matthiessen 2004: 470), are considered 'ready packaged in projected form' (Halliday & Matthiessen 2004: 470) since, contrary to what happens with nouns of projection, they do not derive from a congruent process. They are presented as already established knowledge and have also been referred to as semiotic abstractions (Hood 2010).

Thompson (1994a) suggests an alternative way to the study of projection. His point of departure is the analysis of how we convey experiential meaning and its representation through Propositions, Facts and Things. He states that the congruent encoding of a process together with its participants and circumstances is through a Proposition. However, it is also possible to 'package' meaning through the resource of grammatical metaphor (Halliday 2004: 172–176) by treating a process and its participants as something belonging to the world (a nominalization) so that it can be talked about and can become a participant in a new process. What Thompson suggests is that – in the same way that we can study the nominalization and packaging of information directly coming from our experience – we can also encapsulate and nominalize the information coming from a previous representation of experience. We can not only pack the world, but we can also pack a previous representation of the world. He proposes that the same cline for conveying meaning experientially is applied in the subsequent projection of that meaning. Hence, the cline of projection suggested by Thompson runs as follows:

- the projection of a Proposition is a quote, e.g. *'**That's right,**' the guard said;*
- the projection of a Fact is indirect speech, e.g. *Mrs Carstairs explained **that Sybil had a nasty sore throat**;*
- the projection of a Thing entails cases where the information has already been partially packaged, i.e. cases of Narrator's Representation of Speech Act (with Topic) (Leech & Short 2007; Semino & Short 2004), or fully packaged, i.e. nouns of projection and nouns of fact (Halliday & Matthiessen 2004), e.g. *They have declared **an end to violence**.*

Thompson suggests that we can track meanings in a text and see how they are projected in order to explore how the dynamics of projection work and how writers encode meanings that have been previously represented. Thompson focuses on how meaning develops logogenetically since he is interested in studying how meanings are integrated in text and how they are shaped as the text unfolds. He states that in order to do so, we can either track a single meaning within a text to see if it is projected as a Proposition, Fact or Thing, or we can study the relative frequency, distribution and function of Propositions, Facts and Things in a single text or group of texts. Ideally, meanings entering a text would run along the cline of packaging of propositions, first entering the text as a free-standing meaning, then being partially packaged and, finally, appearing as a nominalization (Thompson 1994a: 14). In his study, Thompson focuses on scientific discourse (research articles) and finds that new meanings typically enter as Facts, as partially packaged meaning '"framed" with a commentary by the writer' (Thompson 1994a: 17). Semi-packaged meaning enters the scientific discourse when writers detach themselves from the integrated information to 'perform the academically valued functions of commenting, labelling [and] ascribing' (Thompson 1994a: 18). Conversely, Propositions would be seen as parallel to raw data where the writers' positioning is not visible, while Things would be seen as already established phenomena that are not open to questioning from the readership. Nevertheless, when new meaning is brought into the text as partially packaged, the writers are indicating that their interpretation is still open to questioning. Consequently, this type of meaning is more dynamic in interpersonal terms as it has not yet been encapsulated. As the article progresses, writers can decide to pick up a Fact as already established knowledge and thus make it 'available for complete packaging as a nominalization' (Thompson 1994a: 19).

One of the main features of popularization articles is their polyphonic nature. In order to make scientific knowledge available to a non-expert readership, journalists rely on external sources of information that validate and give credibility to their mediated report. Unlike other genres of scientific discourse, such as research articles, we find little narration of scientific events in popularization articles. Instead, what we find is the representation of previous narrations of scientific events, either in form of projected meanings coming from external sources or in form of the journalists projecting their own voice to narrate what others have said. In other words, what can be found in the written dissemination of science in the press is a projection of meaning rather than a direct presentation of scientific knowledge. Hence, we are working with a double layer of meaning representation (Thompson 1994a).

In the study presented in the next section, I will explore not only how scientific meaning is projected in the dissemination of science in the written press but also how this meaning is conveyed and which modes of projection are used by the journalists. I will show how journalists pass on information by exploiting the 'lexicogrammatical cline of mediation', and I will investigate whether they prefer to construe scientific meaning by means of grammatical structures (mode of projection) or by means of lexis (nominalized forms of projection). The latter is seen as the most delicate and fine-grained representation of meaning in the cline.

7.3 The study

To study how scientific meaning is projected in science popularization articles in the British press, a sample corpus was compiled consisting of ten popularizations published between July and August 2015 on the webpage *theguardian.com/science* (see Table 7.1).

Table 7.1 Corpus of articles used in the study (*Proj_Sci* corpus)

Code	Headline	Author	Date
Proj_Sci_01	Parkinson's and depression drugs can alter moral judgment, study shows	Hannah Devlin	02/07/2015
Proj_Sci_02	Old before your time? People age at wildly different rates, study confirms	Ian Sample	06/07/2015
Proj_Sci_03	Smoking tobacco might increase risk of schizophrenia, say researchers	Sarah Boseley	10/07/2015
Proj_Sci_04	Huge and ancient underwater volcanoes discovered off coast of Sydney	Oliver Milman	13/07/2015
Proj_Sci_05	Large Hadron Collider scientists discover new particles: pentaquarks	Ian Sample	14/07/2015
Proj_Sci_06	Regularly taking the pill 'helps prevent two forms of cancer' decades after use	Sarah Boseley	05/08/2015
Proj_Sci_07	Frequent spicy meals linked to human longevity	Haroon Siddique	05/08/2015
Proj_Sci_08	Plague grave excavations contradict tales of naked bodies piled in pits	Maev Kennedy	12/08/2015
Proj_Sci_09	Fossilized remains of world's oldest flower discovered in Spain	Helen Thomson	17/08/2015
Proj_Sci_10	Daily glass of wine raises risk of breast cancer in women	Sarah Boseley	18/08/2015

The ten texts were analyzed manually, and a total number of 115 occurrences of projected meanings were tracked. As a first step, a distinction was made between the cases where journalists narrate in their own voice and the cases where they project meaning coming from external sources of information. Once the different voices were identified, the cases of projection were categorized as projected Propositions (quotations), Facts (reports) or Things (into this category fall, e.g. all cases of Narrator's Representation of Speech Act (with Topic), 'nouns of projection' and 'nouns of fact'). Using a corpus-based approach (Tognini-Bonelli 2001), the different cases of projection were tagged according to Thompson's (1994a) taxonomy and put into three different categories.

The first category, projection of Proposition (quote), includes all cases containing a literal reproduction of the words coming from external sources, as is the case in example (1).

(1) **'The overwhelming majority are biologically in their mid-40s or younger, but there are a handful of cases who are in pretty bad shape. In the future, we'll come to learn about the different lives that fast and slow ageing people have lived,'** said Daniel Belsky at Duke University in North Carolina. (Proj_Sci_02)

The second category, projection of Facts (report), comprises cases of hypotactic projection, which are not literal reproductions but reformulations or paraphrases of previous utterances. This is the category traditionally known as indirect speech. Consider the following example in (2).

(2) Beral said **that the overall number of women with endometrial cancer would have dropped further if it had not been for obesity, which increases the risk.** (Proj_Sci_06)

The third category, projection of Things (Halliday & Matthiessen 2004; Semino & Short 2004; Semino, Short & Culpeper 1997), comprises ten different types of cases (see Table 7.2).

NRSA (item i), as given in example (3), encompasses those cases where meaning has been more packaged than in the category of Fact (indirect speech). It is mainly integrated in verbal or mental processes, which typically present illocutionary force. NRSAT (item ii) in example (4), on the other hand, comprises those cases which, apart from having a verb with illocutionary force, give the reader some idea of the topic of the previous utterance, even if the information is not rephrased.

Table 7.2 The ten different types of projection of Things

i	Narrator's Representation of Speech Act (NRSA)
ii	Narrator's Representations of Speech Act with Topic (NRSAT)
iii	Nouns of projection
iv	Nouns of projection with embedded fact
v	Nouns of fact
vi	Nouns of fact with embedded fact
vii	Material participant acting as noun of fact
viii	Attributive clauses with embedded fact
ix	Cognitive mental processes projecting meaning
x	Elaborating clauses in journalists' narration

(3) Prof Sir Ian Gilmore, chair of the Alcohol Health Alliance UK, **called for health warnings on bottles of alcohol like those on cigarettes**. (Proj_Sci_10)

(4) Kevin McConway, professor of applied statistics at the Open University, **warned against reading too much into the results**. (Proj_Sci_07)

In example (3), the verbal process *called for* is used to integrate meaning, but there is no further information given on the actual words which the expert calling for the health warning used. Example (4) presents a case of NRSAT since the verbal process *warned* is followed by a non-finite embedded nominal clause (*reading too much into the results*) to integrate the interpretation of the expert's words as a warning.

As shown above, 'nouns of projection' and 'nouns of projection with embedded fact' (items iii and iv in Table 7.2) are nominalizations of former verbal or mental processes, and some of them can include an embedded fact with the nominalization as the Head. Nouns of projection present the world as already 'packaged'. They are considered grammatical metaphors of the ideational type (Halliday & Matthiessen 2004: 638) since they have agnate congruent verbal or mental processes. In fact, the noun which serves as Thing or Head represents a nominalized version of a previous verbal process, as in example (5), where the noun of projection *revelation* is a nominalization of the verbal process *reveal*.

(5) **The revelation** comes from two years of measurements by an international team of astronomers who installed a telescope and a sensitive camera at the Mauna Loa Observatory [...] (the *Guardian*, 10 January 2014).

'Nouns of fact' and 'nouns of fact with embedded fact' (items v and vi in Table 7.2) are manifested as already packaged information in projected form. They are impersonal projections that do not have any agnate congruent processes since they are not the result of somebody's cognitive achievements or have not been emitted by a signal source. The fact that they are not nominalizations leads us to conclude that they cannot be considered grammatical metaphors because they are already presented as Things which can act as participants of a new process. Although this process is typically a relational one, as in example (6), it can also be verbal or mental, as in example (7).

(6) You've said that **one of your editorial rules is not to publish your buddies** (Halliday & Matthiessen 2004: 479),

(7) She **liked the snow falling.** (Halliday & Matthiessen 2004: 480)

In addition, there are also cases in which nouns of fact with embedded fact act as Existent in an existential process, as epitomized by the noun *evidence* in example (8).

(8) **There is evidence** of pollen dispersed in fossils that are around 140 million years old, he says. (Proj_Sci_09)

Material participants acting as noun of fact (item vii in Table 7.2) represent those cases where there is a material participant which projects new meaning and which, at the same time, represents a noun of fact packaging information which has been previously presented or which will be elaborated on later in the text, as in example (9):

(9) Drinking one glass of wine a day increases a woman's chances of getting breast cancer, according to **new research.** (Proj_Sci_10)

Attributive clauses with embedded fact (item viii in Table 7.2) are clauses containing a relational attributive process where the Carrier is typically realized by a nominal group and the Attribute is a nominal group with an embedded fact clause. In Example 10, the relational process is intensive with an adjective as Head of the nominal group.

(10) Researchers are not completely **sure** what makes the core of Enceladus hot, but part of the warmth could come from what scientists call tidal heating (the *Guardian*, 11 March 2015).

Cognitive mental processes projecting meaning (item ix in Table 7.2) represent those cases where there is a mental process which is projecting the words stated by scientists, as in example (11):

(11) A beautiful aquatic plant, dating back to the start of the Cretaceous period**, is believed** by scientists to be the oldest flowering plant on Earth. (Proj_Sci_09)

Finally, elaborating clauses in journalists' narration (item x in Table 7.2) represent those situations in which the journalist, who is construing knowledge in the form of projection, elaborates on the information through expansion by the use of elaborating clauses:

(12) Oxford University researchers say in the past 10 years, taking the pill has prevented 200,000 cases of womb cancer in high-income countries. In 2008, the Oxford epidemiologists, **analysing the data from 45 studies involving 100,000 women,** found that regular use for 15 years can halve the risk of ovarian cancer. (Proj_Sci_06)

Once the different projections of meaning were classified, the texts were analyzed logogenetically to see how the projected meanings unfolded in the texts. Specifically, single meanings were tracked to see how they were projected and, at the same time, the different modes of projection were accounted for to gain a deeper insight into how scientific meaning is typically integrated when journalists popularize science. Moreover, by analyzing the different modes of projection displayed in this sample corpus, we can also obtain information on whether cases of packaged meaning act as participants in subsequent projections or simply as packaged scientific meaning which journalists present as such. This is especially salient in the case of nouns of fact since they are impersonal projections that are already available as a Thing that can play the role of a participant in a new process. In addition to this, studying the logogenesis of scientific meaning also allows us to complement previous studies analyzing how epistemological positioning is conveyed by journalists when popularizing science.

7.4 Results

The analysis of the logogenesis of popularized scientific meaning revealed a total number of 115 cases of projection in the ten popularization articles in the corpus. This means that journalists attribute information to external sources of expertise 115 times in the texts analyzed. Out of these 115 occurrences, there are 23 cases where scientific meaning is conveyed either as fully-packaged or semi-packaged information, which is subsequently expanded and presented to the readership typically in the form of projected Propositions (cf. Thompson 1994a).

Table 7.3 Tokens of projected Propositions, Facts and Things in the *Proj_Sci* corpus

Cline of projection *(cf. Thompson 1994)*	*Tokens of projection* *in the* Proj_Sci *corpus*
Propositions	41 (35.6%)
Facts	51 (44.4%)
Things	23 (20%)
Total	**115 (100%)**

As is shown in Table 7.3, Propositions, i.e. projected scientific knowledge presented without a journalist's mediation, make up 35.6% of all projections, while cases where journalists have already started to interpret the world by integrating information in the form of projected Facts make up almost half of the total number of projections (44.4%). In contrast, projected Things – the most mediated type of projection – represent 20% of all projections. Through Facts and Things, the journalists' presence in an article is more prominent since they are interpreting data and are acting as mediators for the readers. Propositions are used where the journalists totally detach themselves from the information presented. However, sometimes, as illustrated in examples (13) to (17), Propositions are used when journalists want to transport their own claims in other more packaged forms of information, and then they elaborate on that previously packaged knowledge through Propositions.

Where scientific knowledge is presented in fully-packaged or semi-packaged form, there are several ways in which journalists construe these meanings, as shown in Table 7.4.

Table 7.4 Types and tokens of Things in the Proj_Sci corpus

Types of Things in the Proj_Sci *corpus*	Tokens of Things in Proj_Sci *corpus*
NRSA (i)	2 (8.9%)
NRSAT (ii)	1 (4.3%)
Noun of projection in anaphoric position (iii)	3 (13.1%)
Noun of projection in relational process (iii)	1 (4.3%)
Noun of projection with embedded fact in cataphoric position (iv)	3 (13.1%)
Noun of fact in relational process (v)	1 (4.3%)
Noun of fact with embedded fact in existential process (vi)	1 (4.3%)
Noun of fact with embedded fact in anaphoric position (vi)	1 (4.3%)
Noun of fact with embedded fact in cataphoric position (vi)	1 (4.3%)
Material participant acting as noun of fact (vii)	4 (17.4%)
Attributive clause with embedded fact (viii)	1 (4.3%)
Cognitive mental processes projecting meaning (ix)	3 (13.1%)
Elaborating clauses as part of the journalist's narration (x)	1 (4.3%)
Total	**23 (100%)**

The results in Table 7.4 show that Things (or fully-packaged nominalizations) tend to appear in cataphoric position, and the journalist elaborates on this packaged meaning as the text develops. These nominalizations can act as participants in verbal, mental, relational and existential processes. The following examples (13) to (17) illustrate some of the ways in which scientific meaning is fully-packaged in popularizations:

(13) In a commentary in the journal on the paper, Nicolas Wentzensen and Amy Berrington de Gonzalez, from the National Cancer Institute in the US, say that **the important question now is** whether this allows women to better balance the benefits and the potential harms of taking the pill – and also to work out whether the pill might be useful in some circumstances specifically to prevent cancer. (Proj_Sci_06)

Example (13) shows a noun of projection as part of a relational process. Specifically, the noun of projection *question* is part of an indirect speech presentation (a projected Fact according to Thompson's classification). This noun of projection is the core of the Value in a relational identifying process, whose Token identifies what the question is. Furthermore, the noun *question* is pre-modified and evaluated by the adjective *important*. It is, therefore, not open to challenge by the audience since it is presented as already established knowledge (cf. Hoey 2000). In example (14), on the other hand, we have got a case of a noun of fact with embedded fact in an existential process.

(14) **There are biologically plausible reasons why smoking may be linked to psychosis.** 'Excess dopamine is the best biological explanation we have for psychotic illnesses such as schizophrenia,' said Murray. 'It is possible that nicotine exposure, by increasing the release of dopamine, causes psychosis to develop.' A number of other drugs can stimulate dopamine production, including amphetamines, cocaine and cannabis. (Proj_Sci_03)

Here, the noun *reasons* is the Existent in an existential process, and it incorporates an embedded fact providing information about the reasons. Additionally, the journalist makes use of the adjective *plausible* to identify the *reasons* as potentially those that link smoking to psychosis. In turn, the choice of the noun *reasons* to package meaning and the choice of the adjective *plausible* to evaluate these reasons are justified by the journalist by including a case of direct speech (projected Proposition in Thompson's terms) where the reasons are made explicit so that the audience can conclude that the choice of the noun and the choice of the adjective are well-justified.

(15) People who request an extra kick to their curry could also be adding years to their life, according to **a large study which linked frequent consumption of spicy food to longevity**. (Proj_Sci_07)

Example (15) shows a material participant acting as a noun of fact. It epitomizes cases of material participants which typically act as fully-packaged nominalizations that are later expanded or as nominalizations that can become participants of a new process. Journalists sometimes choose to elaborate on the meaning packaged in material participants by post-modifying them through elaboration. This is the case with the participant *a large study*, which is post-modified by *which linked frequent consumption of spicy food to longevity*.

> (16) Cannabis is known to cause psychosis and schizophrenia. The authors say they could not be **certain** that all the studies they looked at had completely accounted for cannabis use. However, they are **certain** there is a modest effect caused by tobacco alone. (Proj_Sci_03)

Example (16) presents two attributive clauses with embedded fact expanded as projected Proposition. Indeed, the Carriers are realized by a nominal group, in this case *they*. Following Halliday and Matthiessen's analysis (2004: 474) the Attributes are also both nominal groups with an embedded fact clause, in this case 'intensive'. The adjective *certain* represents the Head of these nominal groups. The two embedded fact clauses are later elaborated through the inclusion of projected Propositions to support the previous packaging of information in the form of an adjective integrating embedded meaning.

> (17) Smoking cigarettes might increase people's risk of psychosis, say researchers **who believe tobacco as well as cannabis could play a part in causing schizophrenia.** (Proj_Sci_03)

Finally, example (17), an elaborating clause in the journalist's narration, represents a projected Fact (indirect speech), whose verbal process *say* and participant *researchers* are also integrated. The journalist describes who these researchers are by giving further information in an elaborating clause. This clause, in turn, also projects meaning that presents the journalist's narration of events in indirect speech.

7.5 Conclusions

This paper has delved into the question of how the dynamics of projection work in science popularization articles by focusing on how scientific meanings are construed logogenetically throughout the text. The main aim was (a) to explore the degree of packaging of meanings as they develop in the text and (b) the extent to which some of the 'packagings' in turn act as participants of new processes which project meaning. In addition, this study has also examined the interdependency between the way journalists project meaning and the way these projections contribute to the journalists' support or challenge of the narrated information. In doing so, I followed the taxonomy of projection proposed by Thompson (1994a) to classify the types of 115 cases of projection of meaning found in the *Proj_Sci* corpus, their frequency of appearance and their distribution in the texts. As a result, the analysis of all occurrences of projection has revealed how scientific knowledge is encoded, how it evolves logogenetically and how meaning is construed and conveyed in science dissemination.

In the light of these results, we can conclude that the two main modes of projection preferred by journalists to integrate meaning are projected Propositions (35.6%) and projected Facts (44.4%) (cf. Table 7.3). In agreement with Thompson's findings, new scientific meaning is mainly integrated as Fact, as an intermediate stage between fully-packaged meaning (Thing) and faithful reproduction of original meaning (Proposition). Facts are presented as semi-packaged knowledge, which is partially mediated by the journalists. This partial mediation of knowledge is caused by the fact that journalists present it in the form of a rephrasing of knowledge, i.e. by the use of indirect forms of speech presentation. Projected Facts logogenetically develop in the text in the form of projected Propositions, which journalists use to support or challenge information that has previously been presented as partially mediated or to just introduce their own alignment.

Conversely, there are also cases of projected information presented as Thing (20%) (cf. Table 7.3), as a fully-packaged integration of scientific knowledge. Contrary to expectations and to Thompson's findings in scientific discourse (where Things tend to appear at the end as fully-packaged and mediated knowledge), it is typical in science popularizations that packaged information as Thing appears at the beginning of text to be later developed as Fact or Proposition and explained to the reader. Results also indicate that Things can be construed by various modes of projection, including nouns of projection as ideational metaphors encapsulating cases of projection clause nexuses, nouns of fact as impersonal projections and attributive clauses with embedded fact. These fully-packaged nominalizations can in turn become material participants, which take part in various processes, including mental, relational and existential ones, to project meaning. In the category of Thing, occurrences of Narrator's Representation of Speech Act and Narrator's Representation of Speech Act with Topic were found, through which scientific meaning is packaged to be later developed in fully-projected forms, typically as Propositions.

The fact that scientific meaning is construed as Thing in the first paragraphs of the popularization articles asks for some interpretation. The presentation of packaged or summarized versions of previous scientific explanations makes the beginnings of texts shorter. As a result, it is easier for the audience to decide whether the article is worth reading. This can be viewed as a symptom of the journalists following press conventions to attract enough interest from the readers. Furthermore, popularizations aim at presenting science to a non-expert audience, so the journalists' first interaction with their potential audience is through the presentation of packaged knowledge, which is later explained as the text develops.

The use of fully-packaged forms of projection at the beginning of texts can also be related to the journalists positioning themselves towards the information from the very beginning. As Halliday and Matthiessen (2004: 625) posit, these fully-packaged forms represent the most mediated type of projection since the writers construe the encapsulated meaning according to their interpretation of the original utterance. The journalists' presence and their mediation of the information is also reinforced by cases where the fully-packaged presentations of knowledge are evaluated by adjectives placed in pre-modifying position. This strategy makes them difficult to challenge for the readership so that they are taken for granted since they are not open for evaluation (cf. Hoey 2000).

Alternatively, the journalists' liability to these mediated forms of knowledge is challenged when they integrate some of them into their own narration in the form of nominalizations. In this way, the journalists are still making reference to the fact that the information is coming from external sources and that they are not responsible for it. At the same time, they are playing with the fact that these fully-packaged nominalizations of previous representations of experience are the most mediated forms of knowledge. So even if the journalists acknowledge the existence of the external sources by giving them voice in the text, it is also the case that they often present the information to the readers in a mediated way, i.e. through the use of lexical forms as the most delicate forms in the lexicogrammatical cline of mediation.

An issue that has not been covered in this chapter and that is relevant for future research is the analysis of how scientific meaning is construed and how it unfolds in text genres other than popularizations. This will allow us to see whether scientific meaning enters text as semi-packaged meaning that is only later taken as established and not open to challenge or whether meaning is presented by scientists as already accepted, which is the case in popularization articles. Further research is also needed to explore how popular scientific meanings are construed in other cultures in order to shed light on the question of whether the construal of scientific meanings has to do with the context of culture or whether it is more linked to press conventions independent of cultural issues.

Acknowledgements

Thanks are due to the Spanish Ministry of Education and the Program for the Training of University Professors (FPU) for financial support.

About the author

Miriam Pérez-Veneros holds a PhD in Advanced English Studies from the University of Salamanca (July 2017) and is an associate lecturer at the University of Salamanca, where she teaches courses on syllabus design, the classroom context and English for Specific Purposes. Her research focuses on discourse analysis, systemic-functional linguistics and the teaching of English as a second language. In addition, she works on science popularization articles and their potential application as learning tools in CLIL approaches in different academic settings and on children picture books and their presentation of different family structures and family roles. She has also completed academic activities at the Centre for Language and Communication Research (CLCR) at Cardiff University (Wales).

References

Calsamiglia, H. (2003) 'Popularization discourse'. *Discourse Studies* 5(2), 139–146.

Calsamiglia, H. & López Ferrero, C. (2003) 'Role and position in scientific voices: Reported speech in the Media'. *Discourse Studies* 5(2), 147–173.

Calsamiglia, H. & Van Dijk, T.A. (2004) 'Popularization discourse and knowledge about the genome'. *Discourse & Society* 15(4), 369–389.

de Oliveira, J.M. (2007) 'Las Voces de la Ciencia: La Representación del Discurso en Textos de Divulgación Científica y en Artículos de Investigación'. *Universitas Tarraconensis: Revista de Ciències de L'educació* 2, 77–93.

de Oliveira, J.M. & Pagano, A.S. (2006) 'The research article and the science popularization article: A probabilistic functional grammar perspective on direct discourse representation'. *Discourse Studies* 8(5), 627–646.

Elorza, I. (2011) 'The encoding of authorial voice in science popularizations in the press: A corpus-based cross-cultural text analysis'. Paper presented at the *12th International Pragmatics Conference*. Manchester, 3–8 July, 2011.

Elorza, I. & Pérez-Veneros, M. (2014) 'Constructing stance by means of attribution: How is the "Space for Evaluation" filled in science popularization articles in English?' In: Glynn, D. & Sjölin, M. (eds.) *Subjectivity and Epistemicity: Corpus, Discourse and Literary Approaches to Stance*. Lund: Lund University Press, 281–301.

García Riaza, B. (2012) *Attribution and Thematization Patterns in Science Popularization Articles from The Guardian Newspaper*. Unpublished PhD dissertation. University of Salamanca.

Gil Salom, L. (2000–2001) 'El Discurso de la Ciencia y la Tecnología: El Artículo Científico de Investigación vs. El Artículo de Divulgación Científica'. *RESLA* 14, 429–449.

Gotti, M. (2014) 'Reformulation and recontextualization in popularization discourse'. *Ibérica: Journal of the European Association of Languages for Specific Purposes* 27, 15–34.

Halliday, M.A.K. (2004 [1993]) 'Some grammatical problems in Scientific English'. In: Webster, J.J. (ed.) *The Language of Science. The Collected Works of M.A.K. Halliday.* Vol. 5. London/New York: Continuum, 159–180.

Halliday, M.A.K. & Matthiessen, C.M.I.M. (2004) *An Introduction to Functional Grammar.* 3rd edition. London: Edward Arnold.

Hawes, T. (2014) 'The ambiguous discourse participant: Building a sense of reader "community" in The Sun'. *Linguistics and Literature Studies* 2(3), 79–85.

Hawes, T. & Thomas, S. (2012) 'Theme choice in EAP and Media Language'. *Journal of English for Academic Purposes* 11, 175–183.

Hoey, M. (2000) 'Persuasive rhetoric in linguistics: A stylistic study of some features of the language of Noam Chomsky'. In: Hunston, S. & Thompson, G. (eds.) *Evaluation in Text: Authorial Stance and the Construction of Discourse*. Oxford: Oxford University Press, 28–37.

Hood, S. (2010) *Appraising Research: Evaluation in Academic Writing*. London: Palgrave Macmillan.

Hunston, S. (2000) 'Evaluation and the planes of discourse: Status and value in persuasive texts'. In: Hunston, S. & Thompson, G. (eds.) *Evaluation in Text: Authorial Stance and the Construction of Discourse.* Oxford: Oxford University Press, 176–207.

Klein, P.D. & Unsworth, L. (2014) 'The logogenesis of writing to learn: A systemic functional perspective'. *Linguistics and Education* 26, 1–17.

Leech, G. & Short, M. (2007 [1981]). *Style in Fiction: A Linguistic Introduction to English Fictional Prose.* 2nd edition. London: Longman.

Liardét, C. (2016) 'Nominalization and grammatical metaphor: Elaborating the theory'. *English for Specific Purposes* 44, 16–29.

Moyano, E.I. (2015) 'Patrones de Realización de la Proyección en la Discusión de Artículos de Investigación Producidos en Español'. *D.E.L.T.A.* 31(1), 143–183.

Pérez-Veneros, M. (2017) *Narrative Voice in Popular Science in the British Press: A Corpus Analysis on the Construal of Attributed Meanings.* Colección Vítor 430. Salamanca: Ediciones Universidad de Salamanca.

Semino, E., Short, M. & Culpeper, J. (1997) 'Using a corpus to test a model of speech and thought presentation'. *Poetics* 25, 17–43.

Semino, E. & Short, M. (2004) *Speech, Writing, and Thought Presentation in a Corpus of English Writing.* London: Routledge.

Sušinskienė, S. (2012) 'Nominalization as a lexico-grammatical cohesive device in Science Popular texts'. *Filologija* 17, 133–144.

Thompson, G. (1994a) 'Propositions, Projection, and Things'. Paper presented at the *21st International Systemic Functional Conference.* Gent, 1–5 August, 1994, 1–22.

Thompson, G. (1994b) *Collins Cobuild English Guides 5: Reporting.* London: HarperCollins Publishers.

Thompson, G. & Ye, Y.Y. (1991) 'Evaluation in the reporting verbs used in academic papers'. *Applied Linguistics* 12(4), 365–382.

Tognini-Bonelli, E. (2001) *Corpus Linguistics at Work.* Amsterdam/ Philadelphia: John Benjamins Publishing Company.

Unsworth, L. (1998) '"Sound" explanations in school science: A functional linguistic perspective on effective apprenticing texts'. *Linguistics and Education* 9(2), 199–226.

8 English news texts in the light of authorial orientation: A classification of subjective and objective text types based on the system of modality

Martin Kaltenbacher
University of Salzburg, Austria

8.1 Introduction

Newspaper articles can be broadly divided into texts focusing on the dissemination of fact (story, report) and on the dissemination of opinion (editorial, comment, letters/emails). A text type positioned somewhat in between these two is the analysis, which tries to explain how news effects the interests of the general public. The type a text belongs to has significant consequences on the stylistic features an author can use in the text. Evaluations of behaviour, for instance, (Judgement in terms of Appraisal Theory) can only be made in opinion pieces (Martin & White 2005) but not in reports. This has to do with the subjective nature of evaluations, which are – by convention – banned in news reporting but allowed in all kinds of news commenting. Reports have to be objective texts where all authorial intervention has to be kept at a minimum, while all types of comments can and have to integrate a certain degree of subjectivity (cf. Lüger 1995; Reuters 2012; Burger & Luginbühl 2014).

The present chapter shall analyze how opinionated texts differ from neutral, objective texts in terms of the grammatical structures used to express subjective or objective authorial stance. It will be shown how British authors writing texts in the categories of 'report', 'analysis', 'editorial', 'comment' and 'letter/email to the editor' exploit interpersonal resources of modality and how a differentiation between these text types can be made on the basis of the lexicogrammatical structures employed.

The study of objective and subjective writing styles and of the linguistic features that can be used to make a text appear either objective or subjective has been the focus of linguistic investigation for some time. Kane (1988: 254–263), for instance, identifies the features listed in Table 8.1 as typical objective or subjective features in descriptions.

Table 8.1 Objective versus subjective description (based on Kane 1988: 254–263)

Objective description	Subjective description
detailed description of the subject matter, going from the general to detail	personal, emotional reactions of the author
exactness of denotation	impressionistic and connotational terminology
precise terminology	ample use of metaphors, similes, exaggerations and evaluations
impersonal style	personal and direct style

The interpretation of meanings expressed through the use of the linguistic features listed here often depends on a semantic or pragmatic reading of them. They can be ambivalent and may not always be easy to decode by a reader. Often it cannot be said precisely whether writers pick a particular word for its exact denotative meaning or for some connotative associations which they may want to share with their readers. It is strongly dependent on the personal and cultural experience and knowledge shared between author and readership whether the associations are understood by the recipients. The following study is, therefore, grounded in an analytic method that is based on grammatical structure rather than on semantic or pragmatic criteria. The grammatical system used for analysis here is Modality (Halliday 1994), and the primary focus will be on the choice of modal expressions in terms of their orientation and manifestation in the four categories *subjective, objective, explicit* and *implicit*.[1] Section 8.2 will give an overview of this with a focus on how Modality can be exploited to manifest different kinds of authorial orientation. Section 8.3 contains an overview of the data and presents the quantitative results of the study, which will then be discussed in 8.4 with regard to the authorial choices favoured in different journalistic text types. A concise conclusion will be given in 8.5.

8.2 The system of Modality

8.2.1 Modal categories and their realizations

The system of Modality comprises all those linguistic resources that allow a speaker to posit a proposition on a cline between two polar ends. Examples are the utterances *Perhaps he is at work* or *He might/may/will/must be at*

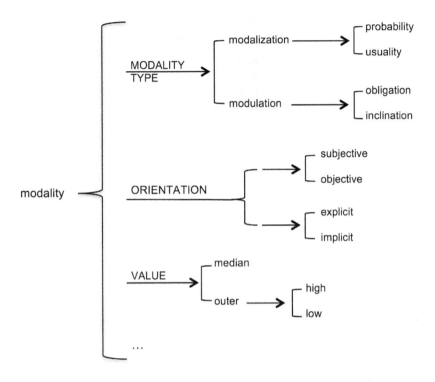

Figure 8.1 The system of *Modality* (after Halliday & Matthiessen 2014: 182)

work. In these utterances the speaker makes a proposition whose truth value lies somewhere between the two opposite poles *He is at work* and *He is not at work*. Modality can be subdivided into the two categories 'modalization' (epistemic modality) and 'modulation' (deontic/dynamic modality), both of which can be further divided into the four types of 'probability', 'usuality' and 'obligation', 'inclination'. Figure 8.1 displays the system network of modality according to Halliday & Matthiessen (2014: 150).

Although newspaper texts generally contain modal expressions of all four types, epistemic modal instantiations of the type 'probability' are most frequent. They can be used by an author to suggest how likely a proposition is to occur. Modal expressions can also be graded in terms of their value (high, median or low) so that they allow a proposition to appear very likely, equally likely, or unlikely to be true. An example is shown in Table 8.2, in which two polar propositions have been modalized to different degrees of value.[2]

Table 8.2 Modalizations of the type 'probability' with high, median and low value

End/value	Probability → here realized through modal verbs
positive	*The tax on deposits brings down the entire Eurozone.*
high	*The tax on deposits must bring down the entire Eurozone.*
median	*The tax on deposits can bring down the entire Eurozone.*
low	*The tax on deposits might bring down the entire Eurozone.*
negative	*The tax on deposits does not bring down the entire Eurozone.*

The second type of epistemic modality is 'usuality'. Typical modalizations, here realized in form of adverbs of frequency, are presented in Table 8.3.

Table 8.3 Modalizations of the type 'usuality' with high, median and low value

End/value	Usuality → here realized through modal adverbs
positive	*We see the pound fall.*
high	*We always see the pound fall.*
median	*We regularly see the pound fall.*
low	*We rarely see the pound fall.*
negative	*We don't see the pound fall.*

'Obligation' is one of the two types of modulation, which comprises all deontic and dynamic modal expressions. 'Obligation' includes linguistic resources that allow speakers to express a directive or – in case of low value – to grant a permission. Examples are given in Table 8.4.

Table 8.4 Modulations of the type 'obligation' with high, median and low value

End/value	Obligation → here realized through modal verbs
positive	*An agreement is reached.*
high	*An agreement must be reached.*
median	*An agreement should be reached.*
low	*An agreement may be reached.* [permission]
negative	*An agreement is not reached.*

The second type in the category of modulation is 'inclination'. It subsumes all those modal expressions that allow a speaker to express the willingness or the ability of a person to take an action. Examples of this type are listed in Table 8.5.

Table 8.5 Modulations of the type 'inclination' with high, median and low value

End/value	Inclination → here realized through modal adjectives
positive	The Eurozone is crossing the Rubicon
high	The Eurozone is determined to cross the Rubicon.
median	The Eurozone is keen on crossing the Rubicon.
low	The Eurozone is willing to cross the Rubicon.
negative	The Eurozone is not crossing the Rubicon.

8.2.2 Modality and authorial responsibility: subjective/objective and explicit/implicit orientation

Orientation (Halliday & Matthiessen 2014: 692–693) is a subsystem of modality that allows authors to reveal or conceal the source of a proposition or a proposal and also to take on a more objective or subjective stance against the claims made. In other words, orientation shows whether writers identify themselves as the originators of a proposition or whether they want to disguise their responsibility as authors. Thompson (1996: 60–61) calls this the author's 'modal commitment' or 'modal responsibility'. For example, with a clever choice of modal structures of probability, authors can express an impartial or even critical stance on a proposition even though it may reproduce their own opinion. In doing so, they can obscure the fact that the proposition reflects their own beliefs and may discourage the readers from challenging or dismissing their claims. Likewise, authors can manipulate their readers' reactions as in *This country is required to cut public spending*. Here the author conceals the source of the directive and pretends the obligation was a public duty without identifying who commissioned this duty.

In addition to modal verbs, there are an enormous number of other linguistic expressions that allow speakers to modalize or modulate an utterance. According to Halliday (1994: 354), these 'metaphors of modality' can take several ten thousands of representational forms in roughly 140 subcategories. A primary classification criterion for all these forms is the classification into 'subjective' vs. 'objective' and 'explicit' vs. 'implicit' modal expressions (Halliday & Matthiessen 2014: 692–693). Examples for these four categories are listed in Table 8.6.[3]

A detailed classification of the four categories has been given by Martin (1995: 40–45) and by Halliday and Matthiessen (2014: 693). According to them, an explicit-subjective expression contains a projecting mental clause that has a first person subject and projects a noun clause as its object. The

136   *Analyzing the Media: A Systemic Functional Approach*

Table 8.6 Modal expressions according to explicit-subjective, implicit-subjective, implicit-objective and explicit-objective orientation[4]

	Explicit-subjective (es)	*Implicit-subjective (is)*	*Implicit-objective (io)*	*Explicit-objective (eo)*
Probability	**I'm sure** our EU poll 'promise' **has** more to do with …	Savers **will** no doubt be nervous.	Cyprus **clearly** has a duty to try to put things right.	**There were fears that** UK service personnel in Cyprus could be among those to lose cash.
Usuality	–	They **would** never ever come together.	**Once again**, it exposes the rifts within the single currency.	*It's quite common for savers to be worried.*
Obligation	**We don't want them to help** us at all.	They **should** not have agreed to share a currency.	The country **is required to** cut public spending.	Cyprus clearly has **a duty to try to** put things right.
Inclination	–	But you **will** not once voice the slightest doubt about …	The Russian authorities **are willing to** bail out Cyprus.	–

first person subject identifies the author of the text as the source of the proposition or the proposal. The reader can, therefore, challenge not only the content of the projected noun clause but also the authority of the writer:

> **I'm sure** our EU poll 'promise' **has** more to do with it.
> *Are you?* (challenge of writer's authority) vs. *Has it?* (challenge of proposition)
> **We** don't **want them to help** us at all.
> *Don't you?* vs. *Well, do they really help you?*

Implicit-subjective sentences, on the other hand, are characterized by always containing a modal verb. The author's responsibility can only be inferred implicitly. While readers can challenge the modal expression, they cannot challenge the writer's authority:

> Savers **will** no doubt be nervous.
> *Will they?*

In implicit-objective sentences, modalizations (probability/usuality) are realized in the form of modal adverbs, e.g. *perhaps, normally*. Modulations (obligation/inclination) are realized as periphrastic verbs (i.e. a form of *be* is followed by a passive verb or a modal adjective) which are followed by a non-finite verbal group, e.g. *is supposed to do, is keen on doing*. Here the modal expression itself cannot be challenged by the reader anymore. Only the proposition can be called into question:

> **Once again**, it exposes the rifts within the single currency.
> *Does it really expose the rifts?*

Finally, in explicit-objective sentences, the modality is usually expressed metaphorically as a modal nominalization in an existential clause (*there is a chance that*) or as a modal complement in a relational clause (*it is likely that*). While the explicit manifestation of these expressions can be challenged by the reader, their origin remains invisible, and the source of the utterance is, therefore, not open to challenge:

> **There were fears that** UK service personnel in Cyprus **could be** among those to lose cash.[5]
> *Were there?* vs. *Could they?*

8.3 Data and results

For this study, 5 reports, 9 editorials, 13 comments, 3 analyses and 14 emails to the editor were extracted from the original database of the 'Helsinki corpus of newspaper comments' (Lenk 2016a) and then analyzed in terms of the authorial orientation manifested in the modal expressions chosen by the writers. The texts were published in the print versions of eight British daily newspapers in the week from 18–22 March 2013 and focus on the so-called 'bailout' in the Cypriot bank crisis in spring 2013. Table 8.7 gives an overview of the data, highlighting the word count for each text and text type. The texts were then analyzed according to the quantitative distribution of modal expressions across the four categories of modal orientation, i.e. explicit-subjective (ES), implicit-subjective (IS), implicit-objective (IO) and explicit-objective (EO). It is important to note that only non-mediated instantiations of authorial modality were considered in the present analysis. This means that a modal expression had to be attributable to the author of the text and not to an external source, such as an eye-witness, a spokesperson, a quoted politician, etc. References to external sources in the form of direct quotes or indirect paraphrases are particularly common in news reports. Such instantiations of 'mediated modality' had to be excluded from analysis for the present study as they do not reflect the writers' stance but that of their sources.

Table 8.7 Word count for each text within each text type

	Report	Analysis	Editorial	Comment	Email
Express	640		260	295	660
Daily Mail			115	1135	
Telegraph			330		
Financial Times	1135	2930	830	2255	
Guardian	1000	730	480	740	600
Independent			270	1140	
Herald				1010	
Times			1240	670	
Total	**2775**	**3660**	**3525**	**7245**	**1260**

Table 8.8 Results for all categories of modal orientation across text types in absolute numbers (normalized to reflect the sample size of the text type 'comment')

Text type	Sample size	Multiplication factor	ES	IS	IO	EO	Total
report	2775	× 2.610	0	8	23	52	**83**
analysis	3660	× 1.980	0	48	48	36	**132**
editorial	3525	× 2.055	6	164	82	90	**342**
comment	7245	× 1.000	9	144	84	66	**303**
email	1260	× 5.750	40	178	63	6	**287**

Table 8.8 presents the distribution of the four types of modal orientation across the different text types in absolute frequencies. As the individual samples for each text type differed in size, the absolute numbers found for each individual category were multiplied by a relative factor normalizing the figures against the largest text type of 'comment' with a total of 7,245 words. This made the figures comparable across all text types. The results have further been converted into two graphs, the first of which illustrates the absolute results in a line chart (Figure 8.2), while the second depicts the relative results in an area chart (Figure 8.3).

The results reveal that modal expressions occur very frequently in so-called opinion pieces (editorial, comment, email), while they are sparingly used by writers of analyses and hardly at all by authors of news reports. The

English news texts in the light of authorial orientation 139

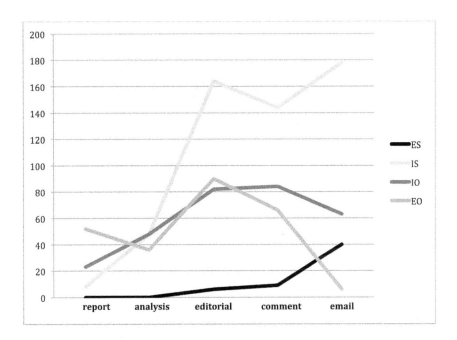

Figure 8.2 Results for categories of modal orientation per text type in absolute numbers

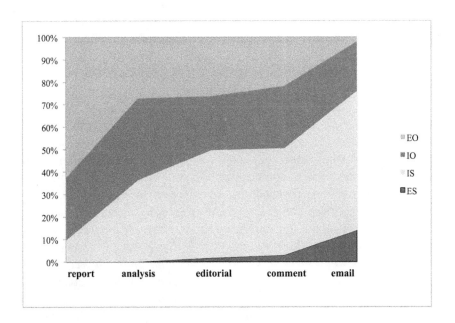

Figure 8.3 Relative results for categories of modal orientation per text type as a percentage

latter category contains only 83 modal expressions (calculated for a sample size of 7,245 words), while editorials, comments and emails incorporate up to four times as many instantiations of modality. Analysis writers use about twice as many modals as report writers, but not half as many as comment writers do, which positions the analysis somewhere in between the reporting and the commenting text types.

The distribution of the four kinds of modal orientation illustrates that newspaper text types can be clearly divided into objective and subjective types, which was however, to be expected. Reports are the most objective texts and have a strong preference for explicit-objective expressions, like *it became clear that; there was speculation that*. If subjective modality occurs in reports, which is rarely the case, it is always implicit. The reason that we can find modality structures in reports at all reflects the fact that even reporting cannot be completely devoid of subjective interpretation (Burger & Luginbühl 2014: 229). The dissemination of factual news, particularly if it is of a more complex nature, requires a minimum of explanation and, therefore, of interpretative commenting.

At the opposite end of the spectrum we find – as one would expect – the readers' emails to the editor. This text type is dominated by a preference for subjective modality and contains the largest number of both implicit-subjective and explicit-subjective expressions. Examples for the latter are *I doubt it will stop there; I used to think Karl Marx's definition of banks ... as cheap and polemic; How long before it's our turn, I wonder?* Explicit-objective modal forms, in contrast, hardly occur in emails to the editor at all.

One question that is central to the present study is where the other three text types, the analysis, the editorial and the comment, are positioned on this continuum between objective and subjective authorial stance. Editorial and comment are frequently considered to be manifestations of the same text type (for a detailed discussion of this controversial issue, see Lenk 2012). For both text types, a similar quantitative distribution of the four types of modal orientation can be observed. Both of them contain an equal amount of subjective and objective expressions of modality. In the subjective categories, both show a clear preference for implicit manifestations of modality, i.e. for the use of modal verbs in the verbal group. Examples are *the Eurozone will not only collapse, but the ghosts of the past will come to life; Cyprus's Eurozone 'bailout' should more properly be called blackmail*. Furthermore, explicit-subjective forms are rare in both and occur at a rate of only 2% (editorials) and 3% (comments). The only difference between the two text types emerges in the distribution of implicit-objective and explicit-objective modality. As the editorial is the slightly more formal and prestigious text type – after all, it voices a newspaper's official stance on important political and social issues – it indicates a slight preference for explicit objectivity, while the comment prefers implicit objectivity. Yet the differences are too marginal here to support the suggestion that editorials and comments differ in their selection of expressions of modal orientation.

The pattern of authorial orientation found for the text type 'analysis' takes a position somewhere between the stance patterns found for objective reporting and subjective commenting. As in the reports, explicit-subjective expressions of modality do not occur at all in the analyses under investigation. Objective expressions clearly prevail over the implicit-subjective ones. Yet instantiations of implicit-subjectivity are far more frequent than in the reports so that their relative frequency closes in on the frequency found for the commenting text types. In addition, the prevalence of implicit formulations (more than 70%) over explicit ones also suggests that authors of analyses adopt a more commenting stance. On the other hand, the text type analysis incorporates the highest number of implicit-objective expressions (35%), as in *Life is going to be grim; Tourists are likely to stay away; It would probably not make a great deal of difference*. This is a unique distinguishing feature of the 'analysis' which sets it apart from the other four text types.

8.4 Discussion and future research

Two trends have been observed in the development of journalism, in general, and of newspaper genres, in particular, in the relevant and recent literature. The first trend concerns a change in the standards of news reporting, which seems to incorporate a transformation from neutral, objective reporting to an increasingly subjective, opinionated and commenting kind of reporting. The second trend concerns the confluence of formerly different types of opinionated texts into one unitary, indiscriminate text type 'opinion', which surfaces without any or only little structural or stylistic differentiation under different headings like 'editorial', 'comment' or 'column'. The first trend has been observed, for example, by Schudson (1982) and Barnhurst & Mutz (1997) for the press in the USA (for a good overview, see Giessen 2013) and by Ward (2007) and Williams (2010) for the British daily national papers. One explanation for this change is ventured by Conboy (2007):

Readers appear to approve of newspapers as places to turn to, not just for reports on what has happened – most of this is available at least a day earlier through other channels – but for explanations from trusted sources, the columnists, of what the news means, and to suggest a range of appropriate opinion for their readers to engage with. (Conboy 2007: 87)

The second observation has been made in particular by researchers in the German tradition of media-linguistics and has been discussed by scholars collaborating on a research project entitled *Styles of Persuasion across Europe* (for details, see Lenk 2016a; 2016b). Giessen (2016), for example, has shown that the traditional 'explanatory comment', which used to share similarities with the analysis, can no longer be distinguished from other forms of comment. Another question that has been discussed among German media-linguists recently is the question as to whether the editorial is a text type in its own right or whether it is just a name for a prominent comment that does not differ from other comments in terms of text-linguistic parameters (Lenk 2012). The results of the present study on the distribution of categories of modal orientation support the latter assumption. As far as the authors' expressions of stance are concerned, editorials and comments are indeed manifestations of the same text type.[6]

This result needs further quantification and research including other linguistic categories. It may well be that editorials and comments differ in other lexicogrammatical aspects, such as in the distribution of low-frequency words, loan words and foreign words. A similar study to the one presented here investigates the quantitative and qualitative distribution of tokens of Appraisal in editorials, comments and columns in the British press (Kaltenbacher forthcoming). This study comes to the same conclusion that editorials and comments are manifestations of the same text type.

The first observation, according to which news reports are becoming increasingly subjective and opinionated, is not supported by the results of this analysis. Beder (2004: 208) identifies depersonalization, balance and accuracy as the three main criteria of journalistic objectivity. The results of the present study show a clear difference between depersonalized reports, in which no explicit-subjective and only very few implicit-subjective modal expressions have been found, and commenting texts, where half of all the instantiations of modal orientation fall into these two categories.

The journalistic analysis does indeed seem to be an ambivalent text type bridging the gap between the objective report and the subjective comment. Malmquist & Von der Heiden (2016: 48) consider the analysis (in Swedish newspapers) to be a special type of comment. Lüger (1995: 119) puts it in the class of informative (reporting) text types but acknowledges that it goes beyond the passing on of news as it also contains the author's reflections, interpretations and discussions of the news reported. Also Reuters (2012) warn against counting 'analysis' among the opinion-based text types, while highlighting the importance of a journalist's judgement when writing an analysis:

> Analysis is a valued part of our news file and **should not be confused with items like Columns**. Whether in spot copy or as a stand-alone item tagged ANALYSIS (sic), we provide valued insight into events or issues and cast light on them from a new angle **without compromising our standards of impartiality** or commitment to fairness. The **writer's professional judgment** has a large part to play in good analysis though we must take care **not to stray into the realm of opinion**. Good analysis is **supported by the established facts or available data and rests on the use of named sources** and the writer's expertise. (Reuters 2012: 8–9; emphasis added)

In spite of this clear rejection of any expression of *opinion*, it remains the main object of good analysis to interpret, explain and classify the news. This may be the reason why analysts take on an implicit-subjective stance to a similar extent as they do when they write a comment. While they completely abstain from the use of explicit-subjective modality, they make use of implicit-subjective modal verbs to almost the same extent as in editorials and comments. Again, further research and additional quantification of these results is needed. In addition, a diachronic study integrating older newspaper texts would be desirable to confirm some of the claims made here, as a general shift of objectivity patterns cannot be validated on the basis of a synchronic study of newspaper articles alone.

8.5. Conclusion

The most tangible result of the study presented here is that the boundaries between informative and commenting newspaper genres remain solid and intact. They can be clearly delineated in terms of the subjective/objective modal orientation patterns chosen by the authors of the respective texts. The frequently described decline of standards of news reporting towards a more and more subjective, commenting kind of reporting cannot be validated here. What can be confirmed is the observation that formerly different kinds of commentary seem to merge into a prototypical form of comment. While the editorial remains the most prestigious text a journalist may be asked to write, the orientational stance taken by its authors is in no way different from the modal stance expressed in less prestigious newspaper comments.

Acknowledgements

Thanks go to OLMS Verlag for giving permission to publish this English version of the originally German book chapter: Kaltenbacher, M. (2017) 'Was macht den Kommentar zum Kommentar? Auktoriale Orientierung als Textsortenindikator in englischen Zeitungstexten.' In: Lenk, Hartmut & Giessen, Hans (eds.) *Persuasionsstile in Europa III: Linguistische Methoden zur vergleichenden Analyse von Kommentartexten in Tageszeitungen europäischer Länder*. Hildesheim: OLMS, 57–75.

About the author

Martin Kaltenbacher studied English and Classics in Salzburg and Oxford. Since completing his doctoral dissertation on *Universal Grammar and Parameter Resetting in Second Language Acquisition* (published by Peter Lang in 2001), he has held a permanent post-doc research position at the University of Salzburg. While he has kept a keen interest in Syntax and Language Acquisition, he soon shifted his scholarly focus onto Systemic Functional Linguistics, Discourse Analysis and Social Semiotics, within which fields he has conducted studies on web-design, on the discourse of tourism and, more recently, on journalism. He co-edited books on Multimodality (Ventola, E., Charles, C. & Kaltenbacher, M. (2004) *Perspectives on Multimodality*, Amsterdam: Benjamins) and on Discourse Studies (Gruber, H., Kaltenbacher, M. & Muntigl, P. (2007) *Empirical Approaches to Discourse Analysis*, Frankfurt: Peter Lang). For the past four years he has been collaborating on a corpus based, international project called 'Styles of Persuasion in Europe', the aim of which is to explore similarities and differences in newspaper commentary across more than 200 European newspapers from 13 different European countries.

Notes

1. For a similar study on subjectivity/objectivity in travel reports in English newspapers, see Kaltenbacher (2012).
2. All examples are based on data taken from the newspaper texts this study is based on.
3. Most of the examples listed here are taken from the 'Helsinki corpus of newspaper comments' (Lenk 2016a). Invented examples are printed in italics.
4. Note that not all categories of modality can be realized in all four types of orientation. The types 'usuality' and 'inclination' cannot be realized with an explicit-subjective orientation in English; nor does inclination have an explicit-objective realization.
5. As can be seen in this example and in the example *Savers will no doubt be nervous* before, sentences and clauses can contain more than one modal expression at the same time. This is, in fact, quite frequently the case. In the present study, such instances were coded multiply; in these two cases as explicit-objective (*there were fears that*) and implicit-subjective (*could be*), and as implicit-subjective (*will be*) and implicit-objective (*no doubt*).
6. There are still formal differences in the positioning and the layout of editorials and comments in British newspapers. The most conspicuous difference is that British newspapers do not, as a principle, name the author of an editorial, while they always disclose the name of the author of a comment. As regards the choice of lexicogrammatical patterns, however, a systematic difference between the two text types cannot be confirmed. For a general overview of the formal differences between different opinion texts in the British press, see Kaltenbacher (2016)..

References

Barnhurst, K.G. & Mutz, D. (1997) 'American journalism and the decline in event-centered reporting'. *Journal of Communication* 47/4, 27–53.

Beder, S. (2004) 'Moulding and manipulating the News'. In: White, R. (ed.) *Controversies in Environmental Sociology*. Melbourne: Cambridge University Press, 204–220.

Burger, H. & Luginbühl, M. (2014) *Mediensprache. Eine Einführung in Sprache und Kommunikationsformen der Massenmedien*. 4. Auflage. Berlin/Boston: de Gruyter.

Conboy, M. (2007) *The Language of News*. Abingdon/New York: Routledge.

Giessen, H.W. (2013) 'All the news that's fit to understand. Über mögliche Gründe für interpretatorische und emotionale Darstellungsformen in der Qualitätspresse'. *Beiträge zur Fremdsprachenvermittlung* 53, 23–30.

Giessen, H.W. (2016) 'Nur noch Kommentare? Zum Verschwinden eines Genres – am Beispiel der *Süddeutschen Zeitung*'. In: Lenk, H.E.H. (ed.) *Persuasionsstile in Europa II. Kommentartexte in den Medienlandschaften europäischer Länder*. Hildesheim/Zürich/New York: OLMS, 149–168.

Halliday, M.A.K. (1994) *An Introduction to Functional Grammar*. 2nd edition. London: Arnold.

Halliday, M.A.K. & Matthiessen C.M.I.M. (2014) *Halliday's Introduction to Functional Grammar*. 4th edition. London: Arnold.

Kaltenbacher, M. (2012) 'Modalität im englischen Zeitungsreisebericht'. In: Grösslinger, C., Held, G. & Stöckl, H. (eds.) *Pressetextsorten jenseits der 'News'*. Frankfurt: Peter Lang, 281–296.

Kaltenbacher, M. (2016) 'Meinungsbetonte Textsorten in der britischen Tagespresse: Differenzierung, Verortung, Vernetzung'. In: Lenk, H.E.H. (ed.) *Persuasionsstile in Europa II. Kommentartexte in den Medienlandschaften europäischer Länder*. Hildesheim/Zürich/New York: OLMS, 93–126.

Kaltenbacher, M. (2017) 'Was macht den Kommentar zum Kommentar? Auktoriale Orientierung als Textsortenindikator in englischen Zeitungstexten.' In: Lenk, Hartmut & Giessen, Hans (eds.) *Persuasionsstile in Europa III: Linguistische Methoden zur vergleichenden Analyse von Kommentartexten in Tageszeitungen europäischer Länder*. Hildesheim: OLMS, 57–75.

Kaltenbacher, M. (forthcoming) 'Evaluierungsmuster in der britischen Tagespresse. Eine Textsortenabgrenzung'. In: Giessen, H. & Lenk, H.E.H. (eds.) *Persuasionsstile in Europa III*. Hildesheim: OLMS.

Kane, T. (1988) *The New Oxford Guide to Writing*. Oxford/New York: Oxford University Press.

Lenk, H.E.H. (2012) 'Methodologische Probleme des Textsortenvergleichs am Beispiel des Kommentars'. In: *Tekst i dyskurs/Text und Diskurs* 5, 155–171.

Lenk, H.E.H. (2016a) 'Zur Entwicklung des Projekts Persuasionsstile in Europa und des Helsinkier Kommentarkorpus'. In: Lenk, H.E.H. (ed.) *Persuasionsstile in Europa II. Kommentartexte in den Medienlandschaften europäischer Länder*. Hildesheim/Zürich/New York: OLMS, 7–20.

Lenk, H.E.H. (ed.) (2016b): *Persuasionsstile in Europa II. Kommentartexte in den Medienlandschaften europäischer Länder*. Hildesheim/Zürich/New York. (Germanistische Linguistik.

Lüger, H.H. (1995) *Pressesprache.* 2nd edition. Tübingen: Niemeyer.

Malmquist, A. & von der Heiden, G. (2016) 'Der Kommentar in Tageszeitungen Schwedens'. In: Lenk, H.E.H. (ed.) *Persuasionsstile in Europa II. Kommentartexte in den Medienlandschaften europäischer Länder*. Hildesheim/Zürich/New York: OLMS, 21–57.

Martin, J.R. (1995) 'Interpersonal meaning, persuasion and public discourse: packing semiotic punch'. *Australian Journal of Linguistics* 15, 33–67.

Martin, J.R. & White, P.R.R. (2005) *The Language of Evaluation: Appraisal in English.* London/New York: Palgrave Macmillan.

Reuters (2012) *Handbook of Journalism*. Thomson Reuters. Online: handbook.reuters.com

Schudson, M. (1982) 'The politics of narrative form: The emergence of news conventions in print and television'. *Daedalus* 3/4, 97–112.

Thompson, G. (1996) *Introducing Functional Grammar*. London: Arnold.

Ward, G. (2007) 'UK National Newspapers'. In: Anderson, P.J. & Ward, G. (eds.) *The Future of Journalism in Advanced Democracies*. Aldershot: Ashgate, 73–87.

Williams, Kevin (2010) *Read all about it! A History of the British Newspaper.* London/New York: Routledge.

9 Interpersonal aspects of an English language Internet travel forum

David Banks
Université de Bretagne Occidentale, France

9.1 Background

In 2015, I presented a paper[1] which analyzed interpersonal aspects of a French language Internet travel forum. The study was carried out using the concepts and terminology of Systemic Functional Linguistics (Halliday 2014, Banks 2005a, Thompson 2004). The paper analyzed two small samples from the Routard website, one dealing with a close destination, Brittany, and one with a distant destination, Namibia. The results showed that the Namibia sample represented a smaller, more closely-knit community. Participants in the Brittany sample used more examples of epistemic modality and more mental than material processes, showing that they were concerned with what they feel and think. In contrast, participants in the Namibia sample used more examples of dynamic modality and more material than mental processes, showing that they were more concerned with practicalities. The vast expansion of the use of electronic means of communication, and of the Internet in particular, make such studies of interest since it is here that we find new forms of communication and hence language development in the making (Crystal 2001).

The object of this paper is to carry out a parallel study on an English language travel forum. The website chosen was that of Tripadvisor; the close destination was Northumberland, and the distant destination, again, Namibia. The choice of places is purely personal: Northumberland is where I was born, Brittany is where I have been living for the last 35 years, and I visited Namibia in 2015.

In what follows, I shall first describe my data (9.2), giving details of the corpus (9.2.1) and elaborating on the nature of the exchanges (9.2.2). I shall then deal with three aspects of the interpersonal metafunction (9.3): first, I shall discuss mood, dealing mainly with direct and indirect questions (9.3.1); second, I shall consider modality in terms of its forms and functions

(9.3.2); third, I shall look at the process types of the finite verbs (9.3.3). This is usually considered to be a question of the ideational metafunction, but I think it has some bearing on the interpersonal stratum of the message since the choice of the ideational content depends on the audience which the speaker intends to address, and the speaker's relationship with that audience falls within the domain of the interpersonal metafunction. I shall close this section with a short discussion of how criticism is voiced among participants (9.3.4) before I conclude the paper with some final remarks (9.4).

9.2 The data

9.2.1 The corpus

Ten exchanges were taken for each destination. Where exchanges consisted of more than ten responses, only the first ten were taken; thus the maximum number of turns in an exchange is eleven (the initial posting, plus up to ten responses). However, this only happened in the Namibia sample; exchanges in the Northumberland sample never exceed ten responses. The total number of words in the Northumberland sample (including headings, names and dates) is 2896. The number of words in the Namibia sample is 8616. Hence the Namibia sample is roughly three times longer than the Northumberland sample.

9.2.2 The nature of the exchanges

The exchanges in the Northumberland sample contained between two and nine turns. The following is the outline of a simple example headed 'Nightlife in Alnwick'.

    (a) Nightlife in Alnwick
        Q1   Heather D   Nov. 16
        A1   starpyrowhittle Nov. 16
        A2   lbj 1963   Nov. 16
        A3   apt 22   Nov. 17

Heather D posts a question (coded Q1) on 16 Nov. This elicits three responses (coded A1, A2, A3), two on the same day and one the following day. The following is a slightly more complex example.

(b) Does anyone know the name of this hotel
    Q1   Travelling_Gem   Oct. 6
    A1   starpyrowhittle   Oct. 6
    A2   pausilypon   Oct. 7
    Q2   Travelling_Gem   Oct. 7
    A3   pausilypon   Oct. 7
    A4   starpyrowhittle   Oct. 7
    A5   libby1   Oct. 13

This has a total of seven turns and four participants. Travelling_Gem posts his initial question on 6 Oct. Starpyrowhittle replies the same day and pausilypon the following day. The same day, Travelling_Gem intervenes again (subsequent postings by the initial questioner are coded Q2 etc., whether or not they are actually questions). The same day, there are further responses from pausilypon and starpyrowhittle. There is then a fairly long pause until 13 Oct, when there is an additional response from libby1.

Table 9.1 gives details of the number of turns by each participant in each exchange, either as questioner (Q) or responder (A).

There is a total of 25 participants, some of whom take part in more than one exchange. Starpyrowhittle takes part in six exchanges, lbj1963 in three, five participants take part in two exchanges, and 18 in only one. Most participants contribute one or two turns, but three participants contribute three and starpyrowhittle contributes nine turns.

Table 9.2 presents the equivalent information for the Namibia sample.

Here there are 22 participants. Xelas takes part in eight exchanges, while two participants take part in five, two in four, two in three, and two in two exchanges; 13 of the participants take part in only one exchange. Exactly half of the participants (eleven) contribute one or two turns; at the other end of the scale, desert_explorer83 contributes no less than 17 turns, spread over four exchanges, in all of which he was the person who posted the initial question. Of the other ten participants who contribute more than two turns xelas contributes nine, spread over eight exchanges, and stargaize contributes eight spread over five exchanges.

The average number of words per participant is 86 in the Northumberland sample but 391 in the Namibia sample. The average number of turns per participant is 1.8 in the Northumberland sample and 3.9 in the Namibia sample. Thus the average participant in the Namibia sample contributes twice as many turns and uses four and a half times as many words as does the average participant in the Northumberland sample.

152   *Analyzing the Media: A Systemic Functional Approach*

Table 9.1 Northumbria: exchanges and turns

	1		2		3		4		5		6		7		8		9		10	
	Q	A	Q	A	Q	A	Q	A	Q	A	Q	A	Q	A	Q	A	Q	A	Q	A
Heather D	1		1																	
starpyrowhittle	1		2					2		2								1		1
lbj1963	1					1								1						
apt22	1																			
bobbybonga			1																	
weepo					2															
bsandrs					2															
rbgs					1															
Lou73NorthEast					1															
Morgana					1							1								
pausilypon					1		2													
Travelling_Gem							2													
libbyl							1													
Gemma M									1											
Lisa H										1										
northmole											2								1	
nowhereman64													1							1
marcusNorthumberland														1						
YorkshireTilly																1				
KarenWaugh																		1		
NOthumbrian																		1		
Frank S																		1		
FarneIslands																		1		
Blackdog11																		1		
BleddynE																			1	

One notable fact about the participants is that all of those in the Northumberland sample have addresses in the UK, with one exception, a participant in the USA. Hence all the participants in the Northumberland sample live in an Anglophone country. Participation in the Namibia sample, however, is much more international. Contributions come not only from the UK but also from eleven other countries, seven of which are not Anglophone. These are listed in Table 9.3.

I do not know whether this means that the contributions in the Namibia sample should be classed as some form of 'World English'. It is true that they contain many examples of non-standard use, but then, so do the contributions in the Northumberland sample, which one might presume to

Interpersonal aspects of an English language Internet travel forum   153

Table 9.2 Namibia: exchanges and turns

	1		2		3		4		5		6		7		8		9		10	
	Q	A	Q	A	Q	A	Q	A	Q	A	Q	A	Q	A	Q	A	Q	A	Q	A
Gil G	4														4					
mfuwe	1				3				2						1					
Skimkat	2																			
YaelGr	1								1				1		2		1			
xelas	1		1		1		1		1				1				2		1	
karinmariman			2																	
allantaylorsa					1															
wildlifepainter					1															
desert_explorer83					5				4		4								4	
stargaize					1						1		1		2					3
Gemcap					1				1								1			
bromion							2													
cannuck50									1											
KobusB									1								1			
seniortraveler137											2									
chargedmr2											3									
Nooee											1				2					2
Markus V													1							
John222333													1							
Tomatinho																	3			
lucyjames																	1			
Spad16																			1	

Table 9.3 Other countries represented in the Namibia sample

Australia
Belgium
Brazil
Canada
Germany
Israel
Slovenia
South Africa
Sweden
United Arab Emirates
USA

have been written by native speakers. At all events, it is evident that many participants do not re-read or correct their contributions.

It is rare for participants to address each other by name. In the Northumberland sample this occurs only twice.

> (1) Hi Pausilypon
> No, that's not it but thanks for the suggestion. [Travelling_Gem: Northumberland][2]
> (2) hi Lisa- that sounds so reasonable for Christmas day, and I would certainly recommend there having dined there a few times. [starpyrowhittle: Northumberland]

In 1, Travelling_Gem is the initiator of the exchange or the OP (original poster); in 2, neither of the participants concerned is the OP. In addition, there are two cases where a third party is referred to by name. Again, none of the participants involved is the OP.

> (3) As Nurthumbrian said, it's a great time of year for visiting the area – you get a real Christmas feel – a real white Christmas is almost certain and very special by the sea. [Frank S: Northumberland]
> (4) N0rthumbrian has it spot on. Although choice of B&B's, etc may be less than in the summer months most other things remain open. [FarneIslands: Northumberland]

In the Namibia sample there are eight examples of addressing another participant by name. Three were supplied by desert_explorer83, and of these two are addressed to Gemscap.

> (5) Hi gemcap,
> i totally agree with you! [desert_explorer83: Namibia]
> (6) thanks gemscap! sounds good to me. with authentic i meant its not like a zoo but animals still wild or will be reintroduced to the wild at some point. [desert_explorer83: Namibia]

Hence this seems to be a rare phenomenon, and though the numbers are small, it seems to be a little more prevalent in the Namibia sample than in the Northumbria sample.

A similar result was found in the French study, where there were some examples of addressing by name in the Namibia sample but none in the Brittany sample.

9.3 Aspects of the interpersonal metafunction

9.3.1 Mood

The aspect of mood which I shall consider is the ways in which questions are asked. In the Northumbrian sample, the initiators of the exchange asked a total of 19 direct questions.

(7) is there any Halloween party's in seahouses as I am stopping there for Halloween? [marcusNorthumberland: Northumberland]
(8) Are there any hotels or BB that don't take dogs we both love dogs but my partner has a severe allergy ok around them but no good sleeping in rooms where dogs have been [bobbybonga: Northumberland]

Of the 19 direct questions, three, like 8 above, had no question mark but were otherwise interrogative in form. In addition, initiators asked five indirect questions.

(9) Seems like a lot of driving, but maybe it's not? [northmole: Northumberland]
(10) What would be a good way to get there? We can take a train as far as possible and hire a car? [northmole: Northumberland]

A direct question in 10 is followed by an indirect question. Questions can occasionally occur in series, as in this cascade of five questions in a posting by Weepo.

(11) Would anyone advise AGAINST driving from Edinburgh to Alnwick? Is there ample parking at the castle and gardens? Is it one parking lot for both attractions? Or would we have to park twice? Is there a fare for parking? [Weepo: Northumberland][3]

Questions by responders are much rarer. There are four examples in the Northumberland sample, and, like the following example, they ask for supplementary information to make the original question more precise.

(12) Shops,bars,restaurants all open xxx what kind of things were you specifically thinking of?? [Karen Waugh: Northumberland]

In the Namibia sample, the initiators ask 28 direct questions.

> (13) Does anyone know what is the game viewing quality in the park as of today? Is it still dry(which means good for viewing)? [Gil G: Namibia]

In addition, they ask 17 indirect questions.

> (14) I'm looking for advise if this is a good plan or if we should rather spend more time (~2 nights) in 2 camps. [desert_explorer83: Namibia]

In relative terms, questions by initiators are more frequent in the Northumberland sample, where they occur at a rate of 7.9 per 1000 words. In the Namibia sample they occur at a rate of 5.3 per 1000 words. On the other hand, if one considers direct questions per exchange, they are more frequent in the Namibia sample (2.8 per exchange) than in the Northumbria sample (1.9 per exchange). That the rate is higher per number of words is probably due to the fact that responses tend to be longer in the Namibia sample. The percentage of questions which are indirect is higher in the Namibia sample, where they account for 37% of all questions, compared with 22% in the Northumberland sample. Questions by responders are of the same order in the two samples. It might also be noted that replies to questions are longer and more detailed in the Namibia sample.

9.3.2 Modality

Modal expressions occur at roughly the same rate in both samples: 22 per 1000 words in the Northumberland sample and 25 per 1000 words in the Namibia sample. The forms and the distribution of the modal expressions used are given in Table 9.4.

The modal auxiliary (Aux) is the only form of modal expression used extensively in both samples, accounting for 62% of modal expressions in the Northumberland sample and 67% in the Namibia sample.

> (15) Hi- you **could** have a look at these and see what you **can** find! [starpyrowhittle: Northumberland][4]
> (16) Whilst a lot of rain over a period of time **will** cause dispersal to fresh areas a few showers **won't**. [mfuwe: Namibia]

Interpersonal aspects of an English language Internet travel forum 157

Table 9.4 Modal expressions

	Northumberland n	Northumberland %	Namibia n	Namibia %
Aux = modal auxiliary	40	62%	143	67%
Semi = semi-modal verb	5	8%	18	8%
Verb = lexical verb + modal meaning	6	9%	8	4%
Adv = modal adverb	5	8%	16	7%
Adj = modal adjective	7	11%	23	11%
Nom = noun + modal meaning	–	–	3	1%
GM = grammatical metaphor	2	3%	3	1%

The only other form used to any extent is that of adjectives (Adj), accounting for 11% of the modal expressions in both of the samples. The adjectives which occur are *sure, able, certain* and *possible*.

(17) Hi, sorry about your sad time last year, I am **sure** you and your dad can have a good time this year. [Lisa H: Northumberland]

(18) Here is mine: how much costed you this trip being **able** to get amazing deals? [xelas: Namibia]

Among the less frequent forms, semi-modals (Semi), which here include *need, dare*, and *have* + infinitive, account for 8% in both samples.

(19) Or would we **have to** park twice? [Weepo: Northumberland]

(20) The wildlife **needs** water and this means waterholes until they can get their needs further afield. [mfuwe: Namibia]

Lexical verbs with modal meaning (Verb), such as *seem, require* and *appear*, account for 9% in the Northumberland sample and 4% in the Namibia sample.

(21) Yes, it **seems** I just love doing things the crazy and unnatural way [northmole: Northumberland]

(22) It **seems** chargedmr2 you obviously know your area and have expertise in this regard. Also you **seem** a caring person. [stargaize: Namibia]

Adverbial forms of modal expression (Adv), like *possibly*, *probably*, *certainly*, *perhaps* and *maybe*, account for 8% in the Northumberland sample and 7% in the Namibia sample.

> (23) if we don't drive, is it easy to catch a taxi and/or bus from Alnwick or <u>Alnmouth</u> (as we would **probably** take the train to Alnmouth if we don't drive). [Weepo, Northumberland]
>
> (24) Tomantinho, every one is talking of the Petrified Acacia Trees in the Deadvlei, but **maybe** you are looking for the petrified forest 42km from Khorixas? [Kobus B: Namibiba]

The few nominal examples that occurred were only in the Namibia sample and accounted for only 1%.

> (25) I think given your itinerary and the fact the vehicle will be your home for a month I would say do not rush day 1 ... just give time to that and your food and personal **needs** for your shopping and banking phone SIM etc. [stargaize: Namibia]

Finally, grammatical metaphors are those cases where a clause of the type *I think* is functioning to all intents and purposes as a marker of modality. This is rare and accounts for only 1% of modal expressions in both of the samples.

> (26) **I think** it was a small place with a few rooms. possibly a B&B rather than a hotel. [Travelling_Gem: Northumberland]
>
> (27) **i guess** if they let people walk there without a guide (unlike many other places in namibia) it cannot really be dangerous. or? [desert_explorer83: Namibia]

I shall consider the functions of modality in terms of the traditional distinction between epistemic modality, which concerns questions of the speaker's judgement, and root modality, divided into dynamic modality, which deals with questions of a physical nature, and deontic modality, dealing with questions of a moral nature (Larreya 1984, Palmer 1986, Perkins 1983). Epistemic modality corresponds roughly to Halliday's modalization, and root modality to his modulation (Halliday 2014). Table 9.5 gives the distribution of the functions of modal expressions.

Table 9.5 Modal functions

	Northumberland		Namibia	
	n	%	n	%
Epistemic	36	55%	129	60%
Dynamic	28	43%	72	34%
Deontic	1	2%	13	6%

Of the modal expressions which occur, the majority are epistemic in both samples, with the rate being slightly higher in the Namibia sample, where they account for 60% of modal expressions, than in the Northumberland sample, where they account for 55%. Correspondingly, the rate for dynamic modality is rather higher in the Northumberland sample, where it accounts for 43%, than in the Namibia sample, where it accounts for 34%. Dynamic modality is fairly rare in both samples, though accounting for slightly more in the Namibia sample, 6%, than in the Northumberland sample, 2%.

This contrasts with the results found in the French study, where dynamic modality accounted for the vast majority of the modal expressions, with 88% in the Namibia sample and 78% in the Brittany sample. Epistemic modality was rare in the French study, accounting for only 8% of the modal expressions in the Namibia sample, but for 20% in the Brittany sample. Deontic modality was rare in both. Hence the differences between the two subsamples were rather more marked in the French study.

9.3.3 Process types

I shall use a system of five process types (Banks 2008, 2016):

1. material processes, which are actions or events of a physical nature;
2. mental processes, which are cerebral events, whether they be cognitive, affective or cases of perception;
3. relational processes, which link two entities, or one entity with one of its characteristics, and which can be attributive, identifying or possessive;
4. verbal processes, which are instances of communication; and
5. existential processes, which simply state the existence of an entity.

O'Donnell et al. (2008) identified a cline of possibilities for the analysis of process types, from conceptual to grammatical; my approach would be

160   *Analyzing the Media: A Systemic Functional Approach*

Table 9.6 Process types

	Northumberland		*Namibia*	
	n	%	n	%
Material	70	27%	182	24%
Mental	49	19%	151	20%
Relational	103	40%	331	44%
Verbal	19	7%	64	9%
Existential	19	7%	22	3%

towards the conceptual pole of this cline. I shall consider the processes encoded by the finite verbs. Table 9.6 gives the distribution of the processes found in the two samples.

It can be seen that the commonest process type is relational, accounting for 44% of the processes in the Namibia sample and for 40% in the Northumberland sample.

> (34) Yeah pretty much everything **is** open at Christmas, it**'s** a nice time of year to visit Northumberland. [NOthumbrian: Northumberland]
> (35) Dune 7 near Swakopmund **is** the tallest in Namibia at 383 m. [xelas: Namibia]

This shows the importance of description in both of the samples. This is reinforced by the fact that 69% of the relational processes in the Northumberland sample and 64% in the Namibia sample are of the attributive type. Existential processes might also be considered to be basically descriptive. These account for 7% of the processes in the Northumberland sample, and 3% in the Namibia sample.

> (36) Therefore both can be visited from the one car park for which there **is** a charge of three pounds for the day well worth a trip. [Weepo: Northumberland]
> (37) Since much of the hike follows a canyon, choose this one for the fascinating geology, as opposed to wide open vistas (though there **are** nice vistas at the beginning of the hike). [chargedmr2: Namibia]

Thus relational and existential processes together make up 47% of the processes in both of the samples.

Interpersonal aspects of an English language Internet travel forum 161

The second commonest process type is material, showing that physical actions and events are of some importance, though considerably less than description.

(38) For one of the iconic views of Alnwick Castle ... and assuming you **are driving** south on the A1 ... at Denwick, instead of continuing into Alnwick, **take** the road which heads west. [pausilypon: Northumberland]

(39) We **have stayed** B&B in Otjiwarongo and **visited** CCF for Cheetah Run. [xelas: Namibia]

This is followed by mental processes, which account for 20% of the processes in the Namibia sample and 19% (virtually the same) in the Northumberland sample.

(40) My mam died at home day after boxing day last year, so kinda **want** to take my Dad out for Christmas lunch this year but cheapest I **have found** is £60pp. [Gemma M: Northumberland]

(41) in May 2016 on our self drive itinerary between Epupa -> Etosha -> Waterberg -> Windhoek we'**d like** to fit 1–2 days camping at a Cheetah farm and participate in their activity programs. The opportunity to see these incredible animals from up close **fascinates** us after having watched the African Safari 3D movie:-) [desert_explorer83: Namibia]

The vast majority of mental processes are of the cognitive type, which account for 86% of the mental processes in the Namibia sample and 78% in the Northumberland sample. However, a small minor difference may be found in the case of affective mental processes, which account for 16% of the mental processes in the Northumberland sample but for only 5% in the Namibia sample.

(42) We've also had both lunch and dinner a few times at the Tree House restaurant at Alnwick Gardens and **enjoyed** the food and surroundings! [Morgana: Northumberland]

(43) Most folks **like** the 'morning run' as then you see the cats going full out chasing the equivalent of a Greyhound lure. [mfuwe: Namibia]

However, it must be noted that raw figures here are small, so this result is to be treated with caution.

Finally, verbal processes are relatively rare, accounting for only 9% of the processes in the Namibia sample and 7% in the Northumberland sample.

> (44) Depending on your available time, I **would also recommend** Lindisfarne/Holy Island which is naturally on your route. [bsandrs: Northumberland]
>
> (45) On the way in (or out) you can also visit REST http://www.restafrica.org **ask** them when does the Vulture restaurant opens …? [YaelG: Namibia]

Consequently, talking about communicative acts is not a significant feature in these texts.

These results are fairly similar to those found in the French study. However, there was one notable difference in that in the Brittany sample, mental processes were more common than material processes. Mental processes accounted for 30% of all processes, material processes only for 20%.

9.3.4 Criticism voiced at other participants

It is perhaps worth noting that in general, these postings are written in a friendly tone. Criticism is rare, and when it occurs, it is usually related to the fact that information requested is easily available on the Internet. The following is the strongest example of criticism that I found in this small sample. This occurs in the context of an exchange where the initiator has asked repeated questions about a difficult section of a hike where it is necessary to move along a cliff face holding onto chains above some pools. Only later does he admit that he is asking the questions because his partner suffers from vertigo!

> (46) I have not a clue about such matters relating to hiking but the type and plethora of questions by the OP seems to me given the Vertigo issue is truly perplexing. I think posting? s w/o doing any research,checking the safety consequences and attempting such activities is sheer lunacy. [stargaize: Namibia]

9.4 Final remarks

The differences between the two samples analyzed in this study are less clear-cut than those found in the French study. It is possible that the international nature of the Namibia sample in this English study is a feature to be taken into account. Nevertheless, in comparing the Northumberland and Namibia samples of this English study, we have seen that although addressing other participants by name is fairly rare, it is rather more common in the Namibia sample than in the Northumberland sample. We have also seen that questions have a greater tendency to be indirect in the Namibia sample. The Namibia sample has more cases of epistemic modality, while the Northumberland sample has more cases of dynamic modality. Deontic modality is rare in both but occurs slightly more frequently in the Namibia sample. Relational, material and mental processes occur with similar frequencies in both samples. However, affective mental processes might be a minor feature in the Northumberland sample. In general, the participants in the Namibia sample give the impression of being more involved in the exchanges; they are more prolix and seem to present an image of a more firmly established virtual community than the participants in the Northumberland sample.

It must be admitted that the differences found between these two samples are fairly slight, and while useful information can be gleaned from small or mini-corpora (Banks 2005b, 2015), the possibility that these differences are simply a quirk of the sample cannot be discounted. Nevertheless, they are valid for the sample studied and can provide a basis for further enquiry. This may seem a fairly negative result, but it is offered in the spirit of Francis Bacon, who, in laying the philosophical foundations of modern science in the seventeenth century, claimed that negative experiments should be reported. In his *Parasceve* he says that 'not only those experiments in each art which serve the purpose of the art itself are to be received, but likewise those which turn up anyhow by the way' (Bacon trans. Spedding in Robertson 1905: 405); and perhaps even more forcefully in his *Novum Organum*, where he says 'it is the peculiar and perpetual error of the human intellect to be more moved and excited by affirmatives than by negatives; whereas it ought properly to hold itself indifferently disposed towards both alike. Indeed in the establishment of any true axiom, the negative instance is the more forcible of the two' (Bacon trans. Spedding in Robertson 1905: 266). Consequently, more research is required on corpora of this type, and among the points that need to be considered are the differences, both linguistic and cultural, between French and English, and the implications of an international and multilingual community writing in English.[5]

About the author

David Banks is Emeritus Professor of English Linguistics at the Université de Bretagne Occidentale at Brest in France. He was born in Newcastle-upon-Tyne (UK) in 1943. He has an MA from the University of Cambridge (UK), where he studied philosophy, a doctorate from the Université de Nantes and an HDR from the Université de Bordeaux 2. He is former Head of the English Department at Brest, Director of ERLA (*Equipe de Recherche en Linguistique Appliquée*) and Chairman of AFLSF (*Association Française de la Linguistique Systémique Fonctionnelle*). He is author or editor of 30 books and has published over 100 academic articles. His publication *The Development of Scientific Writing: Linguistic Features and Historical Context* (Equinox) won the ESSE Language and Linguistics book award 2010. His research interests include the synchronic and diachronic study of scientific text and the application of systemic functional linguistics to English and French. His non-academic activities include poetry, choral singing and ocean rowing.

Notes

1. Published as Banks (2017).
2. The content of the square brackets after examples gives the name of the writer of the posting and the sample from which it comes.
3. Hyperlinks, which appeared in blue in the original, are here printed in black.
4. The relevant parts of examples are printed in bold.
5. An earlier version of this paper was presented at the 26th European Systemic Functional Linguistics Conference, Salzburg, 13–15 July, 2016.

References

Banks, D. (2005a) *Introduction à la linguistique systémique fonctionnelle*. Paris: L'Harmattan.

Banks, D. (2005b) 'The case of Perrin and Thomson: An example of the use of a mini-corpus'. *English for Specific Purposes* 24:2, 201–211.

Banks, D. (2015) 'Approaching the Journal des Sçavans, 1665–1695: a manual analysis of thematic structure'. *Journal of World Languages* 2:1, 1–17.
<http://www.tandfonline.com/doi/ful/10.1080/21698252.2015.1010248#abstract>

Banks, D. (2016) 'On the (non)necessity of the hybrid category behavioural process'. In: Miller, D.R. & Bayley, P. (eds.) *Hybridity in Systemic Functional Linguisics. Grammar, Text and Discursive Context*. Sheffield: Equinox, 21–40.

Banks, D. (2017) 'Notes on interpersonal aspects of an Internet travel forum'. In: Burger, M., Fitzgerald, R. & Thornborrow, J. (eds.) *Places, Spaces and Discursive Actions in Social Media and Real Communicative Environments*. Brussels: DeBoeck, 91–108.

Crystal, D. (2001) *Language and the Internet*. Cambridge: Cambridge University Press.

Halliday, M.A.K. & Matthiessen, C.M.I.M. (2014) *Halliday's Introduction to Functional Grammar*. 4th edition. London: Routledge.

Larreya, P. (1984) *Le possible et le nécessaire. Modalités et auxiliaires modaux en anglais britannique*. Paris: Nathan.

O'Donnell, M., Zappavigna, M. & Whitelaw, C. (2008) 'A survey of process type classification over difficult cases'. In: Jones, C. & Ventola, E. (eds.) *New Developments in the Study of Ideational Meaning: From Language to Multimodality*. London: Continuum, 47–64.

Palmer, F.R. (1986) *Mood and Modality*. Cambridge: Cambridge University Press.

Perkins, M.R. (1983) *Modal Expressions in English*. London: Frances Pinter.

Robertson, J.M. (ed.) (1905) *The Philosophical Works of Francis Bacon*. London: Routledge.

Thompson, G. (2004) *Introducing Functional Grammar*. 2nd edition. London: Arnold.

10 Blending SFL and Activity Theory to model communication and artefact use: Examples from Human-Computer Interaction

Rebekah Wegener and Jörg Cassens
RWTH Aachen University, Germany; University of Salzburg, Austria & University Hildesheim, Germany

> Our schematic constructs must be judged with reference to their combined tool power in our dealings with linguistic events in the social process. Such constructs have no ontological status and we do not project them as having being or existence. They are neither immanent nor transcendent, but just language turned back on itself.
>
> Firth, J.R. (1957: 181)

10.1 Introduction

Systemic Functional Linguistics (SFL) and Computer Science have a long history together (O'Donnell & Bateman 2005). This ranges from Winograd's *blocks world* (Winograd 1971), inspired by Halliday's work on grammar, over applications in Natural Language Generation (Bateman 1998) and interactive media (Bateman et al. 2017), through to our own work. For example, we have used concepts from SFL to help model contextualized, ambient intelligent systems ranging from the use of abstract concepts (Cassens & Wegener 2008) and of parameters of context (Wegener et al. 2008) for requirements engineering to a stratified view on context modelling with a special focus on the semantic stratum (Butt et al. 2013) and its practical application in intention-aware automatic doors (Kofod-Petersen et al. 2009).

Activity Theory (AT; see, e.g. Leont'ev 1978; Nardi 1996) is also no stranger to applications in computer science, both in Human-Computer Interaction (see, e.g. Nardi 1996) and in Artificial Intelligence, in particular in Ambient Intelligent Systems (see, e.g. Cassens 2008). In particular the Cultural-Historical Activity Theory (CHAT; see, e.g. Engeström & Vasquez

1997) has proven to be useful for understanding human work practice with computerized systems.

Based on these experiences and our own work on the use of both Activity Theory and of SFL within similar application domains (see, e.g. Cassens & Wegener 2008), we propose an approach to requirements elicitation and modelling of contextualized, ambient systems that combines the tool-centric perspective from the cultural-historic approach to Activity Theory with the communications and meaning-centric perspective of SFL. In so doing, we draw on two distinct ambient intelligent systems that have very different requirements in modelling: behaviour-aware sliding doors and a smart whiteboard and interactive meeting system.

In what follows, we will first explore what SFL and AT can contribute to the modelling of ambient human-computer interaction systems in Section 10.2. We will then discuss how such systems can be viewed as text within a multimodal context in Section 10.3. In Section 10.4, we will illustrate in two examples how SFL and AT can be integrated at a practical level in ambient systems, and we will subsequently show how this successful integration can be modelled on an abstract, theoretical level in Section 10.5. Finally, the chapter will be brought to an end with a conclusion in Section 10.6.

10.2 Motivation and theoretical background

When implementing socio-technical systems that combine both artificial, computerized actors and human actors, it is necessary to really understand why an activity takes place and to explore the functional foundations of the activity unless one intends to merely replicate or mimic human actions or processes in a technical form. If we ignore the functions of the activity, we put ourselves in the position of building Vaucanson's 'mechanical duck': it looks and acts like a duck, but it is no duck. This process of understanding the functional grounding of an activity before building a system is part of any successful requirements elicitation.

Activity Theory is a descriptive tool to help understand the unity of consciousness and activity (Nardi 1996). Its focus lies on individual and collective work practice (Leont'ev 1978). One of its strengths is the ability to identify the role of material artefacts in the work process. An activity is composed of a subject, an object, and a mediating artefact or tool. A subject is a person or a group engaged in an activity. An object is held by the subject, and the subject has a goal directed towards the object he wants to achieve, motivating the activity and giving it a specific direction. In Cultural Historic Activity Theory, the community of actors with their division of labour and governing rules are added to this model (Cole 1996). One basic property of (CH)AT is the hierarchical structure of activity: activities (the topmost category) are composed of goal-directed actions. These actions are performed consciously. Actions, in turn, consist of non-conscious operations. In this chapter, we will focus on the ability of CHAT to identify different activities and actions based on the material setting.

Halliday's systemic functional theory of language (SFL) is a social semiotic theory that sets out from the assumption that humans are social beings who are inclined to interact and that this interaction is inherently multimodal (Halliday 1978). We interact not just with each other but with and through our own constructions and with our natural world. These are all different forms of interaction, but they are all meaning-making processes. Here, we focus on the ability of SFL to identify the different constituents of communicative interaction and their representations in different modalities.

Both SFL and CHAT are approaches that are functional in nature, and both are very useful for requirements elicitation. For applications in ambient systems, SFL is an attractive model of language because it foregrounds language as a social semiotic and thus frames spoken and written communication as just one avenue for meaning making. CHAT is attractive because it has a notion of activity as a definable and describable concept. As both these approaches are socio-material, functional and concerned with situated social practice, they are usefully combined in requirements elicitation.

SFL focuses on human communication and requires cognition for most of the categories that it posits – for the others, it presupposes language.[1] Despite the assumption that language is a social semiotic, SFL is language centric, and the inclusion of other modalities is, in many cases, quite a challenge. SFL assumes spoken or written language as the baseline, and other modalities are often treated as the context. This has interesting implications for how context is modelled. SFL also has an under-developed model of culture and consciousness. Despite being well positioned to capture both aspects, neither has been adequately integrated into the theory, meaning that while we have a model of language as a social semiotic, we have no consistent model of the semiotic agent or the socio-cognitive and material environment of the semiotic agent.

By comparison, Cultural-Historical Activity Theory (CHAT) is activity centric and focuses on action rather than meaning. Because of this, it has no model of semiosis or meaning making and thus no way to analyze action beyond the representation of the action itself. It also lacks an elaborated model of context, a stratified view of interaction and a conceptualization of the dynamic aspects of social activity.

CHAT does however have a strong model of culture that can accept a layered view of context. By focusing on action, it has developed a modelling of the activity sequence that provides clear units of analysis which can then be subjected to Generic Structure Potential and other SFL analyses. Perhaps the greatest strength, particularly from a human-computer interaction perspective, beyond a model of activity, is the explicit inclusion of non-human agents as potential actors.

Interestingly, for an approach focused on activity, Cultural-Historical Activity Theory also has a well-developed model of cognition that is social in focus, and this means that we have an opportunity to integrate a powerful model of language with a similarly focused model of interaction.

Because they share underlying assumptions, it is possible to integrate the two theories at abstract and applied levels. SFL has a history of building on and integrating other theories if the core assumptions are compatible (e.g. Halliday's integration of Bernstein's theory of social organization). Most importantly, they are non-competitive models. That is, they do not seek to explain or model the same sphere of human behaviour, rather they complement each other, meaning that by combining them they together explain and model more than each alone. Here, we set out our integration of the two theories at the abstract and practical level, citing examples from our previous and current projects in human-computer interaction.

Every theory is built on a set of assumptions, and these assumptions shape the questions that the theory sets out to answer. This is not prescriptive, it is merely a case of the categories of language, in this case metalanguage, shaping the way we perceive and think about the world (Whorf 1956). Indeed, all language can be considered a theory of the world, so it is of little surprise that our theories shape our questions about the world (Halliday 1978; see also Parret 1974). In linguistics, what this means is that by adopting a certain view of language, we commit ourselves to asking certain questions and proposing certain types of answers (Cameron 1990). In the case of SFL, those questions and answers are typically social in nature (Halliday 1978).

One such question we can look at in terms of social activities concerns the expressiveness of different means of interaction. Each code carries distinct representational capacities which relate to the means of interaction. So, for example, written (and to a certain extent spoken) language has the capacity to transcend the here and now, with the consequence that its temporal qualities are almost boundless. By comparison, gesture or gaze need some sort of temporal proximity even if this is mediated by technology (for example, technologies such as video-enabled mobile technology have significantly enhanced the communicative potential for many Sign Language users). Where once we would have said that modalities such as gesture required a material proximity as well as a temporal proximity, technology has meant that neither of these restrictions need apply since gestures can be recorded and transmitted across vast spaces. These modes, gaze in particular, are heavily oriented towards interpersonal meanings (Hasan 1980). To see the significance of gesture for interpersonal meaning we need only consider the attempts at iconic representation of aspects of gesture in the form of emoticons.

It follows that we can establish that different means of interaction, different modalities, have different expressive power, or semantic potential, albeit at least partially mitigated by means of technology. Variability in semantic potential is not new, after all; Bernstein's studies showed that different individuals do not share the same meaning potential. The distinction between Bernstein's findings and our argument, however, is that the first refers to individuals using a mode and the latter to the modality itself. Not having equal access to the full range of meanings in a mode is distinct from the mode itself having a limited potential. Individuals may not have the same access to the mode, but the mode has the same potential whether we access it or not. Here the situation is that the modes themselves do not have the same potential. If this is the case, and certainly it would seem to be, then certain ideas and concepts will be limited to certain modalities; for example, Hasan (2001) claims that it is not possible to represent abstract concepts or what she calls decontextualized language through gestures that co-occur with speech. The implication of this limit on the meaning-making potential for different modalities is that they will have a different semantic stratum. They will also have different reactances in the contextual stratum and may not even have a distinct organizing stratum. There is no reason to suspect that each mode should conform to the same dimensional arrangement as language at all.

Linguistics has typically been understood to deal with (written or spoken) language and the nature and behaviour of such. In saying that linguists deal with language, the question of what linguists do has not really been resolved in any meaningful way since it is equally unclear what is meant by language. Is it confined to written or spoken expressions? Most often what comes to mind when mention is made of language is what a child learns or what we might learn as a foreign language. This orientation is more helpful to understanding the nature of our object than it might appear. What we see in language learning is an orientation to the structural aspects of language, and this foregrounding of structure is perhaps more obvious in second language learning. After all, 'form is significant only in so much as we feel ourselves to be in its grip' (Sapir 1928/1999: 559). Language becomes visible when we focus on it, but otherwise it is almost invisible. As Sapir suggests, 'it can be laid down as a principle of far reaching application that in the normal business of life it is useless and even mischievous for the individual to carry the conscious analysis of his cultural patterns around with him. That should be left to the student whose business it is to understand these patterns.' (Sapir 1928/1999: 558). Making language visible and understanding the patterns of language is the concern of the linguist.

Halliday (1974: 86) sees language 'essentially as a system of meaning potential'. So for him, our object of analysis stops at the level of semantics, which is, according to him, the key to language (Halliday 1974: 87). As Halliday suggests, when we view language from an inter-organism perspective,

> language is being regarded as the encoding of a 'behavioural potential' into a 'meaning potential'; that is, as a means of expressing what the human organism 'can do', in interaction with other human organisms, by turning it into what he 'can mean'. What he can mean (the semantic system) is, in turn, encoded into what he can say (the lexico-grammatical system, or grammar and vocabulary). (Halliday 1978: 21)

The semantic system is 'the meaning potential embodied in language' (Halliday 1974: 86).

But this meaning system is itself a realization of something higher, or more specifically, of something outside of language, what Halliday (1974: 86) calls the behaviour system or 'a social semiotic'. Halliday expresses it this way: 'I see language essentially as a system of meaning potential. Now, once we go outside language, then we see that this semantic system is itself the realization of something beyond, which is what the speaker can do – I have referred to that as the behaviour potential.' (Halliday 1974: 86). Interestingly, Halliday has on occasion referred to language as a social semiotic (see, for example, Halliday 1978). However, in his 1974 account and elsewhere, including the same 1978 text, language is represented as being only one realization of a social semiotic, and it is this later account that we see dominate in the theory. These two views create a tension between whether language is modelled as a mode within a social semiotic or as a social semiotic itself with various modes. Although it is the former model which is taken as the primary representation of language within SFL, it is not uncommon to see other modes represented as sitting within language as we see with the system of *mode* in context models (see, e.g. Bartlett 2016 and Wegener 2016). This question over the situation of language is a boundary question (see Wegener 2016 for further discussion of this).

10.3 Language behaviour in context or what makes a text in a multimodal context?

Halliday (1985: 10) defines text as 'language that is functional', where functional is used to mean serving some purpose in context. So context and text are in this view intimately connected. Of course, from the point of view of context this need not be the case since context has undergone a process of idealization with the result that, for many, it is open to analysis completely free of the text/texts with which it is associated. As linguists, when we consider text, we generally view it as a product. We are not typically giving a running commentary on events as they unfold. To say that we are most often concerned with product is not to say that there is no picture of the process. In considering text as product, we are building on a fundamental grounding in text as process. However, there are both theoretical and practical reasons why we typically comment on product and not on process. In practice, it is impossible to consider context free from the text with which it is associated.

In dealing with context, it is necessary to think about the social process that makes it necessary to consider context. Firstly, as Halliday (1985: 11) suggests, if we are to comment on a text as process, we are relying on our understanding of text as product. Because of the relationship between text as product and text as process, to be in a position to make any meaningful comment on the text as an unfolding process, it is necessary to understand the system which produced that process, and that system is a system of products.

Secondly, for very practical reasons, the text is more likely to be studied as a product because this is how we are able to handle it. A text is recorded, written, filmed or otherwise made into a monumental product for the purposes of sharing, analyzing and storing. A slice of social process is made static for the purposes of our analysis, and it is not just within linguistics that it is necessary to break the subject of analysis into manageable units. The text is just such a unit. It is, as Halliday (1985: 10) describes it, 'a semantic unit'.

Having put forward the claim that it will typically be text as product that we will study, it is always necessary to keep in mind that the text is an artefact of our analysis. Texts are carved out of the ongoing flow of social process. Text, if we can use the term for process, has boundaries and a fixedness only to the extent that we give it boundaries, and this is difficult when we consider multimodal texts because significant portions of the things that make it a text may take place in other modalities.

It might well be argued, however, that humans are inclined to divide up process and give it boundaries, and as such, processness is, by its very nature, a rather ephemeral sensation. Nevertheless, to gain a full picture, it is necessary to view the text as both product and process, that is, 'as a social exchange of meanings' (Halliday 1985: 11).

As a contextual theory of language, context in SFL is one of four levels which are related realizationally (rather than causally), meaning that patterns on one level both construe and construct patterns on another level. As Halliday (1992: 358) suggests, meta-redundancy explains the stratal organization and the semiotic principle of realization 'by treating realization as a relation'. This relation, as Halliday (1994) explains, is a dialectic relation:

> A text is created by its context, the semiotic environment of people and their activities that we have construed via the concepts of field, tenor and mode; it also creates that context. The relationship that we refer to as realization between levels of semiosis – situation (doing) realized in semantics (meaning), semantics realized in lexico-grammar (wording), and so on – is a dialectic one involving what Lemke (1984) interprets as n-order meta-redundancies. A semiotic event is an event on many levels. (Halliday 1994: 254)

Hence, the relationship of realization, as theorized through meta-redundancy, is both multifocal and bi-directional, or better dialectic (Hasan 1996: 110–112).

We have focused here on the language as the typical domain of the linguist, but in our case, our object of analysis is not just language but meaning making as a part of some identifiable social process. Can we define this social process as a text with a context, however? With written text as a product, the boundary question, or what counts as text and what as context, seems straightforward: the product has a beginning and an end. Already in spoken language, and probably even more so in other modalities, establishing what is text and what is context becomes even more difficult, since the boundaries have to be established first.

To explore this problem further, we consider two of our application domains: behaviour-aware sliding doors and an interactive whiteboard.

10.4 Applications in ambient intelligent systems

Ducatel et al. (2001) give a definition of ambient intelligence. At the core of an ambient intelligent system lies the ability to appreciate the system's environment, be aware of persons in this environment and respond intelligently to their needs. At the same time, ambient intelligent systems do not react to explicit interaction by human users alone but rely at least partially on observation of the human behaviour and other implicit interaction cues. They disappear and 'weave themselves into the fabric of everyday life until they are indistinguishable from it' (Weiser 1991).

We have previously used Activity Theory to model contextual parameters for ambient intelligent systems (Kofod-Petersen & Cassens 2006). Another use of AT in Human-Computer Interaction concerns the definition of different activities and actions a user is involved with (Nardi 1996). Our question was: can we make use of the hierarchical structure of activities in AT to define those boundaries, to find the semantic units?

The first of our applications has no verbal language and no explicit interaction capabilities at all. It consists of an automated door that is to open not based solely on the proximity of a human user but on the intention of the user to walk through the door, expressed through observable behavioural patterns (Kofod-Petersen et al. 2009; Butt et al. 2013).

Here, the meaning making is entirely behavioural, and the social process is defined by the first and last contact that the user has with the doors. In nature, this social process, this action, is part of some larger social process or activity that might be considered a text. One rarely walks through a door merely for the pleasure of walking through a door (with a few possible exceptions). In this sense, it is always going to be part of a bigger activity cycle, e.g. going to the shops, going to the hospital, etc. Indeed, it is most likely to be part of what we usually consider the mesh between identifiable social processes or activities.

Using the boundaries established with the help of AT, we were able to make use of multimodal indicators of intention suggested from work in SFL (Cartmill et al. 2007), specifically body alignment (hips and shoulders), proximity and visual target in addition to the movement vector, to establish the intention to walk through the door (Figure 10.1). In an evaluation (390 scripted test runs), a prototypical demonstrator (Solem 2011) achieved a specificity/true negative of about 90% (i.e. a door remained closed if the test person did not intend to walk through it) and a sensitivity/true positive of about 70% (i.e. the door opened when the intention was to walk through it). While in particular the sensitivity could be improved, one has to keep in mind that these results were achieved before any significant performance tuning, and part of the results were due to inaccuracies in the sensing, not the model.

By contrast, the second of our applications, an interactive electronic whiteboard called ShareBoard (Figure 10.2), has a wide variety of meaning-making modalities, including spoken language (between multiple participants across non-physically shared space and potentially across different time zones), behaviour and gesture, written language (including typing and handwriting) and drawing. This is likely to constitute the social process or activity itself. When we use an interactive whiteboard, it is usually to have a meeting or a lesson where the whiteboard forms the focus of our engagement and the means of our engagement. This means that participants (subjects or agents) will have a shared focal point. Within this shared activity, we can distinguish several actions, which 'are the processes functionally subordinated to activities' (Kaptelinin 1996).

In contrast to the previous example, where the action was already given and we looked at the meaning-making behaviour within that action (expressing the intention to walk through the door), we now want to use the semantic potential of behaviour to distinguish between different actions, i.e. to establish the boundaries of semantic units within a given context, the meeting.

Although ShareBoard primarily exhibits explicit interaction capabilities, it can take implicit interaction cues into account to identify different actions and adjust its behaviour accordingly. As an example, it is possible for remote locations connected to ShareBoard to overlay a video feed of a user drawing on the whiteboard on top of the drawing. However, such a video feed will cover areas of the whiteboard. To mitigate this, ShareBoard has been tested with a configuration where this overlay is only presented when the user faces away from the whiteboard and towards the audience, be it a local or remote audience. Given such a cue, it can be reasoned that the user is not performing a drawing action but engaging in a discussion (following our arguments in e.g. Butt et al. 2013). When the user turns to the whiteboard, the video feed disappears, and only small indicators show where the user is writing or drawing, giving unhindered view to all content of the whiteboard. More complex reconfigurations of ShareBoard behaviour, e.g. distinguishing between peer-to-peer discussion and lectures, are also investigated.

Naturally, we have not chosen these examples by accident. They represent two contrasting application domains that demonstrate the difficulties of working with naturally occurring language behaviour in context. In both

Figure 10.1 Behaviour-aware sliding doors: demonstrator (Solem 2011)[2]

Figure 10.2 Meeting activity at a whiteboard: conversation with audience (top) and writing on the board (bottom). Images by Fabrice Florin, Aaron Arcos; source: Wikimedia foundation[3]

these application domains, the role of SFL is to provide a model of meaning bearing behaviour in context for the purpose of creating intelligent artefacts, and the role of AT is to establish the boundaries of the semantic units. In our work, the primary role of SFL is to provide a model of meaning making, of a conversation between the different actants, for example, by employing a Generic Structure Potential for given contexts of use, while CHAT has been used to understand the use of artefacts as tools for communication, e.g. by looking at the broader activity and by understanding which technical means are employed by human users to reach the goal of the activity.

10.5 Integrating CHAT and SFL

In seeking to integrate these two approaches to semiotic behaviour, we are by no means alone. Many have brought the two approaches together for the purposes of understanding writing practices and educational behaviour in the classroom, including Russell (1997), who blends Activity Theory with genre theory to understand writing across the curriculum and in society. His research has resulted in some spectacular diagrams that cover the complexity of writing as an activity. This extensive analysis has also been addressed by others, such as Martin (2005), Williams, Davis and Black (2007), Ferreira (2005), and Johns (2008), who also consider writing as a semiotic activity in the classroom, blending Activity Theory with either genre approaches or a combination of genre and SFL. Others, such as Thorne & Smith (2011), have used Activity Theory and SFL in combination to better understand computer mediated second language learning, particularly as it occurs in joint writing tasks. We ourselves have looked at integrated approaches of AT and semiotic theories for requirement elicitation before (e.g. Cassens 2003).

As they share a common theoretical lineage and core assumptions, the theories lend themselves to integration. This is particularly true when we apply aspects of SFL to language behaviour in context, where it becomes necessary to identify some social process to which the language behaviour belongs. As Hasan (2002) argues, 'semiotic mediation by means of language entails language use', and this means it is necessary to have a theory of language use. This is a segmentation problem in that if you want to study something, you need some way to identify your object of analysis. This might be the word, the phrase, the clause, clause complex, text, etc.

In addressing this issue of locating semiotic behaviour in a model of socio-material activity, Hasan (2002) considers blending CHAT[4] and SFL on the basis that 'to the extent that all discursive practices are social practices, the theory of text in context can be taken as a sub-category of activity theory and so logically on the one hand the scope of activity theory should be wider than that of a theory to account for discursive contexts, and on the other hand, the two should be compatible'. However, Hasan rejects the blending of CHAT with SFL for the following reasons:[5]

(1) 'Activity theory is heavily biased in favour of the experiential function; it, therefore, chiefly concerns itself with concepts relating specifically to action, such as goal, motivation, purpose, action, outcome etc, what SFL would refer to as the *field of discourse* – a component in the social context for text.' Hasan (2002)

(2) Activity Theory is 'unhelpful in describing the social practice of discourse, whose complexity requires a theory that goes beyond action into interaction since the selection, management and outcome of action/field depends so heavily on what SFL calls *tenor of discourse*, i.e. the social relations and the positioning of the interactants'. Hasan (2002)

(3) 'The nature of semiotic and material contact between the discursive participants i.e. their *mode of discourse* is an important consideration in understanding the shaping of discourse. The true nature of the process of semiotic mediation cannot be elaborated if any of these aspects of the use of language is ignored.' Hasan (2002)

In summary, the criticism appears to be that CHAT is merely a poor replacement for a model of context as it would appear in SFL. We would argue, however, that this may come from a limited view of Activity Theory as purely a description of the activity system (see Figure 10.3, Section A), which sets out the core participants, their semiotic and material resources and the purpose/motive and desired outcome of the activity. This does indeed mirror SFL's Field, Tenor and Mode, however, it need not be seen as replacing them but rather as a complement. Given the common theoretical roots of the two theories in classical Marxism and the differences in scale, abstraction and object of analysis, it is far more likely that CHAT activity systems are a more abstract representation of the foundations of Field, Tenor and Mode in the socio-cultural fabric.

While we find the activity system approach a useful addition to Field, Tenor and Mode, we also make use of the tripartite hierarchy of activity (see Figure 10.3, Section B), which we argue is more akin to a rank scale of social interaction and engagement. Viewing this as a rank scale means that the entry conditions for each are different; much like the clause is not the same as a phrase or a clause complex. It also means that the nature of interactants is likely to be very different. For instance, activities are

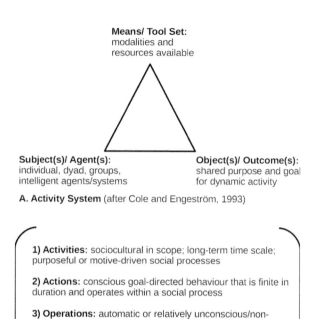

Figure 10.3 Central concepts from CHAT

likely to have institutions or roles as their interactants, whereas actions and operations need individuals (human, animal or machine).

Crucially for our purposes, we find it particularly useful that we are able to map the interactional responsibilities of an artificial intelligence agent at different orders of abstraction, giving it both an institutional position and role (establishing the socio-technical system) as well as likely actions and operations (establishing the technical systems as actors). There is also a difference in temporal duration and time horizon between these aspects. Rather than arguing, as Hasan (2002) does, that Activity Theory is replacing context as set out in SFL, we argue that Activity Theory is extending the rank scale and grounding the notion of context. This means that there is likely to be a tripartite functional arrangement at each rank. Thus, it is possible that there is an ideational, interpersonal and textual function for activities, actions and operations. This also suggests that potentially the functional responsibility or semantic weight will be unevenly distributed across modalities.

In blending the two theories then, we argue that neither theory is replacing or duplicating anything in the other theory. For the purposes of our research, we have found it useful to take the CHAT notion of ACTIVITY as our basis for identifying the boundaries of our application domain context (see Figure 10.4). Within the ACTIVITY we locate two further conceptions of the social process: a distinction made by Wegener (2011, 2016) between the recognizable social process that is the object of our analysis (that which we wish to model) and the individual instances or situations of this social process (our data points or individual texts). The contextual description for the abstract concept of the social process is referred to as the ANTICIPATED CONTEXT (AC), while the actual instances are defined as INDIVIDUAL CONTEXTS (IC) (see Wegener 2011, 2016). Modelling is done on the basis of the ANTICIPATED CONTEXT, and any machine learning (of whatever kind) is done on the basis of the annotated INDIVIDUAL CONTEXTS.

Using this approach allows us to use smart data principles and reduce the amount of learning data required to develop accurate, contextually functional systems. As can be seen in Figure 10.4, we use the anticipated context and anticipated Generic Structure Potential to model both the nature and structure of our activity within the application domain. This enables us to predict the amount and type of variation in the individual instances, thus predicting the likely variation that the system will need to deal with in run time.

(1) **Activity:** identifiable **social processes** within the **application domain of the system**

    A) **Anticipated Context**, outlined through an **Activity System** (after Cole & Engeström 1993) where anticipated **Subject(s)/Agent(s)**, represented through **abstract roles**, are set out in a **Tenor matrix** (after Wegener 2011) that maps the anticipated **tenor relations** between the **roles**. For each **subject/ agent** the available **means/ tool set** and anticipated **object(s)/ outcome(s)** are also mapped.

        A.1) **Generic Structure Potential** for the **Anticipated Context** is developed to model the anticipated unfolding of the activity. This provides a picture of the anticipated logogenesis.

    B) **Individual contexts** outlined using **Field, Tenor and Mode**.

        B.1) **Structure statements** are given for each **individual context** using Moore's (2003, 2005) notion of **phase shifts** that could encompass contextual variation, allowing us to see the degree of individual variation from the anticipated.

    C) A, A.1 and B, B.1 together are used to generate predictions for the structure and semantics that are likely to be at risk in each phase and thus predict both the actions and operations (by other actors) that are likely to occur in the situation and the actions and operations that are required to respond adequately.

(2) **Actions and Operations:** mapped as **multimodal ensembles** set within **phases of individual contexts** including non-system specific individual variations.

Figure 10.4 Integrating CHAT and SFL

Neither of these distinctions are neutral in their nature, and they do not have naturally occurring boundaries. In setting out to analyze these domains, we establish them as social processes and in doing so define their boundaries for the purposes of our analysis. Part of understanding the context is taking account of whose view on context we are taking and how that view or perspective shapes the boundaries and understanding of the social function of the process under analysis. Our understanding of the social process and the subsequent definition of the shape and boundaries of the process will influence the kind of data we collect and the ways in which we use this data for understanding context and the issues in a domain. For example, when we collect instances of walking through doors, we do not take the perspective of the 'walkers' but rather that of the 'doors', and thus our perspective on the social process is shaped by our choice of view point.

The observant reader will notice that for the argument we make in favour of combining SFL and CHAT for requirement elicitation of ambient intelligent systems, we so far have not made use of the distinction between action and operation in CHAT. CHAT distinguishes between non-conscious, automated operations and conscious actions. Both are behaviours supporting the activity at hand. However, since the distinction is on the side of the doer, further work is necessary to assess whether it is possible for an outside observer to reliably distinguish between actions and operations.

Being able to do so would be very beneficial: the border between actions and operations is not static, actions performed often can become operations, and operations can become actions if something goes wrong and conscious attention is needed again. An ambient intelligent system that recognizes these shifts can for example offer help or training functions to make the transition from action to operation smoother and can use the shift from operations to actions as a hint that 'something has gone wrong', i.e. a failure within the socio-technical system has occurred that made the computational system 'appear again' – it is no longer invisible and woven into the fabric of everyday life, but a visible technical artifact.

10.6 Conclusions and future work

SFL already has a strong theoretical structure for looking at language in context, as do a number of other approaches to language. By strong theory we do not refer to what van Dijk (2006) calls the 'weak triple of field, tenor and mode'. Rather, by theory we refer to a means of considering variation at all levels, of separating out difference and similarity, of locating language in the social and of situating it in a biological base. These are the assumptions at the level of theory that make it possible to model context. Without these there is no need and no framework for any consideration of context.

In developing ambient intelligent systems across various domains and for various purposes, we have made several adaptations to both SFL and CHAT that we have found useful and that may also prove useful in other applications. Firstly, we have suggested the division of context into an anticipated or archetypal context and an individual context. This division was motivated by the need to distinguish between an analysis completed with an average view of a situation in mind compared to an analysis done with a specific situation in mind.

Comparisons between these two analyses may prove useful for various research questions, for example, where it is necessary to distinguish between people's conception of a social process and their actual behaviour in a social process. Other research questions might find it more beneficial to compare individual contexts with each other to determine speciation and individual variation or to compare anticipated contexts with each other to determine similarities and differences between social processes. It remains to be seen, however, how well such a conception fits within SFL theory since it is, in effect, a form of stratification at the level of context.

Other developments that we have found useful include changes to the goal orientation network established by Hasan and further developed by Butt and the inclusion of a meta-analysis that considers method as a social process within an Activity and thus has specific and definable contextual settings, as we have laid out in our model. These perspectives take into account the fact that the research method is itself a social process with contextual settings that impact on research outcomes.

About the authors

Rebekah Wegener is a lecturer and senior researcher in linguistics and semiotics at the Institute for English and American Studies at RWTH Aachen University, Germany, and at the Department of English and American Studies at the University of Salzburg, Austria. She is also co-founder of learning technology startup Audaxi in Sydney, Australia. Her research interests include context modelling, theoretical and applied linguistics as well as intelligent learning and teaching technologies. She is currently working on models of context for text understanding and multimodal environments as well as behavioural interfaces for artificial intelligence. She previously worked as a linguist for Appen speech and language technology, doing text analysis for context sensitive software development, and at the Health Information Technology Research Laboratory at the University of Sydney, working on text understanding in medical reports.

Jörg Cassens is a lecturer and senior researcher in media informatics at the University of Hildesheim, Germany. He is working on issues of integrating intelligent systems into human environments with a focus on ambient intelligence, mobile computing, learning and teaching systems as well as awareness systems. His main research interests are the applicability of socio-technical theories for the design of intelligent systems and usability of and user experience with intelligent systems. He has worked on the development of psychologically sound context models and on requirements engineering methodologies for intelligent systems.

Notes

1 For brevity, this has to remain an assertion in this chapter. For the detailed argument, see Wegener (2011).
2 Photos reprinted with kind permission by Anders Kofod-Petersen.
3 The two images in Figure 10.2 are licensed under the 'Creative Commons Attribution-Share Alike 3.0 Unported' licence. They are available at: https://commons.wikimedia.org/wiki/File:Media_Viewer_Launch_Retrospective_Whiteboard_-_April_11_2014_03.jpg https://commons.wikimedia.org/wiki/File:Media_Viewer_Launch_Retrospective_Whiteboard_-_April_11_2014_02.jpg
4 Hasan here draws on the following references for her notion of CHAT: Leont'ev (1978); Wertsch (1981); Minick (1997); Cole, Engeström & Vasquez (1997); and Engeström, Miettinen & Punamäki (1999).
5 Hasan's (2002) arguments have been reproduced in direct quotation here to preserve the nuance of her argument regarding the integration of these theories for the purposes that she was considering at the time of the argument.

References

Bartlett, T. (2016) 'Multiscalar modelling of context: Some questions raised by the category of Mode'. In: Bowcher, W. L. & Liang, J. Y. (eds.) *Society in Language, Language in Society: Essays in Honour of Ruqaiya Hasan.* London/New York: Palgrave Macmillan, 166–183.

Bateman, J.A. (1998) 'Automatic Discourse Generation'. *Encyclopedia of Library and Information Science*, Vol. 62. New York: Marcel Dekker Inc., pp. 154.

Bateman, J. A., Wildfeuer, J. & Hiippala, T. (2017) *Multimodality: Foundations, Research and Analysis.* Berlin/New York: De Gruyter Mouton.

Butt, D., Wegener, R. & Cassens, J. (2013) 'Modelling behaviour semantically'. In: Brézillon, P., Blackburn, P. & Dapoigny, R. (eds.) *Proceedings of CONTEXT 2013.* Annecy, France: Springer, 343–349.

Cartmill, J., Moore, A., Butt, D. & Squire, L. (2007) 'Surgical teamwork: systemic functional linguistics and the analysis of verbal and non verbal meaning in surgery'. *ANZ Journal of Surgery* 77, Suppl. 1, A79.

Cameron, D. (1990) 'Demythologizing sociolinguistics: Why language does not reflect society'. In: Joseph, J. & Taylor, T. (eds.) *Ideologies of language.* London: Routledge, 79–93.

Cassens, J. & Wegener, R. (2008) 'Making Use of Abstract Concepts: Systemic-Functional Linguistics and Ambient Intelligence'. In: Bramer, M. (ed.) *Artificial Intelligence in Theory and Practice II.* Milano, Italy: Springer, 205–214.

Cassens, J. (2003) 'A work context perspective on mixed-initiative intelligent systems'. In: *Proceedings of the IJCAI 2003 Workshop on Mixed-Initiative Intelligent Systems.* Acapulco, 30–35.

Cassens, J. (2008) *Explanation Awareness and Ambient Intelligence as Social Technologies.* Dr. Scient. Thesis. Trondheim: Norwegian University of Science and Technology.

Cole, M. (1996) *Cultural Psychology. A Once and Future Discipline.* Harvard, MA: Harvard University Press.

Cole, M. & Engeström, Y. (1993) 'A cultural-historical approach to distributed cognition'. In: Salomon, G. (ed.) *Distributed Cognitions: Psychological and Educational Considerations.* New York: Cambridge University Press, 1–46.

Cole, M., Engeström, Y. & Vasquez, O. (eds.) (1997) *Mind, Culture and Activity: Seminal Papers from the Laboratory of Comparative Human Cognition.* Cambridge: Cambridge University Press.

Ducatel, K., Bogdanowicz, M., Scapolo, F., Leijten, J. & Burgelman, J.-C. (eds.) (2001) *ISTAG Scenarios for Ambient Intelligence in 2010. Technical Report.* Luxembourg: IST Advisory Group.

Engeström, Y., Miettinen, R. & Punamäki, R.-L. (eds.) (1999) *Perspectives on Activity Theory.* Cambridge: Cambridge University Press.

Ferreira, M.M. (2005) *A Concept-based Approach to Writing Instruction: From the Abstract Concept to the Concrete Performance.* Unpublished doctoral dissertation. The Pennsylvania State University, University Park, PA.

Firth, J.R. (1957) *Papers in Linguistics 1934–1951.* London: Oxford University Press.

Halliday, M.A.K. (1974) 'Discussion'. In: Parret, H. (ed.) (1974) *Discussing Language.* The Hague: Mouton, 81–120.

Halliday, M.A.K. (1978) *Language as Social Semiotic: The Social Interpretation of Language and Meaning.* London: Arnold.

Halliday, M.A.K. & Hasan, R. (1985) *Language, Context, and Text: Aspects of Language in a Social-Semiotic Perspective.* Victoria, Australia: Deakin University.

Halliday, M.A.K. (1992) 'New ways of meaning: the challenge to applied linguistics'. In: Putz, M. (ed.) *Thirty Years of Linguistic Evolution.* Philadelphia/Amsterdam: John Benjamins Publishing, 59–95.

Halliday, M.A.K. (1994) *An Introduction to Functional Grammar.* London: Edward Arnold.

Halliday, M.A.K. (2005) *Computational and Quantitative Studies.* In: Webster, J.J. (ed.) *The Collected Works of M.A.K. Halliday,* Vol. 6. London/New York: Bloomsbury Publishing.

Hasan, R. (1996) 'Semantic Networks: A tool for the analysis of meaning'. In: Cloran, C., Butt, D. & Williams, G. (eds.) *Ways of Saying, Ways of Meaning: Selected Papers of Ruqaiya Hasan.* London: Cassell, 104–132.

Hasan, R. (2001) 'Wherefore context? The place of context in the system and process of language'. In: Shaozeng, R., Guthrie, W. & Fong, I.W.R. (eds.) *Grammar and Discourse Analysis.* Macau: University of Macau Publication Centre, 1–21.

Hasan, R. (2002) *Semiotic Mediation, Language and Society: Three Exotripic Theories – Vygotsky, Halliday and Bernstein.* In: Webster, J.J. (ed.) *Language, Society and Consciousness: The Collected Works of Ruqaya Hasan,* Vol.1. London: Equinox.

Johns, A.M. (2011) 'The future of genre in L2 writing: Fundamental, but contested, instructional decisions'. *Journal of Second Language Writing* 20.1, 56–68.

Kaptelinin, V. (1996) 'Activity theory: Implications for human-computer interaction'. In: Nardi, B.A. (ed.) *Context and Consciousness: Activity Theory and Human-Computer Interaction.* Cambridge, MA: The MIT Press, 103–116.

Kofod-Petersen, A. & Cassens, J. (2006) 'Using Activity Theory to Model Context Awareness'. In: Roth-Berghofer, T.R., Schulz, S. & Leake, D.B. (eds.) *Modeling and Retrieval of Context. Lecture Notes in Computer Science,* Vol. 3946. Berlin/Heidelberg: Springer, 1–17.

Kofod-Petersen, A., Wegener, R. & Cassens, J. (2009) 'Closed doors – modelling intention in behavioural interfaces'. In: Kofod-Petersen, A., Langseth, H. & Gundersen, O.E. (eds.) *Proceedings of the Norwegian Artificial Intelligence Society Symposium (NAIS 2009).* Trondheim: Tapir Akademiske Forlag.

Lemke, J. (1984) 'The Formal Analysis of Instruction and Action, Context and Meaning'. In: Lemke, J (ed.) *Semiotics and Education.* Victoria University, Toronto: Toronto Semiotics Circle Monographs, Working Papers and Prepublications.

Leont'ev, A.N. (1978) *Activity, Consciousness, and Personality.* Englewood Cliffs, NJ: Prentice-Hall.

Llinares, A. (2013) 'Systemic Functional approaches to second language acquisition in school settings'. In: Mayo, M.D.P.G., Mangado, M.J.G. & Adrián, M.M. (eds.) *Contemporary Approaches to Second Language Acquisition.* Amsterdam: John Benjamins, 27–47.

Martin, J.R. & Rose, D. (2005) 'Designing literacy pedagogy: scaffolding democracy in the classroom'. In: Hasan, R., Matthiessen, C.M.I.M & Webster, J.J. (eds.) *Continuing Discourse on Language: A Functional Perspective.* London: Equinox, 251–280.

Miller, E.R. (2009) 'Advanced language learning: the contribution of Halliday and Vygotsky'. *International Journal of Bilingual Education and Bilingualism* 12(3), 348–353.

Minick, N. (1997) 'The early history of the Vygotskian school: the relationship between mind and activity'. In: Cole, M., Engeström, Y. & Vasquez, O. (eds.) *Mind, Culture and Activity: Seminal Papers from the Laboratory of Comparative Human Cognition.* Cambridge: Cambridge University Press, 117–127.

Moore, A. (2003) *The Discursive Construction of Treatment Decisions in the Management of HIV Disease.* Sydney: Macquarie University.

Moore, A. (2005) 'Modelling agency in HIV decision-making'. *Australian Review of Applied Linguistics.* Special Edition S19, 103–122.

Nardi, B.A. (ed.) (1996) 'Context and Consciousness'. Cambridge, MA: MIT Press.

O'Donnell, M. & Bateman, J.A. (2005) 'SFL in computational contexts: a contemporary history'. In: Hasan, R., Matthiessen, C.M.I.M. & Webster, J.J. (eds.) *Continuing Discourse on Language: A Functional Perspective.* Sheffield: Equinox, 343–382.

Parret, H. (1974) *Discussing Language.* The Hague, Netherlands: Mouton.

Russell, D.R. (1997) 'Rethinking genre in school and society: An activity theory analysis'. *Written Communication* 14(4), 504–554.

Sapir, E. (1928/1999) 'The Unconscious Patterning of Behaviour in Society'. In: Darnell, R. & Irvine, J. (eds.) *The Collected Works of Edward Sapir.* The Hague: Mouton de Gruyter.

Solem, J.S. (2011) *Intention Aware Sliding Doors.* Master Thesis. Trondheim: Norwegian University of Science and Technology.

Thorne, S.L. & Smith, B. (2011) 'Second language development theories and technology-mediated language learning'. *CALICO Journal* 28(2), 268–277.

Wegener, R. (2011) *Parameters of Context: From Theory to Model and Application.* Ph.D. Thesis. Sydney: Macquarie University.

Wegener, R. (2016) 'Studying language in society and society through language: Context and multimodal communication'. In: Bowcher, W.L. & Liang, J.Y. (eds.) *Society in Language, Language in Society: Essays in Honour of Ruqaiya Hasan.* London/New York: Palgrave Macmillan, 227–248.

Wegener, R., Cassens, J. & Butt, D. (2008) 'Start making sense: Systemic functional linguistics and ambient intelligence'. *Revue d'Intelligence Artificielle. Special Issue on Modelling and Reasoning on Context* 22(5), 629–645.

Weiser, M. (1991) 'The computer for the 21st century'. *Scientific American* 265(3), 94–104.

Wertsch, J.V. (1981) *The Concept of Activity in Soviet Psychology.* New York: M. E. Sharpe.

Whorf, B.L. (1956) *Language, Thought and Reality.* In: Carroll, J.B. (ed.) *Selected Writings of Benjamin Lee Whorf.* Cambridge, MA: The MIT Press.

Williams, J., Davis, P. & Black, L. (2007) 'Sociocultural and Cultural-Historical Activity Theory perspectives on subjectivities and learning in schools and other educational contexts'. *International Journal of Educational Research* 46.1, 1–7.

Winograd, T. (1971) *Procedures as a Representation for Data in a Computer Program for Understanding Natural Language.* MIT AI Technical Report 235. Cambridge, Mass.: MIT.

van Dijk, T. (2006) 'Discourse, context and cognition'. *Discourse Studies* 8(1), 159–177.

11 Smell as social semiotic: On the deployment and intersemiotic potential of smell

Daniel Lees Fryer
Østfold University College, Norway

11.1 Introduction

Olfaction – our sense of smell – is determined by a complex set of physico-chemical and biological interactions. Odorants, usually in the form of volatile molecules or chemicals, bind with receptors in the nasal cavity and create signals that are sent to the brain.

Many studies of smell relate to the physical, biological and/or psychological nature of olfaction. However, as Classen, Howes and Synnott (1994: 3) note, smell is also a social and cultural phenomenon: 'Odours are invested with cultural values and employed by societies as a means of and model for defining and interacting with the world'. In this paper, I explore some of the social-cultural meanings of smell. I discuss how smell might be considered a socially mediated semiotic system and how some of the resources of such a system can be deployed and integrated with the resources of other semiotic systems.

11.2 The olfactory turn

Smell, it seems, is the least valuable of the human senses, the one we could most do without (Synnott 1993: 183–184, in Drobnik 2006: 2). It is also the sense that is generally given least attention by scholars (Classen, Howes & Synnott 1994: 5). Despite its important role, for example with regard to food, health and disease, sexual relations, social class, gender and power (see Porteous 2006, Rindisbacher 2006, Reinarz 2014, inter alia), the olfactory experience has generally been devalued in 'western culture', in a process that Classen (1993: 15) suggests is concomitant with a rise in the importance of and dependence upon sight.[1] Since the Enlightenment at least, smell, or the cultural importance of smell, has become associated with the 'lower senses', the study of 'primitive cultures' and even the construction of racist ideologies (Classen 1997: 405, Howes 2011: 231).[2] However, the late twentieth century, or more specifically the 1980s, represents a 'watershed moment for [the social and cultural study of] smell' (Drobnik 2006: 3, Reinarz 2014: 2). The publication of Alain Corbin's (1986 [1982]) *Le miasma et le jonquille*, a sociohistorical study of smell in 18th and 19th century France, and Patrick Süskind's (1985) *Das Parfum: Die Geschichte eines Mörders*, a popular novel inspired in part by the work of Corbin, led to 'an olfactory turn' in academia (Reinarz 2014: 3), one that 'sought out the recovery, expression and explanation of smell on its own terms' (Drobnik 2006: 4).

Smell, however, rarely *means* on its own. It is almost always part of a multisemiotic, multimodal or multisensorial activity (Howes 2011, Norris 2013). Smelling flowers in a garden or perfume in a bathroom, for example, is likely as much a tactile, visual and/or aural experience as it is an olfactory one. Compartmentalizing smell (and the sociocultural relevance of smell) from the other senses and from other semiotic resources may be useful for analytic or conceptual purposes, but it risks reducing our understanding of the process of meaning-making to a sense-by-sense or mode-by-mode account (Howes 2011, Norris 2013). While the cultural meaning of smell undoubtedly needs to be studied 'on its own terms' (see Drobnik 2006: 4, above), it also needs to be understood in relation to and in combination with other meaning-making resources to understand its potential in 'multiplying the set of possible meanings that can be made' in any multisemiotic activity (Lemke 1998: 92; see also Royce 2002, 2007; O'Halloran 2005: 159; Baldry & Thibault 2006: 18–19).

Multisemiotic or multimodal accounts of smell tend to focus on perfumery or aromatherapy (e.g. van Leeuwen 2005, Norris 2013, van Leeuwen & Djonov 2015). Perfumery offers a sophisticated and well-established 'language of smell', with its three basic note types (top/head, middle/heart and base) and the complex harmonies created by different combinations of notes and chords. However, this 'language' is not readily accessible to most of us. At best, we might consider smell a 'lexese' (cf. Martin 1992: 15), an inventory of more or less unrelated smell-signs that evoke different moods or memories; but for the perfumer or aromatherapist, smell is a 'grammar', a system of signs that can be used to create complex harmonies and meanings (van Leeuwen 2005: 51–52, van Leeuwen & Djonov 2015: 248). For the latter, smell is undoubtedly a meaning-making system, a semiotic mode; for the former, it may not be (see Kress 2010: 87).

Other studies examine the relation between smell and place (e.g. Porteous 2006, Margolies 2006, Pennycook & Otsuji 2015). When we smell flowers in a garden or perfume in a bathroom, or when we experience the aromas of a city neighbourhood (Margolies 2006, Pennycook & Otsuji 2015), we are potentially engaging with a wide and dynamic range of smell-sources in those spaces. Some of those smells may be propagated for specific reasons; others may not. When analyzing this sensory landscape or 'smellscape' (Porteous 2006), we need to consider the contributions and combinations of both 'intended' and 'unintended' smell-sources (Pennycook & Otsuji 2015: 199).

11.3 Coffee and cinnamon buns

To investigate further the semiotic potential of smell and the relation between smell and place, I undertook a brief, exploratory study. A neighbour who had recently sold her apartment told me that her real-estate agent had asked that she prepare coffee and buns prior to an open-house property viewing 'to make the place smell nice'. I found the idea intriguing. Here, potentially, was an instance of smell being used for part of a very specific purpose: to sell an apartment.

I contacted a local real-estate agency and set up an interview and questionnaires with real-estate agents.[3] I attended and documented property viewings, collected prospectuses and other promotional materials and surveyed potential buyers. In the discussion below, I draw upon data collected from four property viewings, the print and online prospectuses for those properties, approximately one-and-a-half hours of interview, five surveys of real-estate agents and 20 surveys of potential buyers.

11.3.1 Mapping the smellscape

A number of smells (and smell-sources), intended or otherwise, were identified as part of the smellscape of property viewings. These included coffee, cinnamon buns, scented candles, 'green soap' (a detergent for wood floors), hotdogs, fabric conditioner, flowers, trapped or stale air, paint, and stale or rotten food. No single property viewing or smellscape comprised all these smells. Moreover, not all smells were identified by all participants, and some were only mentioned by either potential buyers or real-estate agents. Some potential buyers also remarked that they did not notice *any* specific smells during the viewing.

All the properties were one- or two-bedroom apartments, ranging in size from 38 m^2 to 71 m^2 (*c*. 400–750 sq. ft.). Despite their relatively small size, there was some variation in the distribution of smells throughout the properties. Coffee and cinnamon, for example, were generally discernible throughout the apartment but were particularly noticeable in the kitchen, where they were prepared, and the living room, where they were placed. Scented candles were most discernible in the living room and bathroom; 'green soap' throughout the apartment; hotdogs on the balcony, where they were prepared (as part of a barbeque), and, to a lesser degree, throughout the apartment, where they were eaten; fabric conditioner in the bedrooms; flowers in the living room and kitchen; trapped or stale air in the hallway; paint in the hallway and stairs; and stale or rotten food in the kitchen and throughout the apartment.[4]

11.3.2 Creating, manipulating and responding to the smellscape

Real-estate agents, as sign-makers, select and deploy various smells (smell-sources) to create and manipulate the smellscape. While the intentions of these sign-makers may differ from those of perfumers or aromatherapists, they all share a general desire to elicit certain positive responses in the 'reader'.

For real-estate agents, the smells described above can signify in various ways. The smell of coffee, cinnamon buns, flowers and 'green soap', for example, 'create a homely feeling' and 'a good atmosphere'. They are 'fresh, natural and positive smells' that are not necessarily typical 'house smells'. They elicit a sense of 'cosiness' and 'good feelings'.

Even negatively experienced smells can have potentially positive outcomes. For example, when I asked about possible negative responses to the smell of coffee, cinnamon, or scented candles, one real-estate agent replied that, so long as potential buyers express those dislikes, they can act as prompts or 'ice-breakers' for engaging in further conversation, e.g. 'well, what smells do you like?'

Smell is used intentionally by all the real-estate agents I surveyed, most generally to help create a positive first impression of the property. It also gives the property viewing that 'little something extra', making it stand out or more memorable compared to viewings offered by other real-estate agencies – a form of market branding, according to one respondent. The relation of smell with the subconscious and the way smell might trigger memories and emotions was mentioned by several real-estate agents.

Potential buyers described the smells they encountered and the smellscape more generally as 'clean', 'pleasant', 'summery' and 'homely', and as 'strange', 'unfamiliar', 'potent' and 'tiresome'. Some example responses are given below.

(1) Smells from the candles and smells from the grill [...] Wonderful summer smell.
(2) I thought I smelled scented candles, which I hate. But it was a warm day, so there were lots of different smells. Not horrible, but a bit strange, unfamiliar, so I tried not to smell too much.

In general, responses to coffee, cinnamon, 'green soap' and fabric conditioner were positive, while responses to trapped air and stale/rotten food were negative. Responses to scented candles and hotdogs varied; some respondents liked them, others did not. No evaluative comments were given with regard to the smell of paint.

11.4 Smell as social semiotic

Martin (2011) discusses some of the challenges in treating nonverbal semiotics as kinds of languages in what has essentially become a linguistics-based multisemiotic or multimodal discourse analysis. Martin (2011) poses a series of questions that are useful for us to consider here. For example, how can we deal with various interrelated semiotic dimensions – familiar to those working in a systemic-functional framework – such as stratification, rank, metafunction and axis (see Halliday 1978; Martin 1992; Halliday & Matthiessen 2004; Matthiessen, Teruya & Lam 2010; inter alia), and to what extent are these dimensions relevant or necessary for smell?

With regard to stratification, we might think of the semiotic system of smell as comprising two planes (after Hjelmslev 1947, 1961 [1943]): a content plane, which deals with systems of meaning, and an expression plane, which deals with systems of smells. In the case of language, the content plane is typically stratified into 'grammar' and 'semantics' (Halliday & Matthiessen 2004: 24). But what about smell? For van Leeuwen (2005: 50–53), the answer to this question depends on whose perspective we choose to take. For the perfumer or aromatherapist, the content plane may be stratified ('doubly articulated'). For the (nonspecialist) consumer, the content plane is likely unstratified ('singly articulated'). Real-estate agents' use of smell, however, seems to represent a middle ground or intermediate stage that is neither single nor double articulation but perhaps a bit of both.[5]

Assuming smell does have a 'grammar' – for perfumers and aromatherapists, at least – how might its compositional components be organized? In language, a hierarchy or rank scale is proposed for each stratum. For phonology, we typically have phoneme–syllable–foot–tone group; for (lexico-)grammar, morpheme–word–group/phrase–clause; and for semantics, element–move/message/figure–sequence (Halliday & Matthiessen 2004: 11–20; Halliday & Greaves 2008: 13; Halliday & Webster 2009: 237; Matthiessen, Teruya & Lam 2010: 170, 206–207; see also Hasan 1996: 117–118). As van Leeuwen and Djonov (2015: 248) note and as the work of others suggests (e.g. Dodd 1988, Tisserand 1988, Turin 2006), perfumery and aromatherapy already operate with rank scales. On the content plane, we might formalize this as note–chord–harmony, where a harmony is realized by one or more chords and a chord by one or more notes. On the expression plane, the rank scale could be molecule–mixture–aroma, where an aroma is realized by one or more mixtures or aromatic compounds and a mixture by one or more (typically volatile) molecules. Of course, a more nuanced or fine-grained hierarchy might be possible or necessary. For example, one may wish or need to distinguish between individual smells or smell compounds and the basic note-types they realize, something akin to the distinction between, say, morpheme and word, or clause and clause complex in the rank scale for grammar (see above). The scales proposed above are meant as suggestions rather than as definitive compositional hierarchies.

Halliday and others propose that language and other social-semiotic systems evolve to carry out three basic functions: to enact and maintain social relations (known as the 'interpersonal' or 'interactive' metafunction); to construe and represent the world around us (the 'ideational' or 'representational' metafunction); and to organize those relations and representations into meaningful units or texts (the 'textual' or 'compositional' metafunction). The interpersonal relevance of smell, particularly with regard to emotions and affect, is frequently noted in comparison with the other senses, as the following quote from geographer J. Douglas Porteous suggests:

> olfaction seems to stimulate emotional or motivational arousal […], whereas visual experience is much more likely to involve thought and cognition. Vision […] distances us from the object. […] By contrast,

smells [...] penetrate the body and permeate the immediate environment, and thus one's response is much more likely to involve strong affect. (Porteous 2006: 91)

This also seems to be the case at the property viewings I attended. Real-estate agents and potential buyers variously described their affective responses to, and/or appreciation of, the smells they encountered as 'nice', 'unpleasant', 'appetizing' and so on. However, they also *named* the smells, e.g. 'coffee', 'scented candles' and 'barbeque', connecting their smell-experiences to the objects or activities these smells represent. Compositionally, certain smells in the property-viewing smellscape seem to 'belong together' in a physical, physiological and/or social-cultural sense. Coffee and cinnamon, for example, accord or harmonize in a way that coffee and washing detergent generally do not, even though both smells, individually, may be experienced as 'pleasant'.

Within these three basic strands of meaning, it might be possible to identify distinct paradigmatic systems at different strata.[6] Indeed, like the rank scales discussed above, such systems already seem to exist for perfumery and aromatherapy. Tisserand (1988), for example, provides a number of diagrams, charts and tables that could be developed into system networks and realization statements for smell. One of those diagrams (Tisserand 1988: 179) suggests that odours or perfumes are essentially narcotic–stimulating or erogenic–antierogenic and that those odour-types can be further categorized according to how soothing–exalting or fresh–sultry they are. Another more complex example is of a 'mood cycle' for essential oils (redrawn here as Figure 11.1) that categorizes the interrelations of the supposed positive and negative emotional effects evoked by different plant essences. The diagram shows how these essences can be used as a form of treatment (aromatherapy) to influence mood, suggesting, for example, that feelings of anger might be alleviated with yarrow or that feelings of anxiety might be alleviated with clary sage. Tisserand's (1988) account of the therapeutic properties of essential oils may lend itself as the basis for a simplified model for the moods or feelings typically associated with or evoked by certain smells. A system network for MOOD, based on Tisserand's (1988) mood cycle, is proposed in Figure 11.2. Note the similarity of this system with Martin and White's (2005) interpersonal discourse-semantic system of AFFECT (see also White and Don 2012).[7] Note also that Tisserand's (1988) summary of the mood cycle (see below) can easily be applied beyond aromatherapy, to the context of property-viewing smellscapes. Tisserand writes:

196 *Analyzing the Media: A Systemic Functional Approach*

Essential oils can be used to influence mood in four different ways:

1 To evoke positive feelings (e.g. clarity or vivacity).
2 To counter negative feelings (e.g. anger or depression).
3 To influence our own mood.
4 To influence the mood of others.

We can say that most of the time we are, at some point, travelling around our own complex personal mood cycle, which is affected by so many things, including fragrances. (Tisserand 1988, 179–180)

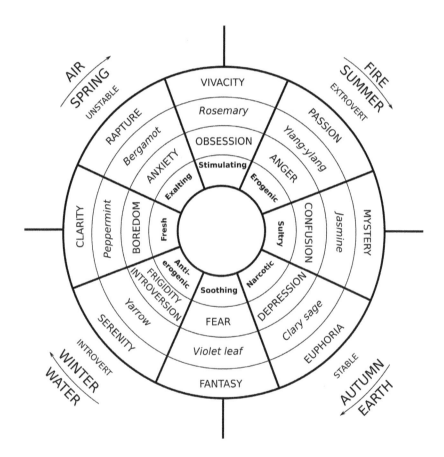

Figure 11.1 'Mood cycle' (after Tisserand 1988: 180, Fig. 9.3); Reprinted/adapted by permission from Springer Nature: Springer eBook, *Essential Oils as Psychotherapeutic Agents*, by Tisserand, R. © (1988)

Smell as social semiotic 197

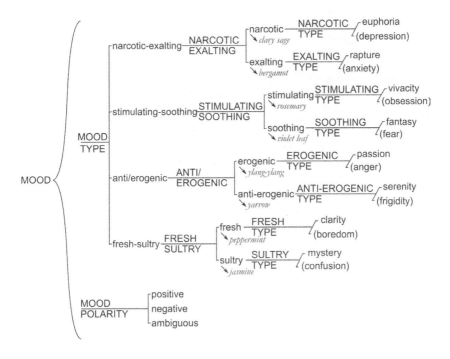

Figure 11.2 System network for MOOD (based on Tisserand 1988: 180; see Figure 11.1 above)

11.5 The intersemiotic potential of smell

Real-estate agents are not perfumers or aromatherapists. They are not specialists in smell, and they may have little or no interest in developing or exploring the olfactory experience. However, their use of smell at property viewings does seem to be quintessentially multimodal. Smell is part of a broader multisemiotic or multisensorial event, part of what several respondents called the overall 'sensory impression' created or curated by the real-estate agent. Our senses of smell, sight, hearing, taste and touch are stimulated in various ways, often simultaneously, to try to ensure a positive (first) impression of the property. Coffee and cinnamon buns, for example, are not only there to produce pleasant smells or to cover up unpleasant smells; they are also there to be seen, touched and tasted. They can act as an 'ice-breaker', they can 'get conversations going' and, 'with a cup of coffee in hand, they [potential buyers] often stay an extra 5–10 mins at the viewing'.

Multisemiotic resources can be integrated in a number of ways. Lim (2004), for example, posits a zone or 'space of integration' that operates across the expression and content planes of two or more semiotics (see also Matthiessen 2009), while Thibault and others (e.g. Thibault 2000, Baldry & Thibault 2006: 23) stress the importance of metafunction in creating synergy between semiotic systems. Martin et al. (Martin 1999, 2008, 2011; Zappavigna, Dwyer & Martin 2008; Painter, Martin & Unsworth 2013), on the other hand, note that regardless of stratum or metafunction, repeated co-patternings of realizations from two or more systems bind or couple these systems in potentially convergent or divergent ways.

With regard to the property viewing as a whole, we might in a very general sense argue that different semiotic resources are integrated simply on the basis of their being deployed in the same context of situation (see, for example, Matthiessen 2009: 12, Halliday & Matthiessen 2014: 42–43). The smell of stale or rotten food, for example, while potentially misplaced or unintended at a property viewing, may still be part of a viewing (see above) and thus part of the way that viewing *means* intersemiotically.

There are also local instances of semiotic cohesion where multisemiotic resources converge or diverge *within* the context of the property viewing, at what we might call the discourse-semantic level of the content plane (cf. Martin 1992). For example, when asked about their first and overall impressions, potential buyers described apartments as 'fresh' and 'clean'.[8] These meaning domains (see Painter, Martin & Unsworth 2013: 139) are likely to be construed through the resources of several semiotic systems, but most of the semiotic work seems to be done visually and olfactively. The smell of flowers, 'green soap' and fabric conditioner couple and converge with the sight of spotless surfaces or a recently painted white staircase to create these kinds of meanings. They are not generally construed verbally. Estate agents and potential buyers do not usually discuss how fresh or clean a property is; nor do prospectuses although they might express this visually.[9]

Another example concerns the property as a potential home. As noted above, several respondents described the smells they encountered as 'home-like' or 'homely'. This is a key meaning domain for the property viewing, but it is one that appears to be enacted predominantly by smell. The contributions made visually, verbally and spatially are somewhat limited and may be consciously constrained or suppressed. Property owners are often asked to remove personal items like pictures, clothing, furniture and books before a property viewing, and the work of 'property stylists', which includes the selecting, rearranging and 'de-cluttering' of furnishings, may lead to a relative depersonalization of living spaces.[10] That is not to say that non-olfactory resources do not contribute to the meaning domain of home. Flowers, music, interviews with property owners (featured in the prospectus), all of these can contribute to the property's potential 'homeliness', helping in various ways to enact the cosiness and good vibes described by real-estate agents and potential buyers (see above). However, for the most part, verbal, visual and spatial resources seem to contribute to other meaning domains, such as property specifications and the bidding process (see endnote 9).

11.6 Smell ya later!

> *I pulled up to the house about 7 or 8, and I yelled to the cabbie, 'Yo, homes, smell ya later!'*
> From 'Yo Home to Bel-Air', theme song
> for the television series *The Fresh Prince of Bel-Air*.

A smell like roasted coffee has the potential to construe a complex set of meanings. When deployed in the context of a property viewing, it can couple with the smell of cinnamon buns to create harmonies that connote feelings of comfort and homeliness. Such meanings can be complemented and multiplied by the sight and smell of flowers or a real-estate agent's verbal account of friendly neighbours. Other resources may construe divergent or potentially conflicting meanings, such as the smell of disinfectant or the sight of a room containing minimal or no furnishings.

Smells have the potential to evoke certain moods, memories, or feelings – what we might call a Proustian response – but they also help situate us in the sensory landscape. At a property viewing, we may not be able to see where the kitchen is, but we might be able to smell it or hear it. Smells like coffee and cinnamon buns can couple with the sound of an extractor fan, an oven door closing or a plate being placed on a table, telling us something about the size, layout and ventilation of a property.

The property viewing as situation-type provides an interesting opportunity for the multisemiotic study of smell. It presents the analyst with a context in which smell appears to play an instrumental role. The theory and application of smell as a socially mediated sign-system or social semiotic, as briefly outlined above, could be broadened and deepened by further examining this and other situation-types. Perfumery and aromatherapy are two obvious examples, but there are a variety of others we might consider, such as olfactory sculpture, environmental fragrancing and four-dimensional cinema or 'smell-o-vision'.[11]

Acknowledgements

I am grateful to participants at the 26th European Systemic Functional Linguistics Conference (13–15 July 2016), at the University of Salzburg, Austria, for insightful comments and questions on the original presentation and discussion of this paper. I am also grateful to the real-estate agents and property-viewing visitors who kindly agreed to answer my questions.

About the author

Daniel Lees Fryer is associate professor of English at Østfold University College, Norway. His research interests include systemic functional linguistics, social semiotics, scientific discourse and the discourse of social movements.

Notes

1. A similar argument is made for the diminished or diminishing value of sound and hearing (Schafer 1994 [1977]: 10, Classen 1997: 15).
2. As one of several examples, Classen (1997: 405) mentions Oken's sensory hierarchy, in which Africans, at the lower end of the scale, are described as 'skin-men', Native Australians as 'tongue-men', Native Americans as 'nose-men', Asians as 'ear-men' and Europeans as 'eye-men'.
3. Real-estate agents are variously referred to as realtors, real-estate brokers or estate agents. In Norway, where I conducted the study, they are generally known as '*eiendomsmeglere*', lit. 'property brokers'.
4. This latter example was provided by a real-estate agent and referred to the unwashed contents of a forgotten dishwasher. It was not a typical smell at the property viewings I attended.
5. An intriguing analogy might be made here with the process of emergent complexity that occurs in the ontogenesis of a human child's language, from a singly articulated proto-form to a doubly articulated adult standard (Halliday 2003 [1974], Matthiessen 2004, Martin 2011: 246).
6. Parametric systems, like those offered by van Leeuwen (1999, 2011) for sound and colour, might also be useful for representing the meaning potential of smell.

7 I have retained the term 'mood' here in line with Tisserand's (1988) terminology. However, 'affect' might be a more appropriate label, considering the association of 'mood' with clause type and speech function in linguistics.
8 Other descriptors included 'good', 'nice', 'great', 'super' and 'pretty'. The only overtly negative comment made by potential buyers on their overall impressions of properties was with regard to size, e.g. 'too small'.
9 Verbal resources, both spoken and written, tend to relate to discussions of price, property specifications such as year of construction and size, the surveyor's report, bidding and insurance forms, prior/future maintenance, reasons for sale and so on.
10 The deployment of certain smells arguably contributes to this process of depersonalization, too. 'Green soap', washing detergent and scented candles may be used to sanitize or cover up certain, let's say, 'less-desirable' home-related odours.
11 For a discussion of olfactory sculpture, see http://www.danielfryer.no/EN/Blog/Entries/2013/8/6_Smell_as_Social_Semiotic.html

References

Baldry, A. & Thibault, P.J. (2006) *Multimodal Transcription and Text Analysis*. London: Equinox.

Classen, C. (1993) *Worlds of Sense: Exploring the Senses in History and across Cultures*. London: Routledge.

Classen, C. (1997) 'Foundations for an anthropology of the senses'. *International Social Science Journal* 49(153), 401–412. doi: 10.1111/j.1468–2451.1997.tb00032.x.

Classen, C., Howes, D. & Synnott, A. (1994) *Aroma: The Cultural History of Smell*. London: Routledge.

Corbin, A. (1986 [1982]) *The Foul and the Fragrant: Odour and the Social Imagination*. London: Macmillan.

Dodd, G.H. (1988) 'The molecular dimension in perfumery'. In: van Toller, S. & Dodd, G.H. (eds.) *Perfumery: The Psychology and Biology of Fragrance*. London: Chapman & Hall, 19–46.

Drobnik, J. (2006) 'Introduction: Olfactocentrism'. In: Drobnik, J. (ed.) *The Smell Culture Reader*. Oxford: Berg, 1–9.

Halliday, M.A.K. (1978) *Language as Social Semiotic: The Social Interpretation of Language and Meaning*. London: Edward Arnold.

Halliday, M.A.K. (2003 [1974]) 'A sociosemiotic perspective on language development'. In: Webster, J.J. (ed.) *Volume 4 in the Collected Works of M.A.K. Halliday. The Language of Early Childhood*. London: Continuum, 90–112.

Halliday, M.A.K. & Greaves, W.S. (2008) *Intonation in the Grammar of English*. London: Equinox.

Halliday, M.A.K. & Matthiessen, C.M.I.M. (2004) *Introduction to Functional Grammar*. 3rd edition. London: Arnold.

Halliday, M.A.K. & Matthiessen, C.M.I.M. (2014) *Introduction to Functional Grammar*. 4th edition. Abingdon: Routledge.

Halliday, M.A.K. & Webster, J.J. (eds.) (2009) *Continuum Companion to Systemic Functional Linguistics*. London: Continuum.

Hasan, R. (1996) 'Semantic networks: a tool for the analysis of meaning'. In: Cloran, C., Butt, D. & Williams, G. *Ways of Saying: Ways of Meaning*. London: Cassell, 104–131.

Hjelmslev, L. (1947) 'Structural analysis of language'. *Studia Linguistica* 1(1–3), 69–78.

Hjelmslev, L. (1961 [1943]). *Prolegomena to a Theory of Language*. Translated by Whitfield, F.J. Madison, Wisconsin: University of Wisconsin Press.

Howes, D. (2011) 'Anthropology and multimodality: the conjugation of the senses'. In: Jewitt, C. (ed.) *The Routledge Handbook of Multimodal Analysis*. London: Routledge, 225–235.

Kress, G. (2010) *Multimodality: A Social Semiotic Approach to Contemporary Communication*. Abingdon: Routledge.

Lemke, J.L. (1998) 'Multiplying meaning: visual and verbal semiotics in scientific text'. In: Martin, J.R. & Veel, R. (eds.) *Reading Science: Critical and Functional Perspectives on Discourses of Science*. London: Routledge, 87–113.

Lim, V.F. (2004) 'Developing an integrative multi-semiotic model'. In: O'Halloran, K.L. (ed.) *Multimodal Discourse Analysis: Systemic Functional Perspectives*. London: Continuum, 220–246.

Margolies, E. (2006) 'Vagueness gridlocked: a map of the smells of New York'. In: Drobnik, J. (ed.) *The Smell Culture Reader*. Oxford: Berg, 107–117.

Martin, J.R. (1992) *English Text: System and Structure*. Amsterdam: John Benjamins.

Martin, J.R. (1999) 'Beyond exchange: appraisal systems in English'. In: Hunston, S. & Thompson, G. (eds.) *Evaluation in Text: Authorial Stance and the Construction of Discourse*. Oxford: Oxford University Press, 142–175.

Martin, J.R. (2008) 'Tenderness: realisation and instantiation in a Botswanan town'. In: Nørgaard, N. (ed.) *Systemic Functional Linguistics in Use*. Odense: University of Southern Denmark, 30–62.

Martin, J.R. (2011) 'Multimodal semiotics: theoretical challenges'. In: Dreyfus, S., Hood, S. & Stenglin, M. (eds.) *Semiotic Margins: Meaning in Multimodalities.* London: Continuum, 243–270.

Martin, J.R. & White, P.R.R. (2005) *The Language of Evaluation: Appraisal in English.* Basingstoke: Palgrave Macmillan.

Matthiessen, C.M.I.M. (2004) 'The evolution of language: a systemic functional exploration of phylogenetic phases'. In: Williams, G. & Lukin, A. (eds.) *The Development of Language: Functional Perspectives on Species and Individuals.* London: Continuum, 45–90.

Matthiessen, C.M.I.M. (2009). 'Multisemiosis and context-based register typology: registerial variation in the complementarity of semiotic systems'. In: Ventola, E. & Moya Guijarro, A.J. (eds.) *The World Told and the World Shown: Multisemiotic Issues.* London: Palgrave Macmillan, 11–38.

Matthiessen, C.M.I.M., Teruya, K. & Lam, M. (2010) *Key Terms in Systemic Functional Linguistics.* London: Continuum.

Norris, S. (2013) 'What is a mode? Smell, olfactory perception, and the notion of mode in multimodal mediated theory'. *Multimodal Communication* 2(2), 155–169.

O'Halloran, K.L. (2005) *Mathematical Discourse: Language, Symbolism and Visual Images.* London: Continuum.

Painter, C., Martin, J.R. & Unsworth, L. (2013) *Reading Visual Narratives: Image Analysis of Children's Picture Books.* Sheffield: Equinox.

Pennycook, A. & Otsuji, E. (2015) 'Making scents of the landscape'. *Linguistic Landscape* 1(3), 191–212.

Porteous, J.D. (2006). 'Smellscape'. In: Drobnik, J. (ed.) *The Smell Culture Reader.* Oxford: Berg, 89–106.

Reinarz, J. (2014) *Past Scents: Historical Perspectives on Smell, Studies in Sensory History.* Champaign, Illinois: University of Illinois Press.

Rindisbacher, H.J. (2006) 'The stench of power'. In: Drobnik, J. (ed.) *The Smell Culture Reader.* Oxford: Berg, 137–147.

Royce, T.D. (2002) 'Multimodality in the TESOL classroom: exploring visual-verbal synergy'. *TESOL Quarterly* 36(2), 191–205. doi: 10.2307/3588330.

Royce, T.D. (2007) 'Intersemiotic complementarity: a framework for multimodal discourse analysis'. In: Royce, T.D. & Bowcher, W.L. (eds.) *New Directions in the Analysis of Multimodal Discourse.* Mahwah, NJ: Lawrence Erlbaum Associates, 63–109.

Schafer, R.M. (1994 [1977]) *The Soundscape: Our Sonic Environment and the Tuning of the World.* Rochester, Vermont: Destiny Books.

Süskind, P. (1985) *Perfume: The Story of a Murderer.* Translated by Woods, J.E. New York: Knopf.

Thibault, P.J. (2000) 'The multimodal transcription of a television advertisement: theory and practice'. In: Baldry, A. (ed.) *Multimodality and Multimediality in the Distance Learning Age*. Campobasso: Palladino Editore, 311–385.

Tisserand, R. (1988) 'Essential oils as psychotherapeutic agents'. In: van Toller, S. & Dodd, G.H. (eds.) *Perfumery: The Psychology and Biology of Fragrance*. London: Chapman & Hall, 167–181.

Turin, L. (2006) *The Secret of Scent: Adventures in Perfume and the Science of Smell*. New York: HarperCollins.

van Leeuwen, T. (1999) *Speech, Music, Sound*. Basingstoke: Macmillan.

van Leeuwen, T. (2005) *Introducing Social Semiotics*. Abingdon: Routledge.

van Leeuwen, T. (2011) *The Language of Colour*. Abingdon: Routledge.

van Leeuwen, T. & Djonov, E. (2015) 'Notes towards a semiotics of kinetic typography'. *Social Semiotics* 25(2), 244–253. doi: 10.1080/10350330.2015.1010324.

White, P.R.R. & Don, A. (2012) 'The appraisal website'. Last modified June 15, 2012 [9.2.2015]. http://www.grammatics.com/appraisal/index.html.

Zappavigna, M., Dwyer, P. & Martin, J.R. (2008) 'Syndromes of meaning: exploring patterned coupling in a NSW youth justice conference'. In: Mahboob, A. & Knight, N.K. (eds.) *Questioning Linguistics*. Newcastle: Cambridge Scholars, 164–185.

Author index

Algoet, B. 90
Ansary, H. 49, 63
Arús, J. 64

Baayen, R.H. 107, 108
Babaii, E. 49, 63
Baker, P. 6, 9, 92, 108
Baldry, A. 198, 201, 204
Banks, D. 7, 149, 159, 163–165
Barnhurst, K.G. 141, 145
Bartlett, T. 9, 173, 185
Barton, D. 10
Bateman, J.A. 167, 185, 188
Becher, V. 89
Beder, S. 142, 145
Bednarek, M. 68, 88
Bell, A. 33, 45, 46
Berry, M. 5, 9
Biber, D. 92, 96–101, 103, 105, 108
Black, L. 178, 188
Blakemore, D. 102, 105, 108
Bogdanowicz, M. 186
Burgelman, J.-C. 186
Burger, H. 131, 140, 146
Burger, M. 165
Burton-Roberts, N. 91, 94, 108
Butler, C.S. 107, 108
Butt, D. 14, 28, 167, 175, 176, 183, 185, 186, 188, 202

Calsamiglia, H. 111, 128
Cameron, D. 170, 185
Cartmill, J. 175, 185
Cassens, J. 7, 167, 168, 175, 178, 183, 185, 187, 188
Christie, F. 113, 28, 65
Classen, C. 189, 190, 200, 201
Cole, M. 169, 184, 185, 187

Collins Cobuild 20, 28
Collins, P. 108, 109
Conboy, M. 141, 142, 146
Connor, U. 33, 45, 65
Conrad, S. 108
Coria, A.M. 5, 13, 27
Corbin, A. 190, 201
Cotter, C. 3, 9, 10
Crystal, D. 149, 165
Culpeper, J. 114, 118, 130

Daneš, F. 52, 64
Davis, P. 178, 188
de Oliveira, J.M. 68, 89, 111, 128, 129
Dehé, N. 91–93, 101, 108, 109
Derewianka, B. 13, 28
Djonov, E. 190, 191, 194, 204
Dodd, G.H. 194, 201, 204
Don, A. 195, 204
Drobnik, J. 189, 190, 201–203
Dubois, B. L. 52, 64
Ducatel, K. 175, 186
Dwyer, P. 198, 204

Eggins, S. 16, 28, 51, 52, 64
Elorza, I. 111, 114, 129
Emonds, J. 94, 108
Engeström, Y. 167, 184–187
Espinal, T.M. 94, 107, 108

Fahey, R. 28
Fairclough, N. 35, 45
Feez, S. 10, 28
Feng, H. 31, 45
Ferreira, M.M. 178, 186
Finegan, E. 108
Firth, J.R. 167, 186
Fowler, R. 32, 33, 35, 45, 64

Fries, P.H. 51, 64
Fryer, D.L. 7, 189, 200, 201
Fuller, G. 68, 88

García Riaza, B. 111, 129
Giessen, H.W. 46, 141, 142, 144, 146
Gil Salom, L. 111, 129
Gotti, M. 111, 129
Greaves, W.S. 9, 194, 202
Gualdo, R. 71, 72, 88

Haegeman, L. 94, 108
Halliday, M.A.K. 1–3, 5, 6, 9, 10,
   15–17, 19, 23, 28, 29, 31, 44–46,
   51, 64, 68, 71, 88, 91, 98, 99, 104,
   105, 109, 112–115, 118–120, 125,
   127, 129, 132, 133, 135, 146, 158,
   165, 167, 169, 170, 172–174, 186,
   187, 193, 194, 198, 200–202
Hand, M. 102, 109
Harcup, T. 73, 83, 88
Hasan, R. 1, 3, 10, 51, 64, 98, 109, 171,
   174, 178–180, 183–188, 194, 202
Hauser, S. 49, 64
Hawes, T. 111, 114, 129
Heine, B. 95, 101, 104, 105, 107, 109
Henriksen, B. 2, 10
Hewings, M. 67, 86, 88
Hiippala, T. 185
Hjelmslev, L. 193, 202
Hoey, M. 124, 127, 129
Hofland, K. 6, 9, 92, 97, 109
Hood, S. 114, 115, 129, 203
House, J. 71, 88, 89
Howes, D. 189, 190, 201, 202
Huddleston, R. 91, 93, 95, 104, 109
Hunston, S. 113, 129, 202

Iedema, R. 3, 10

Jakobson, R. 3, 10
Jewitt, C. 2, 10, 202
Johansson, S. 64, 108

Johns, A.M. 178, 186
Johnson, K. 107, 109
Jones, L.B. 99, 109
Jucker, A.H. 33, 46

Kaltenbacher, M. 1, 6, 9, 131, 142,
   144, 145, 146
Kaltenböck, G. 95, 101, 105, 107, 109
Kane, T. 131, 132, 146
Kaptelinin, V. 176, 187
Kavalova, Y. 91–94, 96, 101, 102, 104,
   108, 109
Keeble, R. 73, 88, 89
Kerschner, M.A. 5, 31, 44–46
Klein, P.D. 112, 114, 129
Kofod-Petersen, A. 167, 175, 184,
   187
Kranich, S. 67, 69, 89
Kress, G. 191, 202

Lam, M. 193, 194, 203
Landert, D. 32–36, 40, 46
Larreya, P. 158, 165
Lavid, J. 5, 49, 51, 53, 63, 64
Lee-Goldman, R. 101, 109
Lee, N.I. 49, 64
Leech, G. 108, 115, 130
Leijten, J. 186
Lemke, J.L. 174, 187, 190, 202
Lenk, H.E.H. 46, 137, 140, 142,
   144–147
Leont'ev, A.N. 167, 168, 184, 187
Liao, M.-H. 67, 89
Liardét, C. 114, 130
Lim, V.F. 198, 202
Lindebjerg, A. 9, 109
Liu, Y. 31, 45
Llinares, A. 187
López Ferrero, C. 111, 128
Lüger, H.H. 46, 99, 109, 131, 143,
   147
Luginbühl, M. 3, 4, 10, 64, 131, 140,
   146

Macdonald, S.P. 67, 89
Mair, C. 97, 109
Malmquist, A. 142, 147
Manfredi, M. 5, 67, 87–89
Mann, W.C. 51, 65
Margolies, E. 191, 202
Martin, J.R. 3, 6, 10, 13, 16, 28, 51, 64, 65, 68–70, 78, 80, 81, 88, 89, 131, 135, 147, 178, 187, 190, 193, 195, 198, 200, 202–204
Matthiessen, C.M.I.M. 1, 2, 6, 9, 10, 16, 17, 19, 23, 28, 29, 31, 44, 45, 68, 88, 91, 99, 104, 109, 112–115, 118–120, 125, 127, 129, 133, 135, 146, 165, 187, 188, 193, 194, 198, 200, 202, 203
Mazeland, H. 102, 109
Miettinen, R. 184, 186
Miller, E.R. 187
Minelli de Oliveira, J. 68, 89
Minick, N. 184, 187
Momigliano, A. 73, 86, 89
Montemayor-Borsinger, A. 5, 13, 28
Moore, A. 185, 187
Moratón, L. 5, 49, 63, 64
Morley, J. 32, 46
Moyano, E.I. 112, 130
Munday, J. 68, 80, 81, 85, 86, 89
Mutz, D. 141, 145
Myers, G. 67, 72, 89

Nardi, B.A. 167, 168, 175, 187
Nelkin, D. 67, 89
Norris, S. 190, 203
Nwogu, K.N. 51, 53, 65

O'Donnell, M. 159, 165, 167, 188
O'Halloran, K.L. 190, 202, 203
OECD 74–76, 89
Olohan, M. 67, 89
Otsuji, E. 191, 203

Pagano, A.S. 68, 89, 111, 129
Page, R. 4, 10
Painter, C. 198, 203
Palmer, F.R. 158, 165
Parret, H. 170, 186, 188
Pennycook, A. 191, 203
Pérez-Veneros, M. 6, 111, 114, 128–130
Perkins, M.R. 158, 165
Perrin, D. 3, 9, 10
Peterson, P. 94, 109
Porteous, J.D. 189, 191, 194, 195, 203
Potts, C. 91, 101, 102, 109, 110
Prado-Alonso, C. 6, 91, 106, 110
Pullum, G.K. 91, 93, 95, 104, 109
Punamäki, R.-L. 186

Qian, H. 89

Ragazzini, G. 81, 89
Reah, D. 14, 29
Reinarz, J. 189, 190, 203
Reinhart, T. 107, 110
Reuters 131, 143, 147
Richardson, J.E. 35, 46
Rindisbacher, H.J. 189, 203
Robertson, J.M. 163, 165
Rose, D. 13, 29, 51, 65, 187
Rothery, J. 65
Royce, T.D. 190, 203
Russell, D.R. 178, 188

Safir, K. 95, 110
Sapir, E. 172, 188
Scapolo, F. 186
Schafer, R.M. 200, 203
Schmitz, U. 3, 10
Schneider, S. 101, 110
Schudson, M. 141, 147
Semino, E. 111, 114, 115, 118, 130
Short, M. 111, 114, 115, 118, 130
Skelton, J. 51, 65
Slade, D. 51, 64
Smith, B. 178, 188

Solem, J.S. 175, 177, 188
Sperber, D. 102, 110
Spinks, S. 28
Spinola, M.C. 5, 13, 27
Squire, L. 185
Stöckl, H. 1, 4, 8, 10, 146
Sušinskienė, S. 112, 114, 130
Süskind, P. 190, 203
Swales, J. 51, 65
Synnott, A. 189, 201

Telve, S. 71, 72, 88
Teruya, K. 193, 194, 203
Thibault, P.J. 190, 198, 201, 204
Thomas, S. 111, 114, 129
Thompson, G. 6, 11, 111, 113–116, 118, 122, 124, 126, 129, 130, 135, 147, 149, 165, 202
Thompson, S.A. 51, 65
Thomson, E. 68, 90
Thorne, S.L. 178, 188
Thunestvedt, J. 9, 109
Tinker Perrault, S. 68, 71, 72, 86, 90
Tisserand, R. 194–197, 201, 204
Tognini-Bonelli, E. 118, 130
Turin, L. 194, 204

Unger, J.W. 10
Unsworth, L. 112, 114, 129, 130, 198, 203

van Dijk, T.A. 14, 29, 35, 42, 46, 49, 64, 65, 111, 128, 182, 188
van Leeuwen, T. 190, 191, 193, 194, 200, 204

Vandenbussche, L. 90
Vandepitte, S. 78, 90
Vasquez, O. 167, 184, 185, 187
von der Heiden, G. 142, 147

Wang, W. 49, 50, 65
Ward, G. 141, 147
Webster, J.J. 9, 28, 31, 45, 46, 129, 186–188, 194, 202
Wegener, R. 7, 167, 168, 173, 181, 184, 185, 187, 188
Weiser, M. 175, 188
Wertsch, J.V. 184, 188
White, P.R.R. 3, 6, 10, 11, 50, 51, 54, 65, 68–70, 72, 75, 78, 80, 81, 88–90, 131, 145, 147, 195, 203, 204
Whitelaw, C. 165
Whorf, B.L. 170, 188
Wikberg, K. 99, 110
Wildfeuer, J. 185
Williams, J. 178, 188
Williams, K. 141, 147
Wilson, D. 102, 110
Winograd, T. 167, 188

Yallop, C. 28
Ye, Y.Y. 111, 114, 130
Yu, H. 51, 65

Zamorano-Mansilla, J.R. 64
Zappavigna, M. 10, 165, 204
Zhang, M. 68, 90
Ziv, Y. 102, 110

Subject index

Acknowledge (s. Engagement: Attribute)
activity 50, 168–170, 175–183, 190
Activity Theory 167–170, 175, 178–180
adjective 120, 124, 125, 127, 135, 137, 157
adverb 79, 82, 134, 137, 157
adverbial 114, 158
Affect 97, 98, 103–105, 194, 195, 201
affective mental process (s. process type)
Ambient Intelligence Systems 167–169, 175, 182, 183
analysis (s. newspaper genres)
and-parentheticals (s. parentheticals)
apartment 191, 192, 198
appendages 93
Appraisal Theory 68, 69, 74, 79, 81, 131, 142
aromatherapy 190, 194, 195, 199
artefact 167, 168, 174, 178
Artificial Intelligence 167, 180, 184
attribute 120, 122
Attribute (s. Engagement)
authorial orientation (s. modality)
auxiliary (s. modality)

Bacon, Francis 163
behaviour 131, 168, 170–173, 175–178, 182–184
behaviour-aware 168, 175, 177
Brittany 149, 154, 159, 162
broadsheet (s. newspapers)

cinnamon 191–193, 195, 197, 199
coffee 191–193, 195, 197, 199
coherence 14, 24
comma intonation 94, 107

communication 31, 33, 34, 67, 69–72, 102, 104, 149, 159, 167–169, 178
community 163, 169
computer science 167
Concur (s. Engagement: Proclaim)
constructional theticals 95, 104
consumer magazine 67, 68, 72–74, 76–78, 82, 84
context 13, 31, 71–74, 85, 86, 102, 104, 128, 162, 167–184, 195, 196, 199
contraction 69
convergent meanings 198
coordinator-marked reduplication 104
corpus 23, 37, 40, 41, 43, 50, 61, 68, 73, 75, 76, 78, 82, 85, 86, 91–93, 96, 97, 104–106, 113, 117, 118, 122, 123, 126, 149, 150
coupling 198, 199
Cultural-Historical Activity Theory (CHAT) 167, 169, 170, 178–184
Critical Understanding of Science in Public (CUSP) 71, 72, 84

deontic (s. modality)
depersonalization 142, 198, 201
dialogism 68, 69, 79, 85
direct equivalence 71, 74, 75, 77, 78, 81, 82, 84, 85
direct question 149, 155, 156
direct speech 34, 36, 75, 112, 124
discourse-semantics 13, 14, 195, 198
Disclaim (s. Engagement)
Distance (s. Engagement: Attribute)
divergent meanings 198, 199
dynamic (s. modality)

editorial (s. newspaper genres)
email to the editor (s. newspaper genres)
emotion 14, 103, 104, 132, 193–195
Endorse (s. Engagement: Proclaim)
Engagement 67–87
   Attribute 69, 70, 75, 77, 79–81, 83–85
      Acknowledge 70, 77
      Distance 70, 77, 81
   Disclaim 69, 70
   Entertain 69–71, 75, 77, 80–85
   Proclaim 69, 70, 77–85
      Concur 70, 77–79, 83–85
      Endorse 70, 77–79, 83–85
      Pronounce 70, 77–80, 84, 85
English 37, 38, 49, 50, 53–62, 67–71, 73, 80, 81, 84, 87, 91, 92, 94, 96, 98, 101, 105, 131, 145, 149, 152, 163
   learning of English 13, 22, 23, 25
Entertain (s. Engagement)
environmental fragrancing 199
epistemic (s. modality)
equivalence 70, 71, 74, 75, 77, 78, 80–82, 84, 85, 88
evaluation 85–62, 68, 69, 72, 124, 127, 131, 132, 193
exchange 31, 149–156, 162, 163
exchange turn 150–153
exclusive *we* 35–37, 44
existential process (s. process type)
expansion 20–24, 69, 122, 124, 125
experiential metafunction (s. metafunction)
experiential metaphor 15, 16, 19, 20

feature article (s. newspaper genres)
finite clause 17, 19–24, 27
French 28, 55, 110, 149, 154, 159, 162, 163
functional equivalence 70, 71, 74, 75, 77, 78, 80–82, 84, 85
functional shift 70

genre 13–15, 26, 27, 32, 34, 36, 44, 49–55, 59–62, 93, 96, 97, 99, 111, 113, 116, 127, 141, 143, 178
generic structure 49–51, 54, 56–62
generic structure potential 51, 170, 178, 181
goal-directed action 169, 180, 190, 191, 195
grammatical metaphor 27, 114, 115, 119, 120, 157, 158

hard sciences (s. science)
headline (s. newspaper genres)
heteroglossia 83, 84, 86
home 158, 161, 192, 193, 198, 199, 201
Human-Computer Interaction 167, 168, 170, 175
hypotaxis (s. taxis)

ideational metafunction (s. metafunction)
inclination 133–137, 145
inclusive *we* 35–43
indirect question 75, 115, 124, 125, 126
indirect speech 75, 115, 118, 124–126
informational production 97–100
integration 126, 168, 170, 178, 198
interaction 31, 33, 85, 96–98, 103, 105, 167–172, 175, 176, 179, 180, 189, 194
internet 149–163
interpersonal metafunction (s. metafunction)
interpolation 93, 94
intersemiosis (s. semiosis)
involved production 97–100, 103, 105

journalistic culture 85
journalistic discourse 49, 50, 62, 67, 68, 75, 85, 96, 104–106
journalistic genres 49, 50, 61, 62, 93, 96, 99 (s. also newspaper genres)

Subject index

journalistic style 80, 83
journalistic text types 96, 99, 132, 142
   (s. also newspaper genres)
journalistic text 43, 49, 50, 61, 62, 67, 68, 72, 85, 99, 101, 106
journalistic writing 96, 99, 101, 106

language of smell 190, 193, 194
lead (s. newspaper genres)
learning of English (s. English)
letter to the editor (s. newspaper genres)
lexese 190
lexical change 14, 23–26
lexical omission 14, 23, 25 (see also: omission)
lexicogrammar 14, 15, 21, 24, 27, 69–71, 74, 81, 113, 117, 127, 131, 142, 172, 174
logico-semantic system 15, 16, 113
logogenesis 111, 112, 116, 121, 122, 125, 126

magazines 67, 68, 71–88
   specialized science magazines 68, 73, 74, 85
manifestation 132, 137, 140, 142
market branding 192
material process (s. process type)
meaning construal 13, 31, 111, 112, 117, 122, 125–128, 198, 199
meaning domain 198, 199
memory 190, 192, 193, 199
mental process (s. process type)
metafunction 31, 71, 74, 91, 96, 193, 194, 198
   experiential 24, 53, 115, 179
   ideational 31, 71, 86, 105, 119, 126, 150, 180, 194
   interpersonal 31, 32, 44, 68, 71, 73, 74, 81, 85, 86, 91, 99, 101, 103–106, 116, 131, 149, 150, 155, 171, 180, 194, 195

textual 31, 57, 61, 70, 71, 78, 80, 83, 86, 180, 194
modality 31, 71, 79, 81–83, 131–145, 149, 156–159, 162
   authorial orientation 131–145
   explicit objective 82, 132, 135–137, 140–143, 145
   explicit subjective 132, 135–137, 140–143, 145
   implicit objective 132, 135–137, 140–143, 145
   implicit subjective 132, 135–137, 140–143, 145
   deontic modality 133, 134, 158, 159, 163
   dynamic modality 133, 134, 149, 158, 159, 163
   epistemic modality 133, 134, 149, 158, 159, 163
   modal auxiliary/operator/verb 82, 83, 134–137, 140, 143, 145, 156, 157
   modal orientation 137–143
   modalization 133–135, 137, 158
   modulation 133–135, 137, 158
   semi-modal 157
modelling 167, 168, 170, 179–182, 193
monoglossia 74, 77–79, 83
mood 31, 149, 155, 190, 195–197, 199, 201
mood cycle 195, 196
multidimensional 98, 199
multimodal 168, 169, 173, 174, 175, 184, 190, 193, 197
multisemiosis (s. semiosis)

Namibia 149–163
news articles 13–15, 17, 20, 27, 36
news culture 32, 33, 36–40, 43, 44
newspapers 32, 50, 51, 67, 68, 67–80, 84, 92, 99, 137, 142–145
   broadsheet newspapers 67, 68, 72–74, 76–78, 84

quality newspapers 5, 31, 32, 44, 73
newspaper genres 36, 49, 50, 52–54, 59, 61, 62, 99, 140, 141, 143
   analysis 131, 138, 140–143
   comment 33, 34, 50, 75, 99, 116, 123, 131, 137–145
   editorial 32–45, 49, 50, 54, 58–63, 91, 92, 96, 97, 99, 101, 103, 105, 131, 137–142, 144, 145
   email to the editor 131, 137–140
   feature article 68, 72–77, 83–86
   headline 14, 26, 54–62, 75
   lead 14, 54, 56, 62
   letter to the editor 131, 49, 50, 54, 60–62, 92, 131
   popular science article 67–73, 75, 85, 86, 111, 112, 116, 122, 125, 127, 128
   report 14, 49–51, 54–58, 61, 62, 91, 92, 96, 97, 99, 101, 105, 131, 137–143
   review 91, 92, 96, 97, 99, 101, 103, 105
nominal example 158
nominalization 14–19, 23, 27, 113, 117, 119, 123, 124, 126, 127, 137
nominal group 16, 20, 23, 82, 114, 119, 120, 125
non-finite clause 17, 19–21, 23, 27, 119
Northumberland 149–152, 154–163

objective/objectivity 72, 73, 75, 82, 83, 97, 105, 131, 132, 135–137, 140–143, 145
obligation 133, 134, 136, 137
olfaction 189, 190, 194, 197, 198, 201
olfactory sculpture 201
olfactory turn 189, 190
omission 14, 15, 19–27, 43, 74, 75, 77–79, 83–86, 91, 94, 95
optimal relevance 102, 105

orientation (s. modality: authorial orientation)

packaging of voices 111–128
parataxis (s. taxis)
parentheticals 91, 92, 94, 96, 97, 101, 107
   and-parentheticals 91–110
participants 26, 31, 86, 111–115, 120–126, 149, 151, 152, 154, 162, 163, 176, 179, 191
perfumery 190, 194, 199
personalization 31–36, 39–41, 44 (s. also depersonalization)
popularization 67–72, 84, 121–127
popularization article (s. newspaper genres: popular science article)
popular science article (s. newspaper genres)
popular science writing (s. newspaper genres: popular science article)
press editorial (s. newspaper genres: editorial)
press reportage (s. newspaper genres: report)
press review (s. newspaper genres: review)
probability 75, 81, 82, 133–137
process type 150, 159–161
   existential process 120, 123, 124, 126, 159, 160
   material process 112, 149, 159–163
   mental process 80, 113, 114, 118–121, 123, 126, 149, 159–163
      affective mental process 159, 160, 163
   relational process 120, 123, 124, 126, 159, 160, 163
   verbal process 24, 26, 55, 80, 113, 114, 118–120, 123, 125, 159, 160, 162

Proclaim (s. Engagement)
projection 16, 17, 20, 24, 25, 80, 111–127
pronoun 31–44, 103, 106
Pronounce (s. Engagement: Proclaim)
property viewing 191, 192, 195, 197–200
Proust 199
Public Appreciation of Science and Technology (PAST) 71, 72, 84, 86
Public Understanding of Science (PUS) 71, 72, 84

rank scale 179, 180, 194, 195
real estate 191–195, 197, 199, 200
reader comprehension 13, 14, 19, 98
relational process (s. process type)
report (s. newspaper genres)
reportage (s. newspaper genres: report)
reported speech (s. indirect speech)
requirements elicitation 168, 169, 178, 182
response 33, 69, 150, 151, 156, 192, 193, 195, 199
review (s. newspaper genres)
rhetorical relations 49–62
Routard 149

science
    hard sciences 74, 76, 85
    science communication 69, 71, 87
    science dissemination 111, 116, 117, 126
    science journalism 68, 72, 87
    science magazines 68, 73, 74, 77, 78, 85
    science popularization 68, 69, 71, 72, 111, 112, 116, 117, 121, 125–128
    soft sciences 74, 75
second language classroom 13, 20, 27

self-reference 36, 39, 40
semi-modal (s. modality)
semiosis 169, 174
    intersemiosis 189, 197, 198
    multisemiosis 190, 193, 197, 198, 199
semiotic cohesion 198
semiotic system 189, 193
senses 189, 190, 194, 197
shift 68–70, 74, 77–87, 143, 182
simplification 13–27
sign-making 192
situated social practice 169
smart whiteboard 168, 175–177
smell 189–201
    smellscape 191, 192, 195
    smell-source 191, 192
social semiotic 169, 172, 189–199
socio-technical systems 168, 180, 182, 183
soft sciences (s. science)
source text 68, 71, 79, 80, 83, 84
specialized science magazines (s. magazines)
Spanish 49–62, 81
stratification 71, 167, 170, 183, 193, 194
subjective/subjectivity 50, 62, 68, 70, 73, 78, 80, 84, 85, 92, 131, 132, 135–137, 140–143, 145
supplementals 91
system network 133, 195

target text 68, 75, 79, 80, 82–84, 86
taxis 15, 16
    hypotaxis 15, 17, 19–22, 24, 27, 95, 111, 113, 114
    parataxis 15, 18–20, 22, 23, 27, 83, 95, 111, 113, 114
technology 67, 71–74, 76, 171, 184
text structure 14
texture 14
thematic pattern 49–53, 56, 57, 59–62

theme 14–20, 22, 23, 27, 51–53, 56, 57, 59–62
thetical grammar 95, 104
translation 67–71, 73–75, 79–81, 84, 86–88
translation studies 67, 68, 87, 88
travel forum 149–163

Tripadvisor 149
turn (s. exchange turn)

usuality 79, 133, 134, 136, 137, 145

verbal process (s. process type)
voices of authority 15, 24, 27

CPSIA information can be obtained
at www.ICGtesting.com
Printed in the USA
BVHW042254161120
593026BV00006B/68